America's Eden

NEWPORT LANDSCAPES THROUGH THE AGES

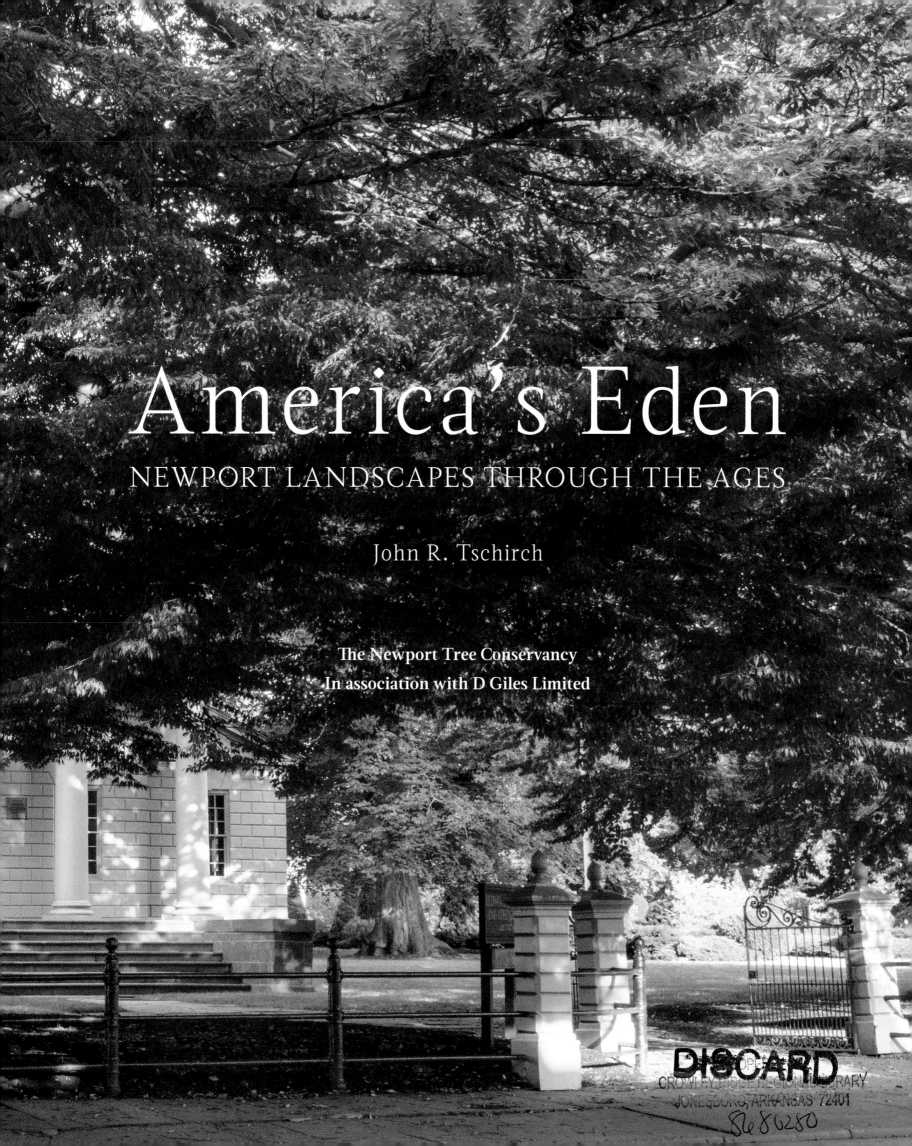

America's Eden

NEWPORT LANDSCAPES THROUGH THE AGES

John R. Tschirch

The Newport Tree Conservancy
In association with D Giles Limited

Dedication

To all of those who have shaped, celebrated,
and preserved Newport's landscapes

We must cultivate our own garden. . . . When man was put in the garden of Eden,
he was put there so that he should dress it, which proves that man was not born to be idle.
—Voltaire, *Candide* (1759)

© 2022 The Newport Tree Conservancy and John R. Tschirch

First published in 2022 by GILES
An imprint of D Giles Limited
66 High Street,
Lewes, BN7 1XG, UK
gilesltd.com

Library of Congress Control Number: 2021913372

ISBN: 978-1-911282-50-1

For the Newport Tree Conservancy:
Project Editor: John R. Tschirch
Photos: Nick Garcia-Belong, Roselle McConnell, and Alexander Nesbitt

For D Giles Limited:
Copy-edited and proof-read by Jodi Simpson
Designed by Caroline and Roger Hillier, The Old Chapel Graphic Design
Produced by GILES, an imprint of D Giles Limited
Printed and bound in Europe

Frontispiece: Roselle McConnell, Fernleaf Beech, 2020, photograph

NEWPORT TREE
CONSERVANCY
plant for the future

FSC
www.fsc.org
MIX
Paper from
responsible sources
FSC® C118234

CONTENTS

opposite:
Frances Benjamin Johnston, Hammersmith Farm Garden Walk, 1917,
photograph
Library of Congress

FOREWORD

The venerable specimen trees, designed landscapes, and works of art inspired by the natural settings of Newport, Rhode Island, form an extraordinary cultural heritage. *America's Eden: Newport Landscapes Through the Ages* is a first, a benchmark publication bringing Newport's landscape history to both scholars and the general reader.

Newport's landscape heritage is fragile and under constant threat from neglect, development, demolition, and lack of awareness. Although much of the city and its landscape retains its historic character, this remarkable legacy is further endangered by a lack of a written and visual record that coherently frames its significance. Unlike its buildings, Newport's verdant architecture—its landscapes—remains generally undocumented. Proper stewardship will only happen when there is a definitive study to guide decision making. Some degree of loss in the built and natural environment is inevitable, but without documentation and its dissemination through a comprehensive publication, Newport's landscape is in peril of disappearing with every passing year. We hope this book will address this issue by informing, entertaining, and inspiring through its prose and pictures.

Lilly Dick, Chairman
The Newport Tree Conservancy

Nick Garcia-Belong, Beech trees, 2017, photograph

ACKNOWLEDGMENTS

The Newport Tree Conservancy thanks the following donors for their vision and generous financial support of *America's Eden: Newport Landscapes Through the Ages.*

FOUNDERS CIRCLE
Ala and Ralph Heyward Isham
Kate C. Gubelmann
Elizabeth "Lisette" Prince

PATRONS CIRCLE
David* and Pamela Ford
Prince Charitable Trusts
*In Memoriam

ARBORETUM CIRCLE
Brittain and John Damgard
Virginia Decker
Bernard and Sarah Gewirz
Virginia and James Purviance
Diane B. Wilsey

GARDEN CIRCLE
Lilly Dick
The Hope Foundation

TREE CIRCLE
Bettie and Jonathan Pardee

GREEN CIRCLE
Lady Romayne Bockstoce
Robert W. Currier
Maureen Cronin and Mark Marosits
Victoria Mele
Janet Robinson
Susan Ruf and Michael Walsh
Kristyn A. Woodland

Gardeners at work (detail), frontispiece from Philip Miller, *The Gardeners Kalendar* (1728)
Redwood Library and Athenaeum

A NOTE FROM THE AUTHOR

The idea for *America's Eden* evolved over many decades as I came to know Newport's landscape in a variety of ways: through its scenery, its designers and their patrons, the gardeners who worked the earth and cared for all growing things, and the artists and writers who interpreted this Edenic place through the ages.

I thank the many people who have both inspired and generously supported this project. With their sense of stewardship, Kate Gubelmann, Oatsie Charles, and Britty Damgard were the first to encourage me many years ago in landscape research in order to inform and guide the preservation of Newport's green places. This set me on the course of a subject that has fascinated me ever since. Lilly Dick and Helen Papp of the Newport Tree Conservancy enthusiastically embraced my vision for this project. Their appreciation for all of the art forms that make up Newport's landscape heritage made this book possible. Holly Collins, Research Associate, has brought her forensic-like skills to her study of important photographic and document archives, unearthing extraordinary treasures on the earthly history of Newport. Kristyn Woodland has lent her insight and invaluable experience with so many of the city's landscapes. I am grateful to Natasha Harrison, Executive Director of the Newport Tree Conservancy, for her assistance and good cheer during the entire production process.

Thank you to the following individuals and organizations for sharing their wisdom and collections: Michelle Farias, Rachel Greggs, Amanda Quink, T.J. Brown, Jeff Curtis, Harry Eudenbach, Kelly Crawford of the Archives of American Gardens/Smithsonian Institution, Michelle Clark of the Frederick Law Olmsted National Historic Site, Danielle Kisluk-Groshiede at the Metropolitan Museum of Art, Martin Chapman at the Legion of Honor, Jim Turenne of the University of Rhode Island, Vartanian and Sons of New York, the Gianfrancesco Gorgoni Estate, Leslie and Mark Hull, Christina Gee Kryca, Betsy Vitton, Chris Fletcher, Christina Connett Brophy, Jennifer Robinson, Rebecca Kelly, Sandy Nesbitt, Roselle McConnell, Nick Garcia-Belong, the Redwood Library and Athenaeum, the Preservation Society of Newport County, and the Newport Historical Society.

I also thank the readers of this book. May it bring you hours of enjoyment, enrichment, and Edenic pleasures.

John Tschirch

Edward L. Hyde, *Map of Cherry Neck* (detail), November 30, 1867
Newport Historical Society, FIC.2015.006

14

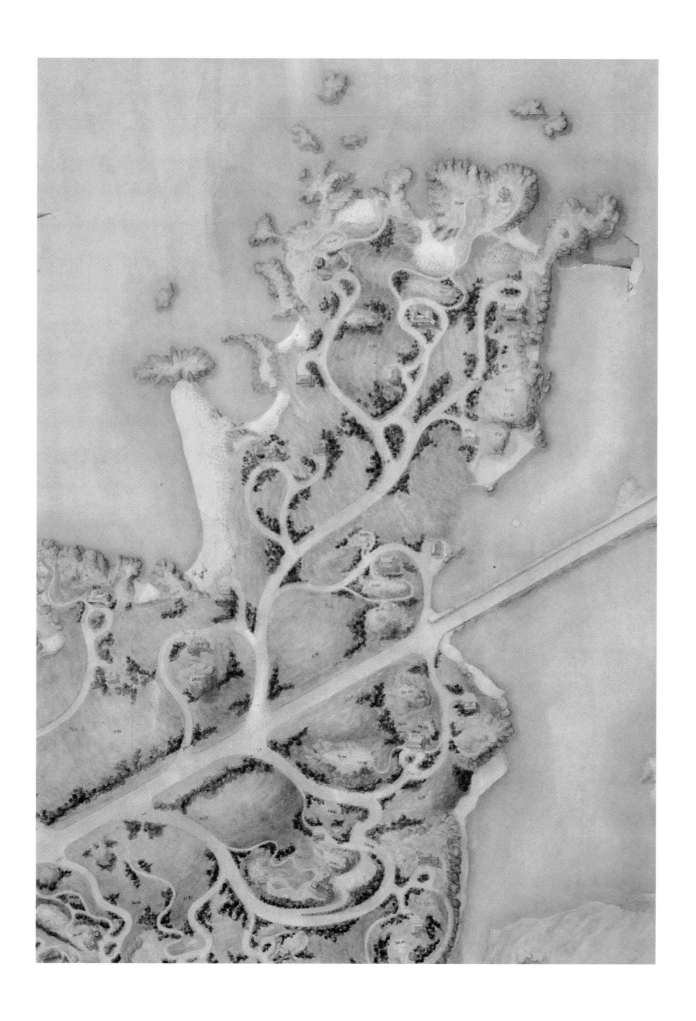

INTRODUCTION: America's Eden

John R. Tschirch

The Island is exceedingly pleasant and healthful . . . Travelers, with propriety, call it the Eden of America.
—Jedediah Morse on Newport and its environs, in *American Geography; or A View of the Present Situation of the United States* (1789)

Newport, Rhode Island, is an Edenic place in fact and fiction. Those who toiled in its soil and those who celebrated its scenery created a paradise both real and imagined. Generations of gardeners, horticulturists, arborists, and landscape architects and their patrons worked with a climate and topography offering conditions at times ideal—but more often challenging. Artists and writers have both documented and invented images of Newport's windswept cliffs, formal gardens, and collections of rare trees. The science-based facts of the botanist and the sense-driven imagery of the aesthete have each played their role as reality and illusion informed and inspired those who approached the landscape from various viewpoints. Time has left its marks upon the land. The result is a cultural landscape that reflects how humankind has shaped nature and how nature, in turn, has shaped humankind's creations.

The idea of Eden itself belies a specific perspective, a European concept projected onto the landscape of North America, proclaimed a New World by those who aimed to inhabit and amend it to serve their needs and appeal to their tastes.[1] This book examines how the act of forming the land in Newport and interpreting it through various art forms produced a physical and cultural record of a place proclaimed an earthly Eden. The idea is a complex and ever-changing one. Eden has its beauties, its bounties, and its boundaries. Every garden maker and landscape-shaper confronts the temptations and limitations of nature. The placement of each tree, plant, and shrub, the color of a flower bed, the contour of a garden path, and the precise cutting of a lawn is evidence of a decision made by a person, or persons, to address an immediate need and to express an aspiration in the pursuit of pleasure, power, or an assortment of other purposes. The scholar and writer Robert Pogue Harrison offers a philosophical view on this relationship between the natural world and our motivations for cultivating the earth:

Our human gardens may appear to us like little openings onto paradise in the midst of the fallen world. . . . History without gardens would be a wasteland. A garden severed from history would be superfluous. . . . The gardens that have graced this mortal Eden of ours are the best evidence of humanity's reason for being on Earth."[2]

Landscapes may be read as aesthetic values written on the land, felt as a manifestation of the human spirit, and gazed upon as the mirror of an age. In the end, however, try as the gardener

C.A. Thiebault, *Almy's Pond*, ca. 1875, pencil on paper
Private Collection

might to rule the earth, nature truly reigns supreme. Herein lies the tension in Newport, as in any landscape, between what is aspired to and what is achieved. Taste tempered by soil, sea, and weather directed the efforts of those who sought their version of Eden in Newport, a landscape bearing the imprint of beliefs, desires, and dreams, those motivating forces of cultural creativity that mark our presence on the earth through time. In 1789, when Jedediah Morse described Newport and the environs of Aquidneck Island as the "Eden of America" in one of the earliest geographies of the United States, it expressed a new nation's search for a compelling cultural identity rooted in its natural environment.[3]

The National Park Service defines a cultural landscape as "a geographic area, including both cultural and natural resources . . . associated with a historic event, activity or person, or exhibiting other cultural or aesthetic values."[4] Newport has these features in abundance. This book explores the character of Newport's landscape in both designed spaces and natural scenery; those who shaped it, from the local gardener to the renowned national designer; and its role as inspiration for works of art. The text and images reveal Newport's layers of history, from a rare eighteenth-century garden pavilion and Victorian arboreta to Gilded Age parterres and tree-lined streets. These natural and human-made features, and the ideas they represent, are documented in period maps, letters, drawings, and photographs and mythologized in paintings, poetry, and prose, comprising a picture of Newport's evolution as a cultural landscape.

A Land Blessed and Cursed

TOPOGRAPHY, GEOLOGY, AND CLIMATE

The air and climate of Newport are secure assets.
—Frederick Law Olmsted Jr., *Proposed Improvements for Newport, Rhode Island*, 1913

Blessed by its location on the southern tip of Aquidneck Island, warmed by the Gulf Stream, Newport is a verdant spot. The city is part of the Narragansett Basin ecosystem encompassing all lands bordering the bay and the eastern half of Rhode Island (Fig. 1). Over fourteen thousand years ago, glacial movements created Long Island, Long Island Sound, and Narragansett Bay. As glaciers retreated, they carved the land with the intense force of nature and the slow and steady act of erosion, leaving Aquidneck Island as a high point isolated among waterways with a configuration of hills, valleys, rocky coves and outcroppings, and coastal ponds.[5] These formations created the topography and microclimates that have dictated the types of agriculture, horticulture, landscape design, and tree propagation practiced for centuries (Fig. 2).

For all of the extolling of its virtues as an American Eden, Newport could justly be described as rich in seductive scenery but poor in fertile ground. This assessment, of course, is based on one's perspective. For the colonial era landowner, acreage was organized for the practical needs of food production. The protected harbor of Newport and a natural spring with its associated rivulets formed the center of the colonial city. Richer soils in the northern sector—including Broad Street, later renamed Broadway—and in the eastern sector—the present-day Bellevue Avenue, Kay-Catherine, and Ochre Point districts—allowed for abundant orchards and field crops. The rock-strewn terrain, exposed to the sea, in the southern part of the city did not lend itself to crop production but was prized as grazing land for sheep and cows during the seventeenth and eighteenth centuries (Figs. 3 and 4). This area is marked by a series of oval-shaped hills, called drumlins, composed of soils with a dense restrictive layer of the till material derived from the Narragansett Basin rocks, which are dark colored shales, sandstone, conglomerates of smaller rocks compacted into "pudding stones," and anthracite coal.[6] Newport's pink- to gray-colored granite is the most venerable of the coast's geological features, assessed as three hundred

Cliff Walk, ca. 1900,
photograph
Library of Congress

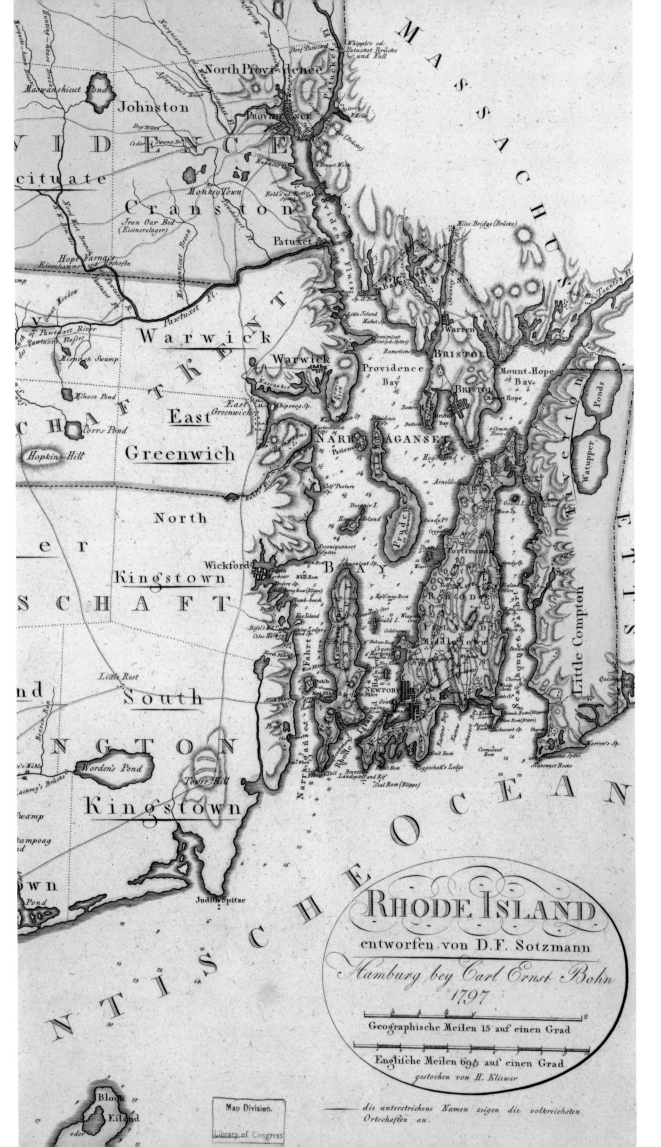

Fig. 1
D. F. Sotzmann,
Heinrich Kliewer,
and Carl Ernst Bohn,
Map of Rhode Island
(detail), 1797
Library of Congress

Fig. 2
John Collins, *Rocks near Purgatory*, ca. 1850, illustration
The Preservation Society of Newport County

overleaf:

Fig. 3 (top)
Map of the city, port and harbor of Newport (detail), 1780
Library of Congress

Fig. 4 (bottom)
Charles C. Hammett Jr., *Map of the Township of Newport, 1860* (detail
of south coastline)
Courtesy of Mr. and Mrs. S. Matthews V. Hamilton, Jr.

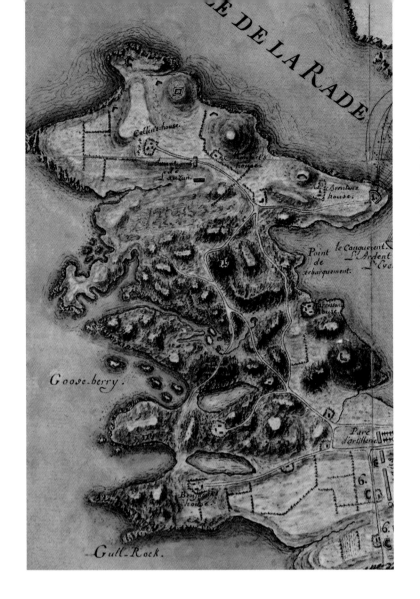

million years old, the remnants of the glacial period known as the Wisconsin.[7] The coastline known today as Ocean Avenue is a combination of granitic material and glacial till capping the rocks at various depths. Rolling hills in this region create several valleys with southerly openings warmed by the currents of the Gulf Stream. These hills present dramatic juxtapositions: the sides oriented toward the sea have barely any soil clinging to their rock faces, creating desert-like conditions, while the land-facing slopes overlooking secluded valleys offer protection to numerous forms of vegetation.

Nineteenth-century romantics valued this irregular windswept territory of glacial erratics (rocks left behind by glacial retreat) not for its soil, but for its picturesque views. Farms and open meadowlands made way for the construction of summer villas. The frequent sea mists nurtured lush lawns—once the right amount of topsoil was duly achieved, after enormous effort. Large-scale grading of the land made the grounds of many of the summer estates some of the most manipulated and reworked in the city (Figs. 5 and 6). Innovation and adaptability were required of any landscape designer working in the varying conditions of Newport. Trees from across the globe were often propagated in this

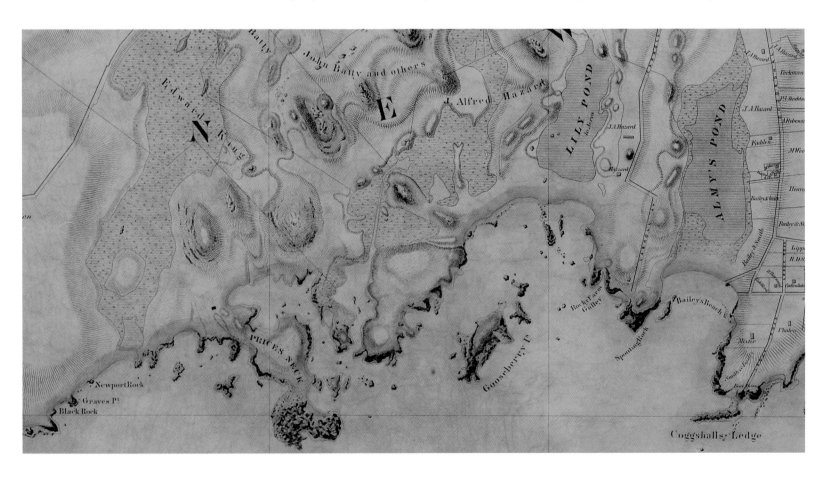

northern growing zone due to its temperate coastal conditions. Varieties of beech, in particular, thrived in this climate and became defining features of the landscape. Many gardeners proudly displayed their triumphs: an exotic cedar or a rare rose that could survive a New England winter.

The unique interface of untamed nature and landscaped artifice is distilled by the novelist Thomas Wentworth Higginson, who in his fiction recast Newport as Oldport, with the Cliff Walk as a prominent setting (Fig. 7):

Along our eastern cliffs it runs for some miles in the rear of beautiful estates, whose owners have seized on it, and graded it, and gravelled it, and made stiles for it, and done for it everything that landscape-gardening could do, while leaving it a footpath still. You walk there with croquet and roses on the one side, and with floating loons and wild ducks on the other.[8]

Fig. 5
Ocean-facing lawn,
Beechwood, ca. 1900,
photograph
Newport Historical Society, P96
Mrs. Astor's perfectly graded
lawn, a flat, manicured carpet
of green with potted plants,
frames views of the sea.

Fig. 6
Re-grading the lawn of Clarendon Court, 1973, photograph
Newport Historical Society, P109

Fig. 7
Cliff Walk, 1880, photograph
Newport Historical Society,
P1994

Mariana Griswold Van Rensselaer, one of the most prominent landscape critics of the late nineteenth century, diligently observed facts and promoted her theories of landscape architecture in her published writings on Newport, commenting, "The soil along the cliffs is, by nature, thin and poor so it requires an immense amount of care and money to make and keep these lawns, although the damp climate favors the work."[9]

The words of Higginson and Van Rensselaer capture the sensibilities of those who luxuriated and the successes of those who labored on the lawns, under the trees, and among the flowers and rocks. In this landscape of climatic and topographical blessings and curses, Eden would be created in various guises. Newport's natural environment provided the canvas, so to speak, upon which humankind expressed its artistic and cultural temper.

From Eden to Eternity
AN HISTORICAL OVERVIEW

A thousand delicate secret places . . . small, mild points and promontories, far away little lonely sandy coves, rock-set lily-sheeted ponds, almost hidden, and shallow Arcadian summer haunted valleys, with the sea just over some stony shoulder; a whole world that called out to the long afternoons of youth.
—Henry James, "The Sense of Newport," 1906

Newport has evolved over the centuries as a landscape both real and mythical. Henry James, inspired by the sense of place, crafted a precise description of the terrain and infused it with the power of personal reminiscences, imposing on it his image of a sublime arcadia and lost paradise. In "The Sense of Newport," (1906), the great novelist as mythmaker endowed Newport with human characteristics: purity, vanity, simplicity, longing, grandeur. He worked in an established tradition of settlers, builders, gardeners, arborists, landscape architects, artists, critics, and property owners, each of whom shaped the land and its art forms, directly or indirectly, according to their tastes, needs, and the cultural forces of their respective ages. As a result, Newport's landscapes present a panoramic view of the development of horticulture, floriculture, art, and design. Classicism and the pragmatic needs of the colonial era dictated the planning of gardens and the organization of orchard and field. Romanticism inspired the picturesque parklands of the Victorian age, while the fusion of the picturesque with a re-emerging classicism characterized the green spaces of the Gilded Age in both private and public places (Figs. 8–10).

Historically, Newport has been a cosmopolitan community with influences from far and wide. As a thriving colonial seaport, merchants had access to ideas and materials as part of a vast trading network within the British Empire. The art and culture of British North America derived its inspirations in landscape organization from a formal tradition established during the Italian Renaissance and interpreted by English architects, painters, and garden makers through the eighteenth century. Symmetry, geometric patterns, and the architectural and decorative language of Greek and Roman design, again adapted to English and then North American conditions, reigned in the garden. In Newport, as in most colonies of the eastern seaboard, the august principles of the orderly landscape in the classical manner shared space with the practical requirements of raising vegetables, herbs, and fruit. Establishing an empire on the edge of a new

Frances Benjamin Johnston,
Hammersmith Farm, 1917,
photograph
Library of Congress

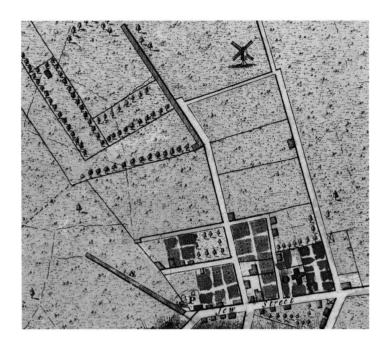

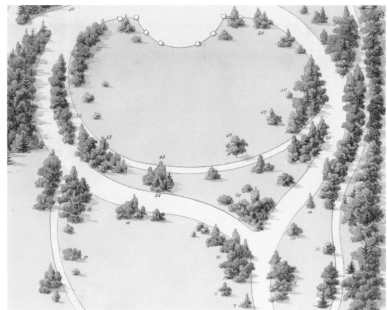

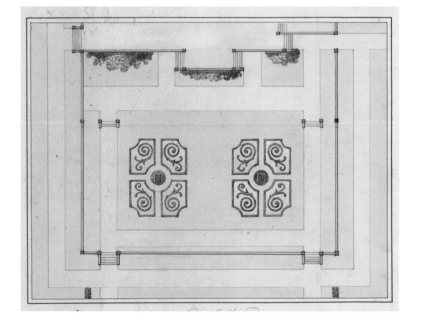

Fig. 8 (above left)
Charles Blaskowitz, *A Plan of the Town of Newport* (detail), 1777
Library of Congress
Gardens in a colonial grid format surround Redwood Library on Jew Street, renamed Bellevue Avenue in 1853.

Fig. 9 (above right)
Estate plan for Beaulieu (detail), from *Beautifying American Country Homes* (1870)
Redwood Library and Athenaeum
This landscape of serpentine lines is laid out in the mid-nineteenth-century picturesque manner.

Fig. 10 (right)
Olmsted, Olmsted and Eliot, Parterre design for Ochre Court, 1893
United States Department of the Interior, National Park Service, Frederick Law Olmsted National Historic Site
The geometric precision of the classical gardens of seventeenth-century France are revived in this Olmsted design.

frontier and across global shipping lanes did not always allow for the luxuries of ornamental horticulture, but Newport's increasing prosperity by the mid-eighteenth century did produce a number of elaborate gardens and an interest in the most current garden-related literature of the day. With the advent of the War of Independence, expert cartographers arrived with the British and French armies, crafting maps of extraordinary geographic detail. Newport at the end of the eighteenth century presented a largely deforested terrain, the result of clearance by the Narragansetts who had lived in the region for centuries, and the subsequent use of the land by European colonists for grazing livestock. This open, windswept topography with expansive views of the ocean set the stage for the next century, a period of new attitudes toward nature, plant collecting, and the meaning of the garden.

The shaping of the landscape in the Victorian age, when Newport rose to become one of the most fashionable seaside resorts in the nation, was defined by the aesthetics of Romanticism

and the realities of real estate speculation. Taste and emerging technologies both played their part in the creation of landscapes intended for the genteel pursuits of leisure. Under the guiding hand of the best-selling author and tastemaker Andrew Jackson Downing, the picturesque landscape would be firmly established in the national consciousness. The conception of nature as the source of beauty and virtue prevailed in the minds of right-thinking Victorians. Downing advocated for the asymmetrical arrangement of trees as central features in the landscape, and envisioned gardens as shadowy, evocative, mysterious places embowered in greenery (Fig. 11). The new technology of mowers and grass rollers produced velvety lawns, for which Newport became famous. The grounds of the summer cottages lining the newly established thoroughfares of Bellevue Avenue (1853) and Ocean Avenue (1867), both the product of Newport's real estate developers, adhered to Downing's landscape principles with their vine-covered trellises, brightly colored flower beds, and trees and plants labeled as "exotics" to appeal to increasing

Fig. 12
Edward Van Altena, Beech tree,
Chateau-sur-Mer, photograph,
ca. 1920
Archives of American Gardens

interest in world-wide collecting (Fig. 12). Newport emerged as a seasonal retreat where a coterie of landscape designers, among them Frederick Law Olmsted and his sons Frederick Jr. and John Charles, Charles Eliot, Ernest Bowditch, and Rose Standish Nichols, met, mingled, collaborated, and critiqued their evolving profession. Writers, such as Harriet Beecher Stowe, Henry James, and Edith Wharton, and painters, including John Frederick Kensett, William Trost Richards, Edward Mitchell Bannister, and Childe Hassam, used Newport's natural scenery and manicured grounds as subjects in their work, which elevated garden, meadow, and coastline from topographical fact to mythologized fiction (Fig. 13).

Much of Newport's nineteenth- and early twentieth-century landscape is inextricably linked to its buildings in the form of estate gardens. Frederick Law Olmsted understood the significance of viewing these sites as an integrated whole, advocating for the primacy of landscape in relation to architecture, writing, "Lord Bacon, three hundred years ago, sagaciously observed: 'God Almighty first planted a garden, and, indeed, it is the purest of human pleasures; it is the greatest of refreshment to the spirits of man, without which buildings and palaces are but gross handiworks.'"[10] This statement is an apt summary of the assertion of the significance of

Fig. 13
Childe Hassam, *Bailey's Beach*, 1901, oil on canvas
Walter H. Schulze Memorial Collection, Art Institute of Chicago

landscape as an art form and a call for it to claim its equal place alongside the practice of architecture. Newport became a rich repository of picturesque gardens serving as frames for an eclectic array of Victorian cottages, and the role of those who designed landscapes gained in prominence as the century progressed.

By the 1890s, a grandeur and opulence descended upon the city, its residents, its architecture, and its gardens. A new spirit and aesthetic sensibility emerged in the United States in the guise of the American Renaissance, a complex artistic and cultural firmament that aimed to recast the nation in the classical model of the Greco-Roman past. Fueled by the fortunes of the Gilded Age, America's financial elite and their architects searched for symbols of their newfound economic power. The villas of Roman emperors, the palazzos of the Medici, and the court of Versailles provided the sources for the imperial splendor of monumental stone houses built on Newport's cliffs and along Bellevue Avenue (Fig. 14). New approaches to landscape were required to integrate these classical structures with their natural settings and the social pageantry they were built to serve.

In support of Newport's flourishing estates, a vibrant community of gardeners fostered and maintained an extraordinary ensemble of landscapes, prompting the writer Lucius Davis to state, "America's great resort . . . is almost literally a city of gardens and flowers."[11] These

Fig. 15
Robert Yarnall Richie, John Jacob Astor's Chetwode estate, 1934, photograph
Robert Yarnall Richie Photograph Collection, Negative Series: 0595, DeGolyer Library, Southern Methodist University
Two forms of landscape design are illustrated in this aerial view: the asymmetrical picturesque plan of Stoneacre (top), created by Frederick Law Olmsted in a style that prevailed from the mid- to late nineteenth century; the straight lines of Chetwode (bottom), influenced by the classical aesthetics of Beaux Arts architecture and landscapes beginning in the 1890s and continuing through the early 1900s. Both houses and landscapes were demolished by the late twentieth century.

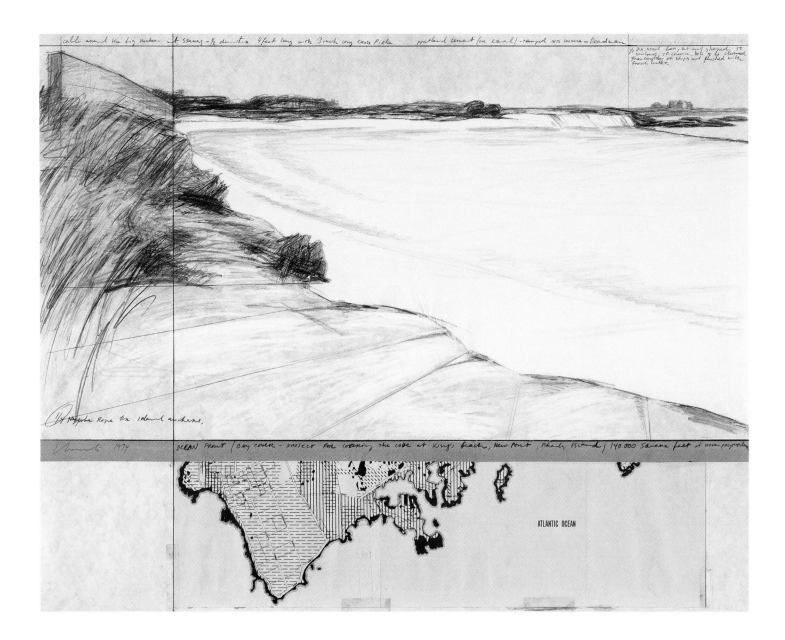

Fig. 16
Christo and Jeanne-Claude,
Ocean Front Project (Bay
Cover—Project for Covering
the Cove at King's Beach,
Newport, Rhode Island), 1974,
collage, fabric, pencil, charcoal,
crayon, and cardboard,
56 × 71 cm (22 × 28 in.)
Private collection, Photo
Archive: Estate of Christo V.
Javacheff
This installation was created
for the *Monumenta* exhibition
of 1974 featuring the abstract
works of leading modern
artists.

words were written in 1899, the year of the founding of the American Society of Landscape Architects by the professionals who had created many of Newport's gardens. Their work would be recorded by pioneering artists of photography who documented this city of greenery in the twentieth century. Photographers Frances Benjamin Johnston, Mattie Edwards Hewitt, Edward Van Altena, and Robert Yarnall Richie each turned their artful eye on the estates of Newport from the early 1900s through the 1950s (Fig. 15). They captured gardens at the height of their glory, producing images of both beauty and utility, delighting the viewer and aiding the historian and preservationist of now lost or time-worn landscapes.

In terms of garden making, the mid-twentieth century appeared to ignore Newport or relegate it to the past. In his *Modern Gardens*, Peter Shepheard wrote of the city as "a seaside resort of roses and marble, familiar to Europeans through the work of Edith Wharton and Henry James; beautiful old gardens abound, and the soft climate is especially kind to vegetation."[12] The author was not intentionally derogatory, but he appropriately framed Newport's

Fig. 17
H. D. Perkins, Mary Street,
1913, photograph
The photograph was part of a
series of streetscapes for the
Olmsted Brothers' *Improvement
Plan for Newport* (1913)
United States Department of
the Interior, National Park
Service, Frederick Law Olmsted
National Historic Site

landscapes as historic, left to simmer in a golden leafy dream. Modernism, however, came to call in its own way. Artists, once again, played their part in reinterpreting the landscape for a new age. The *Monumenta* exhibition of 1974 set large-scale works of abstract sculpture on Newport's rocky shores and in its gardens, a juxtaposition of history and modernity, nature and art (Fig. 16). Fleeting it may have been, but modernism had its moment in the eternal slumber of Newport's natural scenery.

The centuries have left their legacy on the topography of the city. Preserved gardens and trees, remembered gardens and trees—they persist as green spaces the viewer can experience in the present, or encounter in the past through the written word and the artist's brush and photograph (Fig. 17). Newport hosts a landscape of natural and cultural evolution, of design, horticulture, art, and literature. The hand of humankind has made its mark, with nature's assistance in some instances, and its defiance in others. In each case, the story is one of humanity and its relationship with the land.

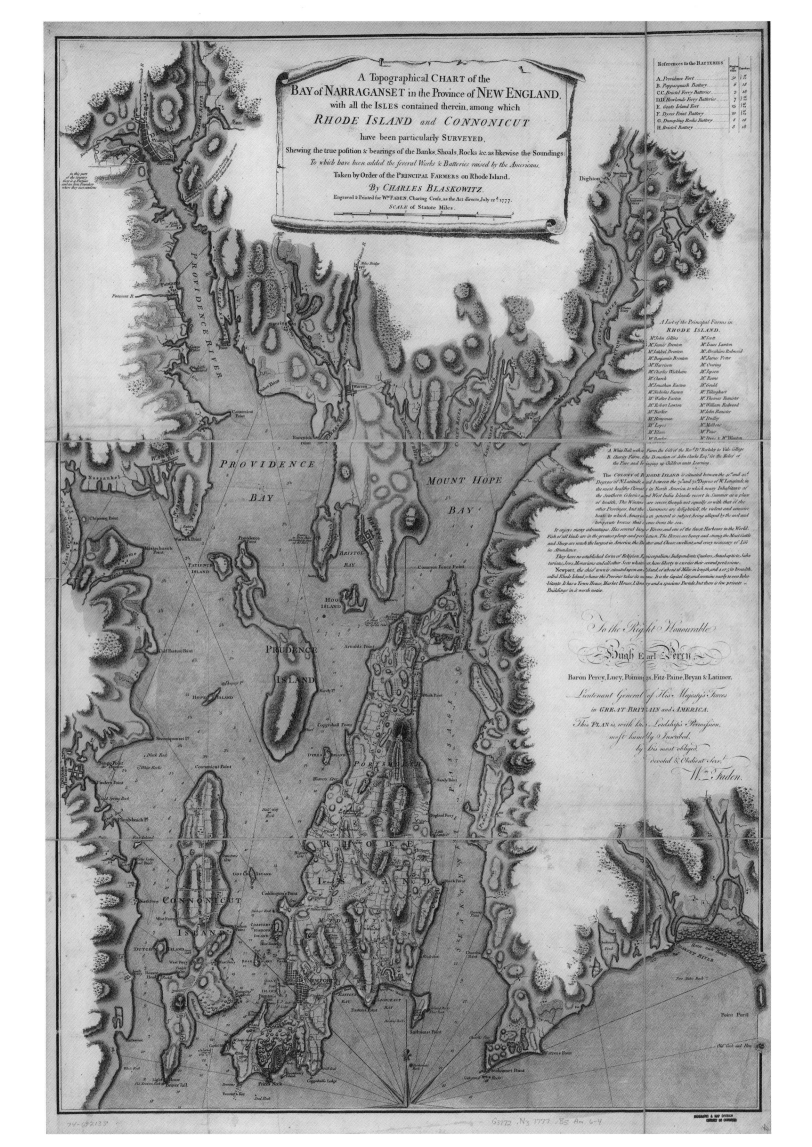

A Topographical CHART of the
BAY of NARRAGANSET in the Province of NEW ENGLAND,

with all the ISLES contained therein, among which

RHODE ISLAND and CONNONICUT

have been particularly SURVEYED,

Shewing the true position & bearings of the Banks, Shoals, Rocks &c. as likewise the Soundings:

To which have been added the several Works & Batteries raised by the Americans.

Taken by Order of the PRINCIPAL FARMERS on Rhode Island.

By CHARLES BLASKOWITZ.

Engraved & Printed for Wm FADEN, Charing Cross, as the Act directs July 22d 1777.

SCALE of Statute Miles.

References to the BATTERIES

A. Providence Fort
B. Pappasquash Battery
CC. Bristol Ferry Batteries
DD. Howlands Ferry Batteries
E. Goats Island Fort
F. Dyers Point Battery
G. Dumpling Rocks Battery
H. Bristol Battery

A List of the Principal Farms in
RHODE ISLAND.

Mr. John Collins
Mr. James Brenton
Mr. Jahleel Brenton
Mr. Benjamin Brenton
Mr. Harrison
Mr. Charles Wickham
Mr. Church
Mr. Jonathan Easton
Mr. Nicholas Easton
Mr. Walter Easton
Mr. Robert Lawton
Mr. Barker
Mr. Honyman
Mr. Lopez
Mr. Ellery
Mr. Bowler

Mr. Scott
Mr. Isaac Lawton
Mr. Abraham Redwood
Mr. James Potter
Mr. Overing
Mr. Jepson
Mr. Rome
Mr. Gould
Mr. Tillinghart
Mr. Thomas Banister
Mr. William Redwood
Mr. John Banister
Mr. Dudley
Mr. Malbone
Mr. Prior
Mr. Davis & Mr. Wanton

A. White Hall, with a Farm, the Gift of the Rev'd Dr. Berkley to Yale College
B. Charity Farm, the Donation of John Clarke Esq'r for the Relief of the Poor and bringing up Children unto Learning.

The COLONY of RHODE ISLAND is situated between the 41st and 42d Degree of N. Latitude, and between the 71st and 72d Degrees of W. Longitude; in the most healthy Climate in North America, to which many Inhabitants of the Southern Colonies and West India Islands resort in Summer as a place of health. The Winters are severe, though not equally so with that of the other Provinces, but the Summers are delightfull, the violent and excessive heats to which America in general is subject, being allayed by the cool and temperate breezes that come from the sea.

It enjoys many advantages. Has several large Rivers, and one of the finest Harbours in the World. Fish of all kinds are in the greatest plenty and perfection. The Horses are boney and strong, the Meat Cattle and Sheep are much the largest in America, the Butter and Cheese excellent, and every necessary of Life in Abundance.

They have no established forms of Religion, Episcopalians, Independents, Quakers, Anabaptists, Sabatarians, Jews, Moravians and all other Sects whatever, have liberty to exercise their several professions.

Newport, the chief town is situated upon an Island, of about 16 Miles in length, and 4 or 5 in breadth, called Rhode Island, whence the Province takes its name. It is the Capital City, and contains nearly 12000 Inhabitants. It has a Town House, Market House, Library and a spacious Parade, but there is few private Buildings in it worth notice.

To the Right Honourable

Hugh Earl Percy,

Baron Percy, Lucy, Poinings, Fitz-Paine, Bryan & Latimer,

Lieutenant General of His Majesty's Forces

in GREAT BRITAIN and AMERICA.

This PLAN is, with his Lordship's Permission,
most humbly Inscribed,
by his most obliged,
devoted & Obedient Serv't
Wm. Faden.

PROVIDENCE RIVER

PROVIDENCE
BAY

MOUNT HOPE
BAY

WARWICK

PRUDENCE
ISLAND

PATIENCE
ISLAND

HOPE ISLAND

CONNONICUT
ISLAND

PORTSMOUTH

RHODE ISLAND

MIDDLETON

Newport

Dighton

Paradise of New England
THE COLONIAL ERA AND EARLY REPUBLIC

It enjoys many advantages. Has several large Rivers and one of the finest Harbours in the World. Fish of all kinds are in the greatest plenty and perfection . . . the Meat Cattle and Sheep are much the largest in America, the Butter and Cheese excellent, and every necessary of Life in Abundance.

—Charles Blaskowitz, *A Topographical Chart of the Bay of Narragansett*, 1777

Newport's primeval landscape—the original Eden, if you will—can only be imagined, for there is no written or visual record. The earliest known European account of Newport and its environs attests not to a virgin wilderness but to a pastoral setting, one of established farming and open meadowlands. When Giovanni da Verrazzano, an Italian explorer on a mission for His Majesty, Francois I, King of France, sailed into the harbor he described as "Porto di Refugio" in 1524, he wrote of Aquidneck Island,

> *We reached a land . . . and found it as pleasant as I can possibly describe, and suitable for every kind of cultivation—grain, wine or oil. For these fields extend for XXV to XXX leagues, they are open and free of any obstacles or trees, and so fertile that any kind of seed would produce excellent crops.*[13]

The Narragansetts, who occupied the island at the time of da Verrazzano's observations, managed the natural resources; they created no permanent built settlements, but they methodically and systematically cultivated the land. The abundant variety of tree and plant life unknown to Europeans was duly noted.

> *On entering the woods, we observed they might be traversed by an army ever so numerous. The trees of which they were composed were oaks, cypresses and others unknown in Europe. We found also apples, plums, filiberts and many other fruits, but all of a different kind from ours.*[14]

Charles Blaskowitz,
A Topographical Chart of the Bay of Narragansett, 1777
Library of Congress

Over a century after da Verrazzano sailed away, colonists from nearby Massachusetts purchased the right from the Narragansetts, in 1639, to found a permanent settlement on the southern portion of Aquidneck Island, at the place they named "Newport," where they established themselves upon terrain that had already been cleared and tilled, at the site of a natural spring at the present-day juncture of Spring and Touro Streets.[15] Immediately, the colonists organized the land on a European model, implementing a town council ordinance to lay out Thames Street along the harbor and Spring Street to its east. They also provided common land at present-day Marlborough Street, and Reverend John Clarke deeded acreage on the outskirts of the town center in 1655 to serve as the burying ground.[16] Salem and Boston, Massachusetts (1626 and 1630); New Haven, Connecticut (1638); and Bristol, Rhode Island (1680), were a few examples of seventeenth-century New England coastal towns that had similarly designated land for communal use, though, like Newport, their political, economic, and social systems were otherwise focused on private property.

Outside of the main town settlement, the founding colonists acquired large tracts of land. William Brenton's property encompassed the southern portion of Newport from Narragansett Bay on the west to Almy's Pond on the east, Nicholas Easton owned lands on the Point and on the western edge of Easton's Pond, and Benjamin Church held over three hundred acres extending from Rough Point to Ochre Point.[17] Elizabeth Brenton, in her family reminiscences, described William Brenton's approximately two thousand acres, with grazing lands on the exposed south coast, and fields and orchards on the protected west- and north-facing acreage of Hammersmith Farm, which possessed the

> *richest soil, and presently the most picturesque scenery, diversified with hills, valleys, bays, and ponds, fields adorned with the most luxuriant grass, jutting rocks fringed with rich foliage, mingled with wildflowers, trees of superior growth, the hemlock, spruce and cedar, the oak, maple and chestnut, crowned the summit of hills.[18]*

With the exception of Brenton's Hammersmith Farm, much of the land had poor soil and, as a result, the agricultural economy of Newport evolved toward the raising of livestock. This resulted in the further deforestation of the southern section of Aquidneck Island and the desire to invest in additional grazing land on Conanicut Island across from the harbor.[19] Newport's landowners adapted their agricultural practices to suit the inherent quality of their acreage, but who labored on this land? Who toiled to create this bountiful Eden? Both large- and modest-scale farms coexisted in Newport. There was a working agricultural community, but it was small compared to the number of residents involved in maritime-related trades and businesses, according to the 1774 census.[20] As a major port in the brutal transatlantic slave trade, Newport was home to enslaved African and African Americans as well as a large number of Native Americans, but most were engaged in crafts or household duties.[21] Newport's colonial-era splendor—its architecture, landscape, art, and culture—was funded by the city's integral role as a commercial center predominantly linked to the enslavement of Africans. Within this community focused on commercial riches, Caesar Lyndon, enslaved by Governor Joseph

Lyndon of Newport, left his own mid-eighteenth-century record of working on the land in an entrepreneurial spirit:

> *November 24th, 1765 sold ½ bushel beets to Cudjo Wanton for £2 0' 0'*
> *December 17th, 1765*
>
> *Friday, June 27th 1766 put five bunches turnups in the market house to sell for Neptune*
>
> *Wednesday, October 29th, 1766 sold 150 roots celery to Aaron Lopez*
> *November 22nd, 1766*
>
> *May 4th, 1769 Caesar finished planting beets in Esq. Ellery's garden*
>
> *Tuesday, May 2nd 1769. Caesar and Hammond hired Mr. Christopher Ellery's garden. What Caesar planted was for ½ the produce at four dollars annum also the same Tuesday paid 8£0 for plowing the same lot.*[22]

Caesar brokered produce at the Brick Market and rented land to supply his own vegetables for sale.[23] After gaining freedom, he and his contemporaries resided in the same landscape as other Newporters, though their daily lives were centered around different places.

> *The Euro American cultural landscape likely focused on areas of market, worship and social interaction for Euro Americans. And although "black" and "white" landscapes intersected in complex ways, the African American cultural landscape was different from Euro American landscape and likely focused on fringes of town, which were the enclaves of home-owning African Americans.*[24]

The fringes of town in the eighteenth century were at present-day West Broadway, to the north, and Pope Street, to the south. Not all residents of Newport were able to define the land in the same manner. Wealthy Euro Americans built houses, laid out gardens, and planted trees. African American and Native Americans, even those who prospered and owned property, did not have the ability to put their imprint upon the earth with the same prominence as their Euro American counterparts. The legacy of racial injustice and social inequality is evident in the absence of physical marks on the landscape made by communities of color.

The northern sector of Newport (Figs. 18 and 19) had far richer soil and became the primary source of produce. By the eighteenth century, most inhabitants turned their attentions to maritime activities and crafts as the city became one of the major seaports of British colonial North America. Many merchants invested their wealth in country estates in the northern sector of Newport and throughout Aquidneck Island. For example, Metcalf Bowler had a house on

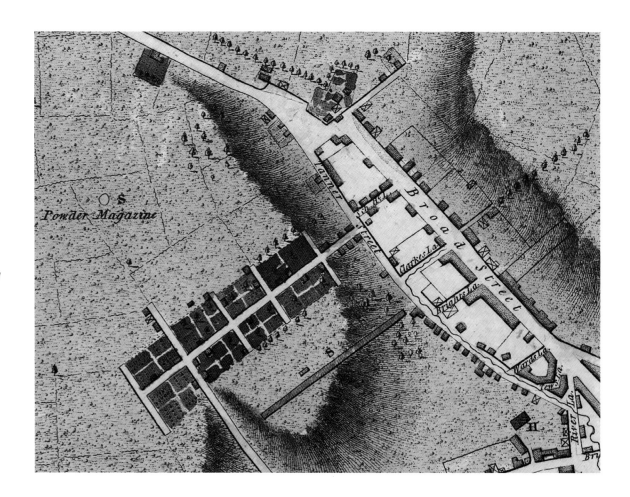

Fig. 18 (right)
Charles Blaskowitz, *A Plan of the Town of Newport* (detail), 1777
Library of Congress
The landscape elements in New Towne, indicated by the dark green grids (left), illustrate the symmetry of eighteenth-century garden plots.

Fig. 19 (below)
Map of the city, port, and harbor of Newport (detail), 1780
Library of Congress
Note the orderly arrangement of trees to define the landscape.

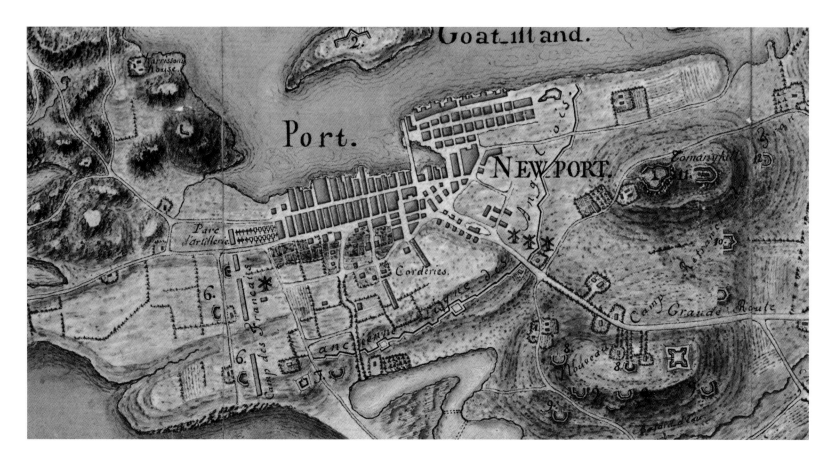

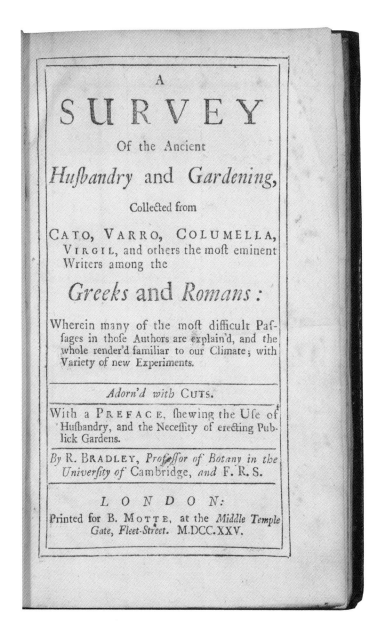

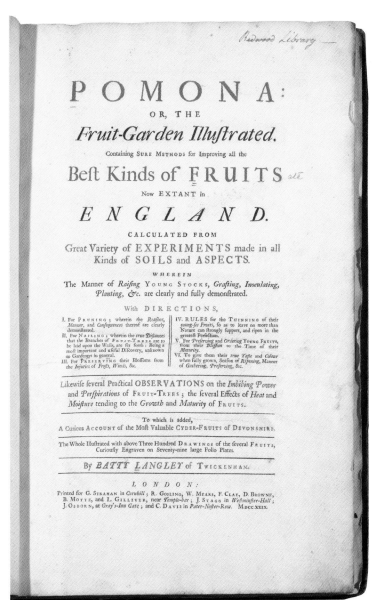

Clarke Street in Newport and large landholdings in Portsmouth, which the Reverend Manasseh Cutler visited on August 16, 1778, and recorded in his diary:

> went in the afternoon with a number of officers to view a garden . . . belonging to one Mr. Bowler, — the finest by far I ever saw . . . contains four acres, has a grand aisle in the middle and its adorned in the front with beautiful carvings. Near the middle is an oval, surrounded with espaliered fruit trees, in the center of which is a pedestal, on which is an armillary sphere, with an equatorial dial. On one side of the front is a hot-house, containing orange trees, some ripe, some green, some blooms, and various other fruit trees of the exotic kind, curious flowers, etc. . . . There are espalieres of fruit trees at each end of the garden.[25]

The classical outlines and presence of fruit trees in Metcalf Bowler's garden were in keeping with seventeenth- and early eighteenth-century British garden planning. These ideas

Fig. 20 (above left)
Title page from Richard Bradley, *A Survey of the Ancient Husbandry and Gardening* (1725)
Redwood Library and Athenaeum

Fig. 21 (above right)
Title page from Batty Langley, *Pomona: Or, the Fruit-Garden Illustrated* (1729)
Redwood Library and Athenaeum

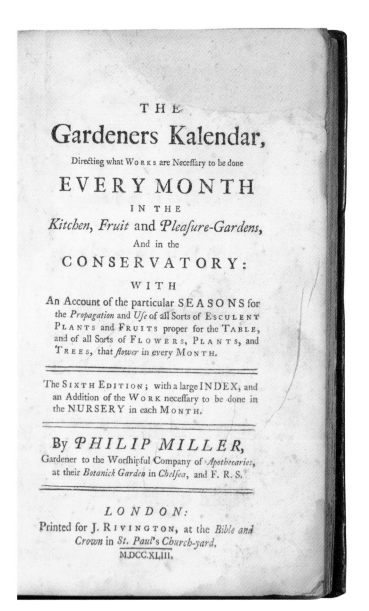

may have been transmitted to the colonies simply by memory or by the common horticultural practices of recent arrivals from England, but there is another vital source for landscape forms and functions in colonial Newport. Books were an essential feature in the visual arts of the age, whether in architecture, furniture, or landscape, and Newport housed its volumes in an august manner. In 1748, the Company of the Redwood Library commissioned architect Peter Harrison to design their new building, located on the former bowling green of the merchant and patron of the arts Henry Collins. The Neo-Palladian-style temple front of this landmark of Western classicism on the shores of North America contained in its original inventory four volumes related to horticulture and garden planning (Figs. 20–23). Among them is Richard Bradley's *A Survey of the Ancient Husbandry and Gardening* (1725), which opens with a description invoking the authority of the classical world:

> *A survey of the ancient husbandry and gardening, collected from Cato, Varro, Columella, Virgil, and others the most eminent writers among the Greeks and Romans: wherein many of the most difficult passages in those authors are explain'd, and the whole render'd familiar to our climate; with variety of new experiments. Adorn'd with cuts. With a preface, shewing the use of husbandry, and the necessity of erecting publick gardens.*[26]

Pomona, or the Fruit-Garden Illustrated (1729) by Batty Langley offered the most current methods of cultivation practiced in England, "the whole illustrated with above three hundred drawings of the several fruits, curiously engraven on seventy-nine large folio plates."[27] Also a leader in the production of architectural pattern books, Langley provided models in his publications that were highly popular in the British colonies. Practical gardening advice was provided in the *Gardeners Dictionary* (1743) and the *Gardeners Kalendar* (1743), both by Philip Miller, gardener to the Worshipful Society of Apothecaries at their Physic Garden in Chelsea, the preeminent center of plant collecting, located on what was at the time the outskirts of London. Both books illustrate archetypal garden plans with four rectangular beds centered upon a sundial, reflecting pool, or fountain, serving as models for Newport. The *Gardeners Dictionary* explained "the methods of cultivating and improving the kitchen, fruit and flower garden, and also, the physick garden," while the *Gardeners Kalendar* directed the reader to relevant tasks on a monthly basis, "in the kitchen, fruit and pleasure-gardens, and the conservatory: with an account of the particular seasons for the propagation and use of all sorts of esculent [excellent] plants and fruits proper for the table, and

Fig. 22 (above)
Title page from Philip Miller,
The Gardeners Kalendar (1743)
Redwood Library and
Athenaeum

Fig. 23 (opposite)
Frontispiece from Philip Miller,
The Gardeners Kalendar (1743)
Redwood Library and
Athenaeum
Gods call upon each other
while cherubs tend topiary and
gardeners prepare plots and
trim trees.

THE GARDENER'S KALENDAR.

J. Pine. Sculp:

all sorts of flowers, plants and trees, every month."[28] All of these books are a window onto the taste and practices of the age that influenced Newport's landscapes.

The abundance of flowers and fruits displayed by Newport's merchants in their garden beds and upon their tables revealed their access to a variety of plants due, in great part, to their trading connections with Europe and the Caribbean. Abraham Redwood's country estate in Portsmouth featured a rich bounty, according to one account (Fig. 24):

In it grows all sorts of West Indian fruit, viz Oranges, Lemons, Limes, Pine-Apples and Tamarinds, and other sorts. It also has West India flowers . . . and a fine Summer House. . . . It has Hot Houses where things that are tender are put in winter, and Hot Beds for the West India fruit. I saw one or two of these gardens in coming from the beach.[29]

Redwood employed Charles Dunham as his gardener, who also conducted his own business in seeds and garden supplies on Thames Street in the 1760s and 70s.[30] No colonial-era urban gardens survive, but the role of flowers in the home is evident in Newport's household inventories, which are filled with porcelain and earthenware vessels; the inventory of Joseph Jacob, for example, cites "one great earthenware flower pot" in the "Great Parlor."[31]

Not only did Newporters enjoy the beauty and bounty of their garden flowers and produce in the sitting rooms and dining parlors of their houses, but the privileged few could create a building wholly devoted to nature. Abraham Redwood built a pavilion on his Portsmouth estate, a rare survivor of this colonial type, today located on the grounds of the Redwood Library and Athenaeum in Newport. The octagonal structure with an eight-part bell-shaped roof features wood surfacing carved with beveled edges to simulate stone blocks. In keeping with tastes in English garden architecture, the builder based the summer house on Plate 28 in James Gibbs's *A Book of Architecture* (1728), one of the most influential pattern books in the colonies (Fig. 25). Beginning in the early 1700s with the Temple of the Four Winds (designed in 1724) at Castle Howard in Yorkshire and the garden follies (circa 1730) of William Kent for Lord Burlington's Chiswick House near London, the classically inspired garden pavilion became established as part of the English landscape. The Redwood summer house is a superlative example of high fashion in garden architecture interpreted through English pattern books (Fig. 26). In a colonized land where survival and sustenance were priorities, the Redwood summer house is evidence of increasing stability, wealth, desire for luxury, and leisure to indulge in the aesthetic appreciation of nature.

From town to country, in letters and books, the propagation of fruit and flowers prompted horticultural invention and a love of display in Newport. This sense of extravagant show is most apparent in the remains of Malbone, a rural estate in Newport's northern sector offering a rare instance of the evolution of a landscape from the colonial period through the early years of the Republic. In 1741, Godfrey Malbone began construction of a large house on his country estate near Miantonomi Hill. Dr. Alexander Hamilton visited in 1744 and wrote in his *Itinerarium*, "Round it are pretty gardens and terraces with canals and basons for water, wence you have a delightful view of the town and harbour of Newport with the shipping lying there."[32] Surviving earthworks are evidence of the existence of formal gardens in the eighteenth century, laid out in a series of terraces leading to a garden plot set in four squares around water channels. Symmetry and the modeling of the land to conform to an overall geometric plan attest to a classical European garden sensibility. James Birket, visiting in 1750, commented, "upon the surface of the Earth before the house is a Handsome Garden with variety of wall fruits And flowers &c: this house and Garden is reckoned the wonder of that part of the country not being Such another in this Government."[33]

Fig. 24 (opposite, top)
Roselle McConnell, Gilded pineapple in the pediment of Colony House, 2020, photograph
Visitors arriving on Long Wharf, on a main axis with the Colony House (1741) at the heart of Newport's main urban square, were greeted with the superbly carved golden pineapple, an exotic fruit from the Caribbean and a symbol of the city's commercial wealth.

Fig. 25 (opposite, bottom)
Plate 28 from James Gibbs, *A Book of Architecture* (1728)
Redwood Library and Athenaeum

Fig. 26 (below)
Abraham Redwood garden house, 2020, photograph
Redwood Library and Athenaeum

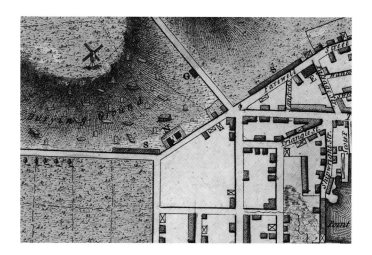

Malbone and its fellow country estates, the fine horticultural books of the Redwood Library, and the rich grazing lands and orchards of landholders such as the Brenton, Easton, and Church families illustrate the prosperity and cultural richness of Newport by the mid-eighteenth century. One feature in the landscape, a tree at the corner of Thames and Farewell Streets, served as a potent symbol of things to come. In 1766, Captain William Read deeded a plot of land, including a mature buttonwood tree, to William Ellery and Newport's Sons of Liberty in response to the Stamp Act (1765) protests that swept through the colonies. In Boston, the Sons of Liberty had first gathered under an elm tree on the city's common, and this sparked a trend that was followed in Newport, Charleston, Philadelphia, and other cities. Captain Read's deed (Figs. 27 and 28) for his Newport land stated, "The said tree forever and hereafter be known as the Tree of Liberty, and that the same stand as a Monument of the Spirited and Noble Opposition made to the Stamp Act in the year One Thousand seven hundred and Sixty-five, by the Sons of Liberty."[34] The British cut down the first Liberty Tree, which Newporters replaced with an oak in 1783, the year the Treaty of Paris concluded the War of Independence. As that tree aged, it was replaced by another oak in 1860 and by a fernleaf beech in 1897 (Fig. 29). The beech tree, which still stands today, and the plot of ground was deeded to the City of Newport by Henrietta Ellery in 1919.[35]

The designation of Newport's Liberty Tree constituted an act of defiance and a defense of the right to freedom—though it did not symbolize liberty for all in the city. At this tree, enslaved and free Africans and African Americans assembled to observe seasonal celebrations, events that preserved cultural ties while in bondage or living within a society that withheld full equal rights.[36] Across from this living tree is a parcel of land that caters to other aspects of life. The Common Burying Ground, established in the mid-seventeenth century on the outskirts of the colonial settlement, is a landscape of eternal rest with superbly carved gravestones, one of the earliest art forms in colonial America. Within this cemetery is a section called "God's Little Acre," one of the oldest known burying places of enslaved and free Africans and African Americans in the United States.[37] Many of the stones commemorating men bear names inspired by Roman generals and orators—Cesar, Cato, Scipio, and Pompe—while such names rarely applied to women, who were often named for flowers.[38] The male names reflect the same classical Greco-Roman imprint evident in the architecture, urban plan, literature, and gardens imposed upon Newport by European colonists. Pompe Stevens, enslaved and working for the John Stevens stonecutting

shop, created the gravestone of his brother Cuffe Gibbs, and many others as well. These stones are some of the oldest hand-crafted objects in the Newport landscape, cultural emblems of the history of enslavement and human persistence in adverse conditions, to develop and practice skills, and to produce art that honors a people in place and time.

The War of Independence radically altered the economic prominence of Newport, no longer a major seaport as nearby Providence had bypassed it in commercial strength. Many of the country estates fell into disrepair through benign neglect or were subdivided into smaller farms. At Malbone, the house had burned to the ground, but in the overgrown landscape there could still be seen the relic of its formal gardens, which took on the mantle of a colonial-era curiosity and a destination for visitors, one noting in 1784,

I went to see a garden a mile distant from the town belonging to Mr. John Malbone . . . The garden is very large and well arranged, with a pretty bathing pool and many and excellent fruit trees, but it is entirely neglected. For 9 pennies or half . . . one can go into it to walk where one pleases and take all the fruits one wants.[39]

While English gardens evolved from formal, axial plans to the serpentine lines of the picturesque in the early 1700s, the gardens of the American colonies generally adhered to a linear, ordered classical formula. Arriving in the United States in the 1790s, the English architect Benjamin Henry Latrobe noted,

Fig. 27 (opposite, top)
Charles Blaskowitz, *A Plan of the Town of Newport* (detail), 1777
Library of Congress
The Liberty Tree is indicated at the tip of the triangle on Farewell Street.

Fig. 28 (opposite, bottom)
Deed of the Liberty Tree, 1766
Newport Historical Society, 2016.073.001

Fig. 29 (above)
Liberty Tree, ca. 1890, photograph
Newport Historical Society, P8788

In America we have been, in our taste in Gardening, a little behind our scale of improvement in other respects. Til very lately we still loved straight unshaded Walks, and called them a Garden, and the few Trees about our dwellings which escaped the axe, we robbed of their best property—that of shading us from the scorching sun. The rage of trimming our trees still subsists.[40]

The earthworks of Malbone, representing the outline of its strict, geometrically arranged garden, illustrate the traditional and classical orientation of colonial Newport landscapes. As this once-grand country estate faded, an already historic piece of land in the bustling center of town became part of Newport's first urban square focused on greenery. Originally known as the "Parade," the open lot between the spring and the harbor was renamed in honor of George Washington after the War of Independence. The earliest depictions of the space in maps by Ezra Stiles in 1758 and Charles Blaskowitz in 1777 defined the triangular shape but gave no account of plantings, since the area

Fig. 30
Unidentified artist, Trees on Washington Square (detail), painting, 1818
Newport Historical Society, 94.4.1

was not originally envisioned as a garden. The builders of cities in British North America did not generally seek to create urban forests.[41] Commerce reigned in Newport's city plan, a complex of wharves and buildings abutting the streets with no room for tree-lined thoroughfares or parks. Space on private property was limited to side yards and kitchen gardens, but, to date, no archaeological or written evidence exists that would allow us to fully reconstruct their appearance. In rare circumstances, colonial American cities were centered around green spaces, such as the malls of Williamsburg, Virginia (1699), and the squares of Savannah, Georgia (1733). In Britain, London's garden squares were the work of land-owning aristocrats speculating in terraced housing; its parks evolved from royal hunting grounds turned over to public access at the will of the sovereign. The masterful connection of green urban spaces with views of the countryside in Bath during the mid-1700s introduced nature to the city in an integrated manner, but this would not influence American urban design until later in the century. Rows of trees, columnar and regular, line the triangular turf of Washington Square in Newport in a painting of 1818, a sign that the city had an early urban green space (Figs. 30 and 31). While the exact species cannot be determined from the picture, elms do appear on that same spot in a photograph of circa 1860. These stately trees could well be the mature version of those in the painting of forty years earlier.

The once generally barren streets of colonial-era cities and towns were being lined with trees by the late eighteenth century, and Washington Square is a prime example. Serving both to beautify and provide shade, trees were beginning to be considered assets in the urban environment.[42]

The town gardens, farms, orchards, grazing meadows, and country estates of the colonial period are largely buried under the surface of modern Newport. Few physical remains are left, but the aesthetics and practices of colonial-era gardening and land use survive in the written word: in horticultural books, in the legal deeds for land transactions, and in the letters and reminiscences of visitors and the descendants of garden makers. These documents reconstruct a view of the tastes and techniques at work in the colonial landscape, one that combined classical inspiration with contemporary function. Open meadowlands and newly planted urban trees at the close of the eighteenth century formed a legacy for the next century. The meadows would serve as the blank canvas for summer villas and gardens; trees would arise as treasured objects and visual focal points. Newport's landscape came to host a vision of Eden in the nineteenth century to suit the tastes and cultural temperament of a new age in which the rational geometries and bright sun of the classical mind bowed to the mysterious serpentine lines and moody shadows of the romantic spirit.

Fig. 31
Elm trees in Washington Square, ca. 1860, photograph Newport Historical Society, P2380
The mature trees in this image were most likely planted in the late eighteenth or early nineteenth century, as indicated in a painting of the square in 1818 (see Fig. 30).

CASE STUDY

SEEING, OR RECORDING, THE LAND

Changing Perspectives on Mapping Newport

Christina Connett Brophy

Senior Director of Museum Galleries and Senior Vice President
of Curatorial Affairs, Mystic Seaport Museum

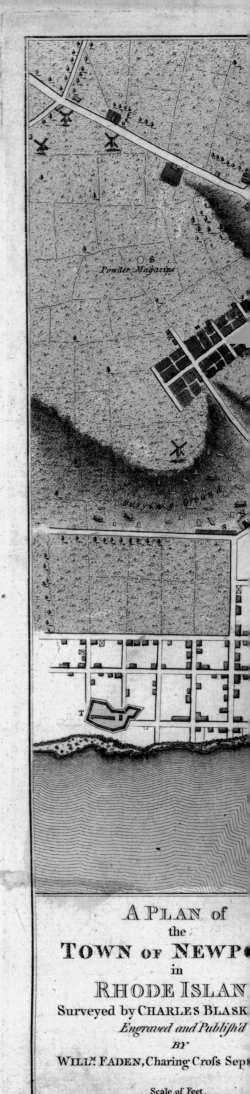

Fig. 32
Charles Blaskowitz, *A Plan of the Town of Newport*, 1777
Library of Congress
This map was part of the systematic mapping program by the British
government to exploit and manage resources and military control
of its colonies. The emphasis on the harbor indicates the importance
of the town as a maritime port and positions the viewer as if
approaching from the sea. Trees are used to delineate domesticated
green spaces, but the absence of wilderness marks this as a map
focused on the human presence on the land.

50

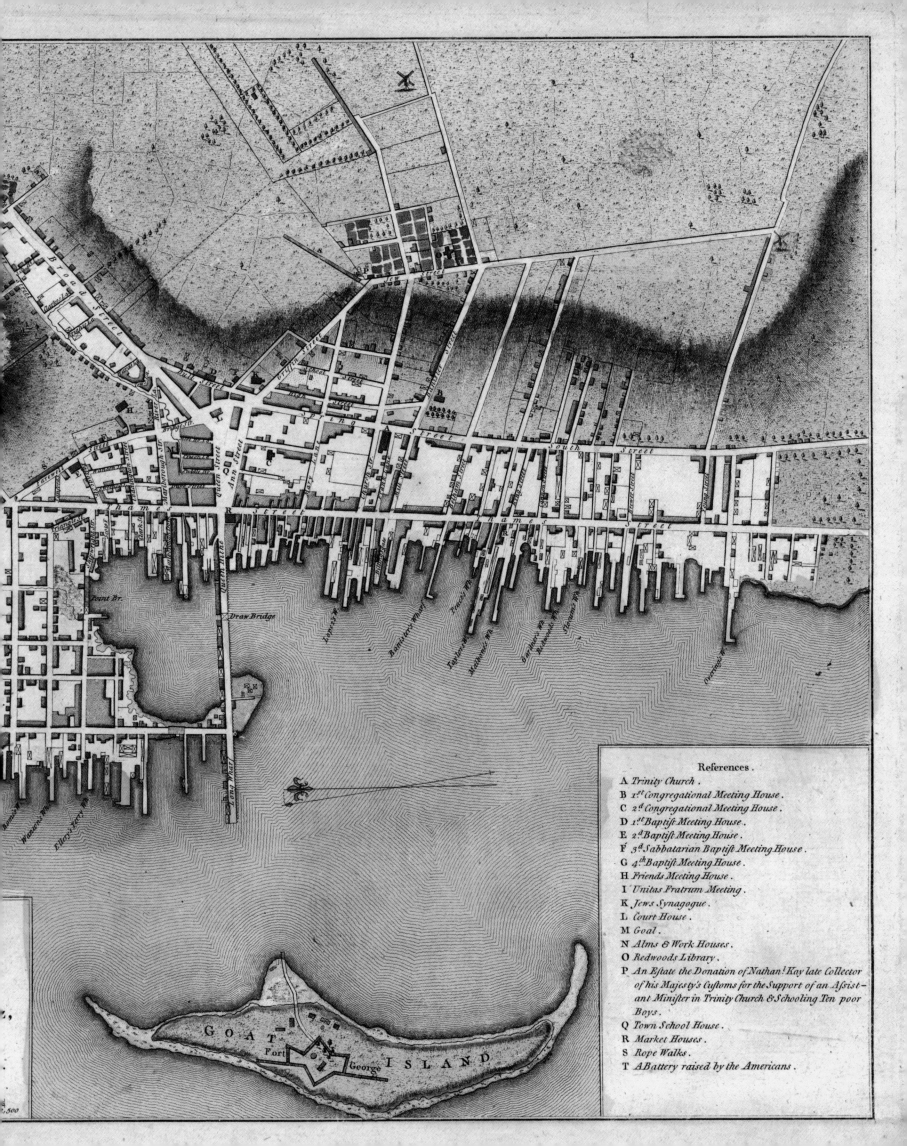

References.

A Trinity Church.
B 1st Congregational Meeting House.
C 2d Congregational Meeting House.
D 1st Baptist Meeting House.
E 2d Baptist Meeting House.
F 3d Sabbatarian Baptist Meeting House.
G 4th Baptist Meeting House.
H Friends Meeting House.
I Unitas Fratrum Meeting.
K Jews Synagogue.
L Court House.
M Goal.
N Alms & Work Houses.
O Redwoods Library.
P An Estate the Donation of Nathanl Kay late Collector
   of his Majesty's Customs for the Support of an Assist-
   ant Minister in Trinity Church & Schooling Ten poor
   Boys.
Q Town School House.
R Market Houses.
S Rope Walks.
T A Battery raised by the Americans.

An interesting way to consider physical geographic space is to look at map production during the period of interest. None of the maps included here is specifically intended to illustrate the landscapes of Newport, yet the landscape is irrefutably integral to their respective programs. Most are focused on matters of possession, several on wartime, and one is a glorious visual souvenir map reflecting wealth and recreation. In these examples, Newport's unique topography plays a role in not only military strategy but also in economics, architecture and urban design, and capitalist celebration.

Maps are obsessive, abstract spatial constructions with at least one agenda, and sometimes several. The best-designed maps eliminate all of the superfluous chaos of geographical information that is not relevant to its purpose, and, if successful, they can represent brilliant economy of design. One cannot include all details on a map, or it would merely be a blanket on top of the known world. Whether these are maps used to navigate the seas or illustrate the nervous system, too much information, or too little, or a lack of clarity in the design confuses the end user. The cartographer must use clear signals and rely on signs, symbols, and language recognizable to the intended audience so they may understand and process the visual, or in some cases tactile, information.

Some exclusions from the map, or "silences," are more important than what is included, and these absences can be quite telling when interpreting maps from a critical perspective. As in any history there are choices of what will be remembered and what will be forgotten, but the prevalence of selective truths, exaggeration, and perhaps embellishment was not unusual. Maps are never neutral or value free or completely scientific: "Each map argues its own case."[1] All of the maps represented here are made from positions of power, as most maps are, and all are from a Eurocentric point of view. Some of their "silences" are significant from the perspective of possession and dispossession. The names, with few exceptions, are English ones, and the visual symbolic vocabulary we take for granted in a post-colonial world is entirely of European origin. Most of the indigenous names are excluded or "silenced," a common practice in any European colonial program: "maps—just as much as examples of literature or the spoken word—exert a social influence through their omissions as much by the features they depict and emphasize."[2]

If we accept the map as a nonverbal sign system, like painting and music, we can deconstruct its symbolism and context in much the same way as we would any other cultural or political expression. Maps seem to describe a landscape scientifically, but they also interpret space according to the categories of knowledge of the audience. Although maps seem an objective enterprise, they are inherently subjective in nature and are rarely—arguably never—objective visual abstractions of space, but they can be important indicators of the social, religious, and personal contexts in which they were created. When looking at any map it is important to consider who made it, for what purpose, and for what audience. A place represented on a map is indicative of more than the geographical location: "It embodies textual sources, imaginary representations, and symbolic values" and can also stand in for a "cultural memory."[3]

Fig. 33
Map of the city, port, and harbor of Newport, 1780
Library of Congress
This manuscript map depicts the topography in detail, with a focus on optimal vantage points for military action. The red arcs depict the range of artillery mounted on the ships labeled and positioned in the entrance to the bay as well as the batteries.

PLAN DE LA VILLE, PORT ET RADE DE NEWPORT, AVEC UNE PARTIE DE RHODE-ISLAND OCCUPÉE PAR L'ARMÉE FRANÇAISE AUX ORDRES DE Mr. LE COMTE DE ROCHAMBEAU ET DE L'ESCADRE FRANÇAISE COMMANDÉE PAR Mr. LE Chr. DESTOUCHES.

Map Division
Library of Congress

PARTIE DE L'ISLE DE KONENIKUT.

ENTRÉE DE LA RADE

Gold island.

Rase island.

Brentons pt.

Coaster island.

Point de débarquement.

Ol. Provence.
Ol. le Jason.
Ol. le Duc de Bourgogne.
Ol. le Neptune.

Goat island.

Coddington Core.

Goose berry.

Port.

NEWPORT

Gull Rock.

Inondation.

Echelle de deux Miles.

Legende.

1. Batterie de brentons pt. de 12. pieces de 24. et de 4 mortiers de 12 po.e fermant la gauche de la position et dont le feu croise celui des Vaisseaux.
2. Batterie de Goat island de 8 pieces de 24.
3. Batterie de Rase island de 20. pieces de 36. et de 4 Mortiers de 12 po.e à laquelle la droite des Vaisseaux est appuyée, deffendant l'Entrée de la Rade, la passe du Sud et tout ce qui auroit pû dépasser cette Isle.
4. Vaisseaux Embossés.
5. Batterie de 8. de Coaster island dont le feu se croise avec le fort de Tomany hill et deffend le debarquement de Coddington Cove.
6. Redoute de 50 hommes couvrant le front du Camp françois et formant la droite du Camp retranché.
7. Redoute et Batterie de 4 pieces de 12. qui deffendent le passage entre la mer et l'Inondation.
8. Redoutes de 100 hommes chacune qui commandent tout ce qui est devant Elles.
9. Redoutes avancées ou flêches de 50 hommes.
10. Redoute de 50 hommes arretant tout ce qui voudroit passer dans la Gorge et protegé par les forts de Tomany
11. forts Contenant deux cens hommes avec 4. pieces de 18. Commandant toute la position.
12. Ouvrages avancés commandés par Tomany hill et dominés par Coaster island.

Terrein propre à déployer les troupes.

Emplacement du Camp.

Point de débarquement.

Point de débarquement.

black pt.

G3774
.N453
1780
.75

53

Fig. 34 (left)
Charles C. Hammett Jr.,
Map of the Township of Newport, 1860
Courtesy of Mr. and Mrs. S. Matthews V. Hamilton, Jr
These maps from 1860 and 1870 (Fig. 35) show a shift in the interests of their makers. Typically absent from maps of possession, such as these, are the dispossessed. Their silence speaks loudly. Indigenous people and their place names are excluded, as they are from virtually all maps made from the first point of European contact, enforcing the idea of an Edenic America, which served the new possessors of the land and erased the dispossessed.

Fig. 35 (right)
Matthew Dripps, *Map of Newport*, 1870
Library of Congress
This map uses Native American names in some instances, but they denote marginalized functions. Weenat Shasitt, or Coaster's Island, now part of the U.S. Naval War College, was used as an asylum; Conockonoquit, or Rose Island, was used for quarantine; and Nante Sinunk, or Coat [sic] Island (Goat Island) is disconnected from the mainland. Dripps celebrates industry by marking the railway and the ferry route to the wharves. Each map is rooted in private property, with the owners noted in each plot large enough to fit a name.

Fig. 36
Galt and Hoy, *Newport 1878*
Library of Congress
The bird's-eye perspective of this map celebrates
Newport's rise as a resort. This style of map design
has been around for hundreds of years, but it gained
enormous popularity in the late nineteenth century in
souvenir or subscriber maps. The perspective focuses
on the picturesque coastline and houses along the
Cliff Walk rather than on the port itself or its industry.

Notes
1 J. B. Harley, *The New Nature of Maps: Essays in
   the History of Cartography* (Baltimore, MD: Johns
   Hopkins University Press, 2001), 5.
2 Harley, *The New Nature of Maps*, 67.
3 Christian Jacob, *The Sovereign Map: Theoretical
   Approaches in Cartography throughout History*, trans.
   Tom Conley, 1st ed. (Chicago: University of Chicago
   Press, 2006), plate 3 text.

The Genteel Landscape
ROMANTIC VILLAS AND REFINED VIEWS

All along Bellevue Avenue . . . are geraniums, roses, begonias, heliotropes, hydrangeas, verbenas,
gladioli, a wilderness of flowers, native and exotic, filling the air with perfume and the eye with beauty.
—J. H. Browne, "The Queen of Aquidneck," 1874

The poetic and the practical merged in Newport's landscapes during the Victorian age. Writer, painter, real estate developer, cottage builder, landscape gardener, and nursery owner—these were the figures who celebrated, envisioned, and implemented the transformation of windswept fields and rocky shores into a premier seaside resort during the course of the nineteenth century. Their motivations may have been varied, but the result was singular: an enclave of picturesque villas embowered in greenery with easy access to ocean views and scenic drives (Figs. 37–40), enlivened by a sparkling social scene. Newport became a place to see and be seen. Bellevue Avenue, established in 1853, served as the stage for this fashionable whirl, as writer and artist George Champlin Mason recorded:

> one sees a succession of beautiful villas and cottages on either hand, embowered in trees,
> shrubs and flowering plants, and in full sight of the ocean, the lawns smoothly rolled and
> carefully cut, and the borders so arranged as to convey the idea of deep vistas with skillful
> combinations of color; here delighting in a sharp contrast, and there blending together in a
> graduation of hues, beautiful to behold.[43]

Mason saw the future success of Newport in its picturesque scenery. As editor of the *Newport Mercury*, he championed the construction of Bellevue Avenue, providing access to the cliffs on the southeastern edge of the city (Figs. 41 and 42). Real estate developers and investors, notably Alfred Smith and Joseph Bailey, George Downing, Edward and Anne King, and John Hazard, subdivided large tracts of treeless meadowlands.[44] Architects began the construction of summer cottages in a variety of popular styles, from Gothic Revival and Italianate to Second Empire French, all in settings inspired by idealized notions of a refined life in nature, tamed and cultivated by the nursery owner and estate gardener (Figs. 43 and 44). Florists and commercial

John Collins, *The Reefs*,
ca. 1850, print
The Preservation Society of
Newport County

Fig. 37 (above)
Kernochan Villa, from *Newport and Its Cottages* (1875), photograph
Redwood Library and Athenaeum

Fig. 38 (right)
Frank Child, Appleton House, ca. 1890, photograph
Library of Congress

Fig. 39 (left)
Cliff Walk, ca.1880, photograph
Library of Congress

Fig. 40 (below)
G. Hayward, *Map of the Farm known as Easton Farm* (detail), 1845
Newport Historical Society
This subdivision plan illustrates the transition from agricultural production (left) to housing lots (right).

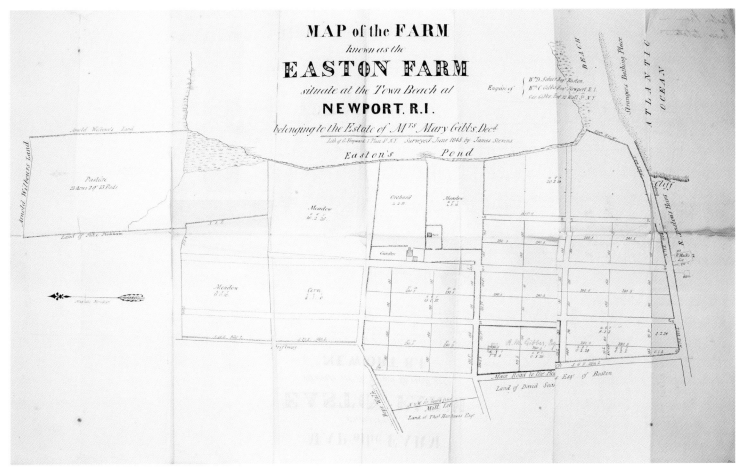

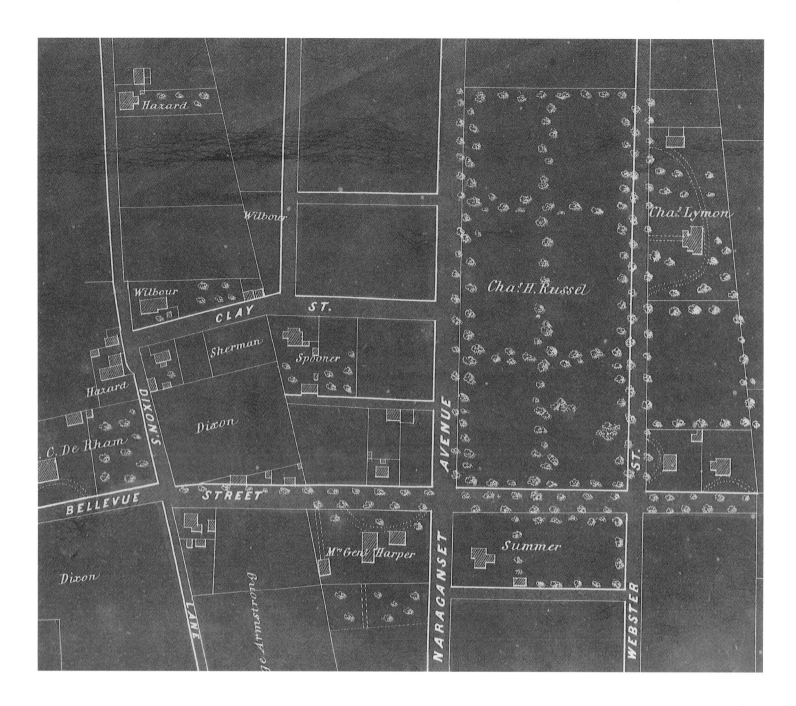

greenhouses were established, and grew in number over the decades, to cater to the needs of this new district, an area where the romantic villa required a genteel landscape, one in which precisely manicured, meandering paths offered picturesque views without the fear of grass stains on delicate silk slippers or dirt on polished leather shoes. At the corner of Bellevue and Narragansett Avenues, Mason found the perfect archetype of the Newport cottage and its grounds:

> Mr. Russell, who is subdividing his land and opening streets, reserved a tract of about thirteen acres for his own estate, now known as Oaklawn, and which is one of the finest spots on Bellevue Avenue. It is deservedly admired; not for its view or natural attractions, but for its superb trees gracefully grouped, its admirably arranged lawn, its succession of flowering shrubs and plants, and its well-appointed Italian villa. Here may be seen the finest specimens of the purple beech, English and Turkey oaks of large size, and a[n] . . . oak of rare beauty, which bids fair in time to claim an acre for its own immediate use.[45]

In planning the landscapes of Oaklawn and its neighbors, Newport's estate owners, gardeners, and nursery owners were influenced, either directly or indirectly, by theories popularized by the horticulturist and writer Andrew Jackson Downing, adapting them to local conditions and practices. If Mason had a vision for Newport, Downing had a vision for the entire nation.

Downing played an extraordinary role as both a horticulturist and a historical figure in the evolution of attitudes towards nature and the burgeoning interest in the gardens of private residences and public parks in the United States. He was a seminal character in the transmission and interpretation, in landscape and architecture, of the picturesque, which had emerged in eighteenth-century England, expressed in compositions of curving lines, natural contours, and asymmetrical placement of trees and shrubs to create an improved form of the natural. From the many at work refining this idiom, Lancelot "Capability" Brown arose as a master, conjuring up parklands of sweeping lawn, lake, and meadow in an idealized version of an English pastoral world.[46] In the latter part of the century, Humphry Repton worked within Brown's formula, developing his version of "landscape gardening," which introduced flower beds and colorful plantings adjacent to buildings to act as a transition zone between house and landscape. Richard

Fig. 42
Bellevue Avenue, ca. 1900, photograph
Library of Congress

Fig. 43
John Knower House, Seacliffe,
from *Newport and Its Cottages*
(1875), photograph
Redwood Library and
Athenaeum

Payne Knight and Uvedale Price then advocated for an ever more rustic, albeit contrived, manner of landscape design in which gnarled tree branches and jagged topographies were treasured features.[47] This certainly appealed to the prevailing tastes of the Romantic movement in art and literature, which sought a range of emotions from the sublime to the sensational in field and forest. This spirit influenced American artists in many media, from painting to literature, all in the pursuit of a distinct identity for the new nation.[48] Culture would be enhanced, ennobled, and enriched by the natural world. Downing entered upon this cultural and horticultural scene at the height of Romanticism's worship of nature and the early Victorian evangelical passion for reform, embracing both of these tendencies combined with a zeal to instruct and guide. A noted nurseryman in the Hudson River Valley, he became a national personality in the 1840s through his articles in the *Horticulturist* and his publication *A Treatise on the Theory and Practice of Landscape Gardening, Adapted to North America; With a View to the Improvement of Country Residences* (1841). The book reflected the influence of the Scottish botanist, garden designer, and author John Claudius Loudon, who used the term *arboretum* in his prolific writing to define the scientific assembly and aesthetic arrangement of trees. Loudon also developed the *gardenesque style*, which incorporated a range of exotic plant materials from potted palms and tubs of ferns

Fig. 44
Kingscote, ca. 1877, photograph
The Preservation Society of
Newport County
The Gothic Revival–style house
is the picturesque ideal of a
romantic cottage.

to flowers from across the globe on verdant lawns. Downing owed a debt to Loudon's ideas. He also had a keen awareness of the historical and cultural associations of landscape, invoking the past in his writings to give weight to his vision of nature shaped by humankind.

In the poetical imagination, indeed, the ideal type of a modern landscape garden seems always to have been more or less shadowed forth. The Vaucluse of Petrarch, Tasso's garden of Armida, the Vale of Tempe of Aelian, were all exquisite conceptions of the modern style. And Milton, surrounded as he was by the splendid formalities of the gardens of his time, copied from no existing models, but feeling that Eden must have been free and majestic in its outlines, he drew from his inner sense of the beautiful, and from nature as he saw her developed in the works of the Creator.[49]

Downing excelled at definitions of the art of landscape. The *ancient* referred to the formal, geometric landscape; the *natural* was divided into the *beautiful*, a manner comprising soft, flowing forms, such as round-headed shrubbery, and the *picturesque*, possessing sharper, pointed features, such as fir trees to evoke the raw power of nature. The garden makers of Newport may

Fig. 45
Relaxing on the porches and lawn of Beaulieu, ca. 1860, photograph
Newport Historical Society, P5783

Fig. 46
Beaulieu, ca. 1870, photograph
Library of Congress

not have always applied these definitions in the strictest ways, but records of their work in plans, photographs, and account books are a testament to their devotion to Downing's general ideas. The arrangement and use of trees and flowers at Beaulieu (1859) in Newport and the Hoppin and Van Rensselaer houses (1860) in nearby Middletown appear to have risen from Downing's writing:

Landscape Gardening differs from gardening in its common sense, in embracing the whole scene immediately about a country house, which it softens and refines, or renders more spirited and striking by the aid of art. In it we seek to embody our ideal of a rural home not through plots of fruit trees, and beds of choice flowers, though these have their place, but by collecting and combining beautiful forms in trees, surfaces of ground, buildings, and walks, in the landscape surrounding us. It is, in short, the Beautiful, embodied in a home scene.[50]

Designed in the Italianate style by architect Calvert Vaux, who worked on projects with Downing, Beaulieu was set in a green lawn perched upon cliffs overlooking the ocean. Eugene A. Baumann created the plan of serpentine drives and paths with groupings of deciduous and evergreen trees to frame views of the main house from the entrance on Bellevue Avenue (Figs. 45–47). Among the selections were English and purple beech, tulip trees, hornbeam,

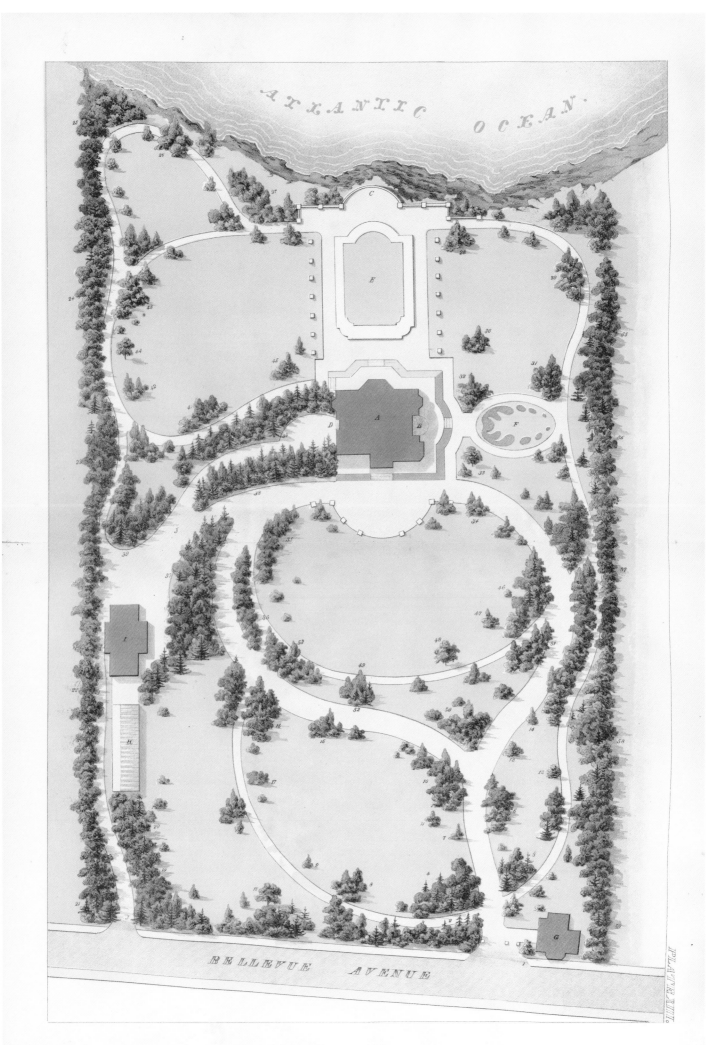

ATLANTIC OCEAN.

BELLEVUE AVENUE

Turkish oak, hemlocks, Austrian pine, Norway spruce, English silver firs, Norway and sycamore maples, horse-chestnut, Scotch larch, and dwarf juniper, gingko, and Chinese arborvitae, representing the Victorian interest in assembling a variety of specimens from across the globe and the practice of giving pride of place to specimen trees.[51] Baumann's scheme for Beaulieu introduced some formal elements into the overall picturesque scene, according to Jacob Weidenmann, who featured the estate plan in *Beautifying Country Homes* (1870). Often serving as an associate on public and private commissions with Frederick Law Olmsted, Weidenmann held a prominent place in the emerging landscape profession, and his publications were highly influential in the dissemination of the picturesque.[52] He wrote of Beaulieu with attention to its combination of many landscape features:

> *The terraces around the mansion and the parterre between them and the sea are very happy combinations of the natural and the artificial style of landscape gardening . . . The seafront is enclosed and decorated by a handsome stone balustrade, while between this and the building on both sides of the parterre is placed a row of elegant flower vases which produces a highly satisfactory effect. The semicircular graveled place in front of the house is also richly ornamented with Venetian candelabras, which tastefully connect the grounds with the building.*[53]

Beaulieu demonstrates Vaux's mastery of integrating architecture with landscape by means of terraces and stairs, elements he had seen in the work of gardeners and architects practicing the art of transition from the formal to the gardenesque to the natural.[54] Facing the ocean was a rectangular lawn edged by clipped evergreens, drawing upon the idea of a *tapis vert*, or green carpet, adapted from the seventeenth-century French formal tradition. As one moves further from the house, the framed geometry of the tapis vert gives way to curving paths that create a dynamic pattern of flowing forms in and around asymmetrical groupings of trees. The flower beds on the lawn were examples of the horticultural extravaganzas of the gardenesque style as a middle ground in design between the strict structure of formal gardens and the rustic quality of the natural. This composition displays the unity of planning achieved by Baumann and Vaux, who commented, "In country houses the design has to be adapted to the location, and not the location to the design, for it is undesirable, and generally impracticable, to make the natural landscape subservient to the architectural composition."[55]

Beaulieu faced the sea, whereas the Hoppin and Van Rensselaer houses were set on a hill in nearby Middletown overlooking field, meadow, and orchard (Figs. 48 and 49). The architect Richard Upjohn devised these Italianate houses in wood for a setting far more rural than that of Beaulieu. The curving drives, paths, and selection of trees, however, mimicked those of Beaulieu with the addition of magnolia (*M. glauca* and *M. conspicua*), red buckeye, shell-bark hickory, and groups of flower beds with rustic vases. Weidenmann featured the two houses as an example of country estate planning, stating,

Fig. 47 (opposite)
Estate plan for Beaulieu,
from Jacob Weidenmann,
Beautifying American Country Homes (1870)
Redwood Library and Athenaeum

Fig. 48 (overleaf)
Hoppin and Van Rensselaer
landscape plans, from Jacob
Weidenmann, *Beautifying American Country Homes* (1870)
Redwood Library and Athenaeum

Fig. 49
Gathering on the porch of the
Van Rensselaer house, ca. 1860,
photograph
Newport Historical Society,
P5837

The handsome country seats of Messrs. Alexander van Rensselaer and Hamilton Hoppin . . . afford an excellent illustration of the principles upon which undivided pleasure-grounds are constructed . . . The somewhat undulating grounds are almost entirely devoted to ornamental purposes. Although absolutely separate in their arrangements and disposition, the two together represent, from whatever point viewed, an extensive and handsome park, which will be handsomer still when the young trees have attained their full growth.[56]

Lawns set with trees intended to grow to their most mature expanse were a leitmotif of the picturesque. The interplay of color, texture, light, form, and space was designed to evoke a romantic picture, an artful expression promoted by Downing, who opined, "as a general rule, the grass or surface of the lawn answers as the principal light, and the woods . . . as the shadows, in the same manner in nature as in painting, and that these should be so managed as to lead the eye to the mansion."[57] The layout of the grounds and collections of trees at Beaulieu and the Hoppin and Van Rensselaer estates fully realized Downing's ideas of picturesque composition

Fig. 50
Beechwood, ca. 1880,
photograph
Newport Historical Society,
P5787
The lush flower beds are typical
of the gardenesque style
and the abundance of plant
material available due to the
burgeoning nursery industry.

and effective scene making in nature. Architecture served as the main object, partly hidden, partly revealed by the trees, the key points in an artful hierarchy. According to Downing's advice, "it will also be seen how much, in the eye of a painter, a tree with a beautifully diversified surface, as the oak, surpasses in the composition of a scene, one with a very regular and compact surface and outline, as the horse-chestnut."[58] Trees in a garden served the same function as paint on a canvas, being combined to create various tones of color and light. Horticultural variety and an air of mystery created through asymmetry in both the natural forms and the arrangement of diverse plantings made for a worthy and enticing landscape experience on the part of the viewer.

In *Villas and Cottages* (1872), which he dedicated to Andrew Jackson Downing and Jane Downing, Vaux wrote of design principles very much in sync with those of the man who had befriended him and invited him to partner on certain projects, such as the Daniel Parrish house (1851), later renamed Beechwood when acquired by Mr. and Mrs. William Backhouse Astor, Jr., only two lots north of Beaulieu on Bellevue Avenue (Fig. 50).

Fig. 51
John Perry Newell, Chateau-
sur-Mer, ca. 1860, print
The Preservation Society of
Newport County

This design was erected for a gentleman residing at Newport, Rhode Island. . . . It was prepared for a fine situation, commanding an uninterrupted view of the sea, including several acres of ornamental ground, that have been well laid out and planted under the superintendence of an experienced landscape gardener.[59]

Vaux and Downing were each developing a template for the unified design of houses and grounds that easily incorporated the formal and gardenesque within the overall framework of a picturesque plan. In 1852, Downing lost his life in a steamboat accident on the Hudson River. Vaux memorialized his partner in *Villas and Cottages*:

tidings of his sudden and shocking death were mournfully received by his family and friends, and almost as mournfully by thousands, who knowing him only through his books, still felt that he was to them a dear and intimate companion.[60]

Downing's death was tragic, but he had set American landscape design on a trajectory that would create a long-lasting legacy. He partnered with Vaux, and he advocated for the creation of what would become Central Park in New York City; Vaux in turn teamed with Frederick

Fig. 52
Chateau-sur-Mer, ca. 1860,
photograph
Library of Congress

Law Olmsted on the plan for that ground-breaking urban amenity. Each of these figures of national repute would have their influence felt in Newport through their writings, buildings, and landscape plans.

Beaulieu, the Hoppin and Van Rensselaer estates, and the Daniel Parrish house were all conceived with master plans, while Chateau-sur-Mer represents the evolution of most Newport landscapes, which were developed over time with additions by several generations (Figs. 51–55). Built in 1852 by the retired China Trade merchant William Shepard Wetmore, the main house in the Italianate style stood out on expansive lawns with nearby fields affording unobstructed views of the sea, framed through a version of a Chinese moon gate. Wetmore was noted as selecting Newport for the "restorative" quality of its climate.[61] He often wrote to his daughter, Annie, advising, "your habit of exercise in the air must be kept up daily . . . give my hugs and my love to the Boys and Yourself."[62] The lawns where the Wetmore children took their exercise were cared for by the Scottish head gardener, Robert Christie.[63] After Wetmore's death in 1862, his son George Peabody Wetmore inherited the estate and continued to enhance the grounds with trees and shrubs. Christie's correspondence with George Wetmore recounts his seasonal activities and attention to detail, from the seeding, fertilizing, and rolling of the turf in spring to tending the nectarines, peaches, and grape vines in the hothouses. Beginning in the

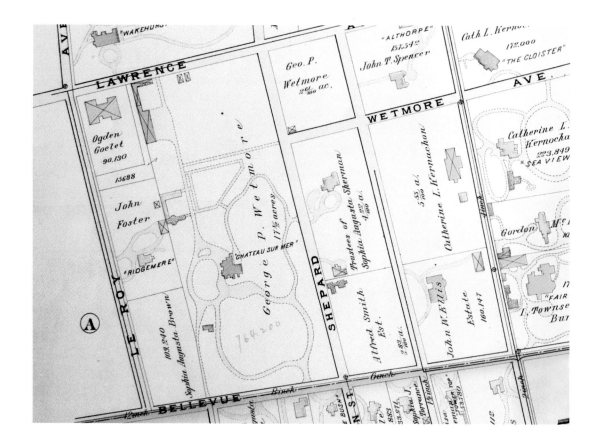

1870s and continuing for the next half century, George and his daughter, Edith, and their head gardeners, Robert Christie followed by John Cairns, transformed the vast lawns of Chateau-sur-Mer into a collection of trees reflecting the Victorian taste for displaying examples from across the globe, including weeping, fernleaf, and copper beech, Japanese sophora, weeping hemlock, Turkey oak, Mongolian magnolia, Kentucky coffee, cryptomeria, tulip trees, and sycamore. These imported specimens were placed in asymmetrical groupings along winding paths and drives, allowing the viewer to travel in and out of shaded groves onto broad lawns, framing scenes of the great house at the center of this green enclave.

The grounds at Chateau-sur-Mer were the setting for a constant round of fetes and dances hosted by the Wetmores. At these parties, the skill of Robert Christie, aided by the florist John Hodgson, was in full view, as at the debutante dance for Miss Maude Wetmore on August 18, 1891:

The floral decorations were more artistic than usual and Hodgson introduced many novel and authentic features. The principal interior decorations were in the ballroom . . . It is a room worthy of the title Grand Salon, and with the delicate decorations by the floral artist, was made especially charming. The room is decorated in Louis XV style with panels in pale lavender and green . . . and the various delicately tinted flowers used harmonized perfectly with the permanent decoration. From the tops of the panels were hung garlands and pendants of natural flowers in white and blue caught up in satin ribbons of pale pink tint, tied with long streamers. Combinations of garlands and pendants were hung with the same shade of ribbon on the two large mirrors, on opposite sides of the ballroom in such a manner as to produce an almost endless reproduction of the garland by reflection. One was of a delicate tracing of pink rose and green and the other was of creamy yellow Perle rose with jasmine.[64]

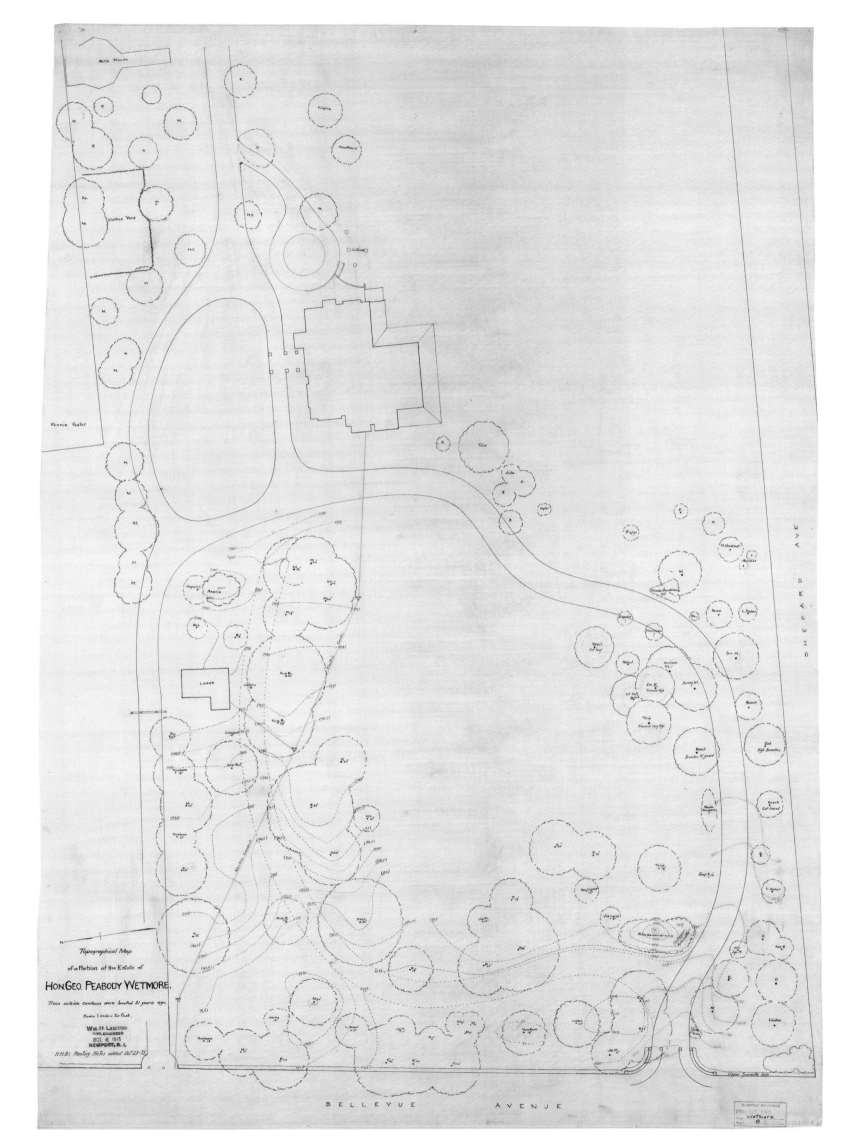

Topographical Map
of a Portion of the Estate of
HON. GEO. PEABODY WETMORE.

Trees outside contours were located 21 years ago.

Scale 1 inch = 20 feet.

WM. H. LAWTON
CIVIL ENGINEER
OCT. 6, 1915
NEWPORT, R. I.

H.H.B) Planting Notes added Oct 23-15

S H E P A R D   A V E

B E L L E V U E   A V E N U E

Fig. 55
Alexander Nesbitt, Weeping
beech and Japanese maple,
Chateau-sur-Mer, 2020,
photograph

In a fashionable Newport summer season, the debutante ball was a high point for a house and its inhabitants, an opportunity to exhibit discernment through display and to present the heiress to society, the ultimate aim being a marriage alliance, hopefully both happy and lucrative. Flowers and fine manners created a veil of gentility to soften the more stark social and financial business at hand. The head gardener was an essential player in the cast assembled to produce such an evening's ornaments, which encompassed house, piazzas, and grounds.

> *At one end of the main piazza were placed large tanks of water containing lotus and nymphae plants in full flower and of the numerous varieties and colors, under cultivation. These were from the private collection of Mr. Robert Christie, Mr. Wetmore's gardener. The archways of the piazza were paneled off with wild grasses and bulrushes. Palms and other plants grouped around the piazzas formed nooks for settees . . . and the ceilings of red and white material were lightly hung with oak boughs. Fine vines were used with rare effect, and the pillars were massed with Japanese maize and tropical leaves alternately, over a wealth of pink, white and (blue) hydrangeas. At one side was made a bed of growing holly hocks, the long stalks burdened with quantities of double pink, yellow and red blooms . . . guests could have a view of the moonlight or of the ground where Landers had made a pretty picture of variously colored fairy lamps about the groups of shrubbery and lanterns in the smaller trees.*[65]

Neither Maude nor her sister Edith chose to marry, regardless of the artfulness of their debutante balls. They remained at Chateau-sur-Mer, assisting their parents with the running of the estate and adding their own horticultural touches. In the period 1915 to 1918, Senator

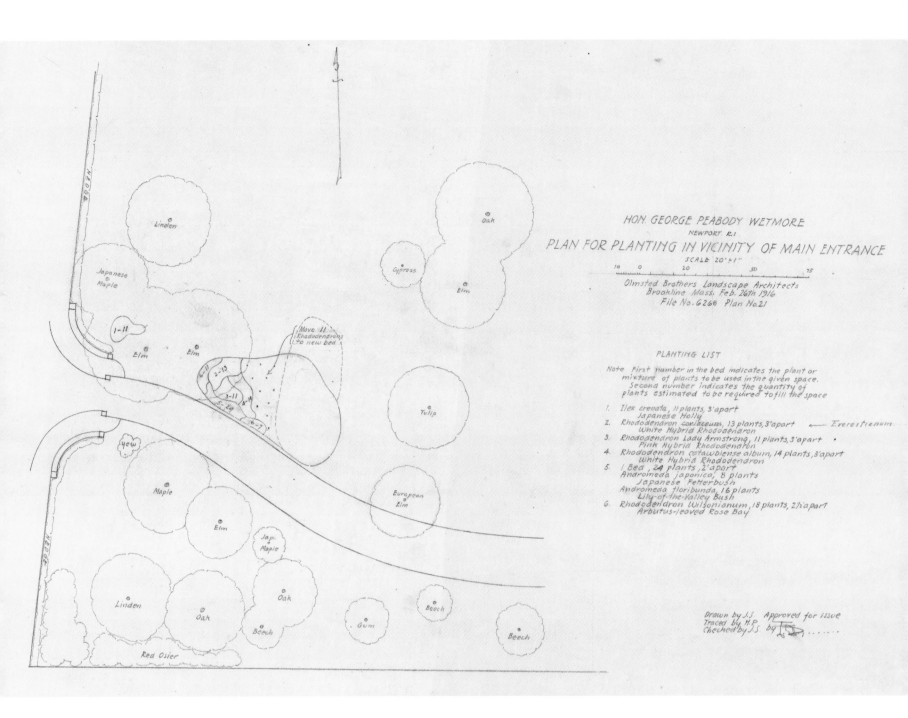

Fig. 56 (above)
Olmsted Brothers, *Plan for Planting in Vicinity of Main Entrance*, Chateau-sur-Mer, 1916
United States Department of the Interior, National Park Service, Frederick Law Olmsted National Historic Site

Fig. 57 (overleaf, top)
Olmsted Brothers, *Plan for Planting in Vicinity of Clothes Yard*, Chateau-sur-Mer, 1916
United States Department of the Interior, National Park Service, Frederick Law Olmsted National Historic Site

Wetmore engaged Olmsted Brothers to redesign the south entrance and the service courtyard.[66] Harold Hill Blossom, the representative from the Olmsted office, filed a report on his survey of the property:

> Mr. Wetmore first took me entirely about the place, which was begun by his father. I inquired if he had not had a landscape architect at some time in the past, as I thought the grounds gave it the appearance of having been designed with a great deal of thought, and he told me that William H. Grant thirty years ago was employed by him; that Mr. Grant had worked on Central Park for a good many years, I suppose under F.L. Olmsted Senior . . . The lawns are very beautiful on the estate and the trees are mostly grouped around the borders. They are in great variety and very fine. Senator Wetmore likes, he says, a simple style of planting, and he is not fond of gaudily colored foliage.[67]

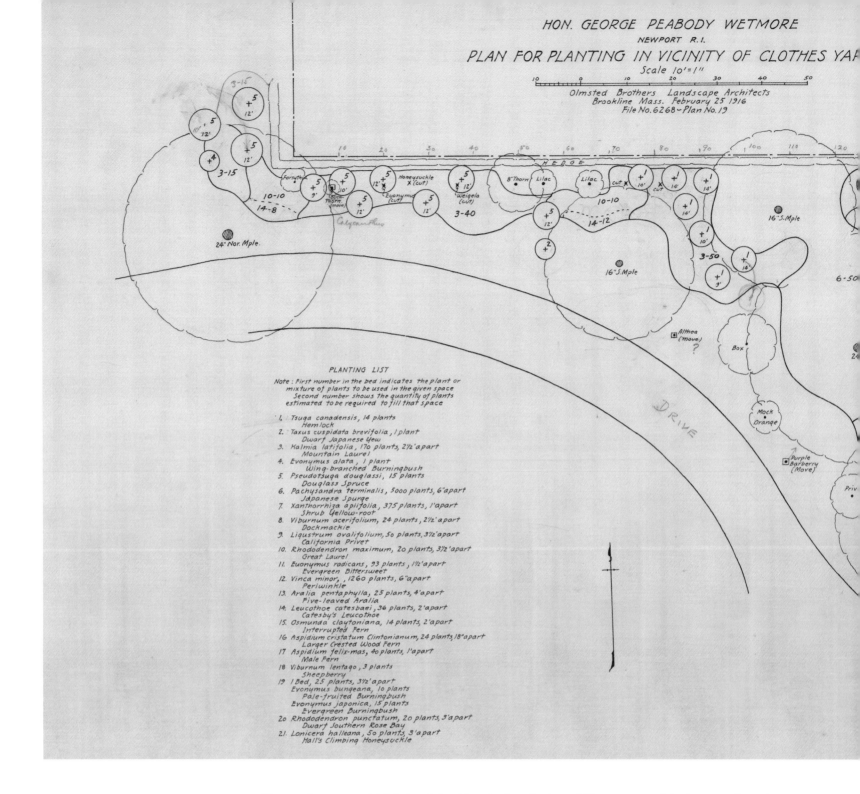

HON. GEORGE PEABODY WETMORE
NEWPORT R.I.
PLAN FOR PLANTING IN VICINITY OF CLOTHES YAP
Scale 10'=1"
Olmsted Brothers Landscape Architects
Brookline Mass. February 25 1916
File No.6268~Plan No.19

PLANTING LIST

Note : First number in the bed indicates the plant or
mixture of plants to be used in the given space
Second number shows the quantity of plants
estimated to be required to fill that space

1. Tsuga canadensis, 14 plants
   Hemlock
2. Taxus cuspidata brevifolia, 1 plant
   Dwarf Japanese Yew
3. Kalmia latifolia, 170 plants, 2½'apart
   Mountain Laurel
4. Evonymus alata, 1 plant
   Wing-branched Burningbush
5. Pseudotsuga douglassi, 15 plants
   Douglass Spruce
6. Pachysandra terminalis, 5000 plants, 6'apart
   Japanese Spurge
7. Xanthorrhiza apiifolia, 375 plants, 1'apart
   Shrub Yellow-root
8. Viburnum acerifolium, 24 plants, 2½'apart
   Dockmackie
9. Ligustrum ovalifolium, 50 plants, 3½'apart
   California Privet
10. Rhododendron maximum, 20 plants, 3½'apart
    Great Laurel
11. Euonymus radicans, 93 plants, 1½'apart
    Evergreen Bittersweet
12. Vinca minor, , 1260 plants, 6'apart
    Periwinkle
13. Aralia pentaphylla, 25 plants, 4'apart
    Five-leaved Aralia
14. Leucothoe catesbaei, 36 plants, 2'apart
    Catesby's Leucothoe
15. Osmunda claytoniana, 14 plants, 2'apart
    Interrupted Fern
16. Aspidium cristatum Clintonianum, 24 plants, 18"apart
    Larger Crested Wood Fern
17. Aspidium felix-mas, 40 plants, 1'apart
    Male Fern
18. Viburnum lentago, 3 plants
    Sheepberry
19. 1 Bed, 25 plants, 3½'apart
    Evonymus bungeana, 10 plants
    Pale-fruited Burningbush
    Evonymus japonica, 15 plants
    Evergreen Burningbush
20. Rhododendron punctatum, 20 plants, 3'apart
    Dwarf Southern Rose Bay
21. Lonicera halleana, 50 plants, 3'apart
    Hall's Climbing Honeysuckle

Blossom's account highlighted the historical evolution of Chateau-sur-Mer's grounds and the task set by Mr. Wetmore for the Olmsteds to make improvements to the south entrance gate and the service courtyard in sympathy with the original character of the landscape (Figs. 56–58). Wetmore's daughter, Edith, made major adaptations to the grounds in the years following World War I, demolishing the greenhouse and palm house, the foundations serving as frames for new projects. Frederick Rhinelander King designed a Colonial Revival garden house (ca. 1920) with a walled garden on the site of the palm house (Fig. 59). John Cairns, the head gardener from the 1920s through the 1960s, created lush floral borders in the English Arts and Crafts manner on the footprint of the greenhouse.[68] These were evolving annual arrangements of varying height, texture, and color composed of anchusa, Canterbury bells, columbine, delphinium, forget-me-nots, foxglove, heliotrope, iris, yellow and white lilies, phlox, plumbago, snap dragons, Sweet

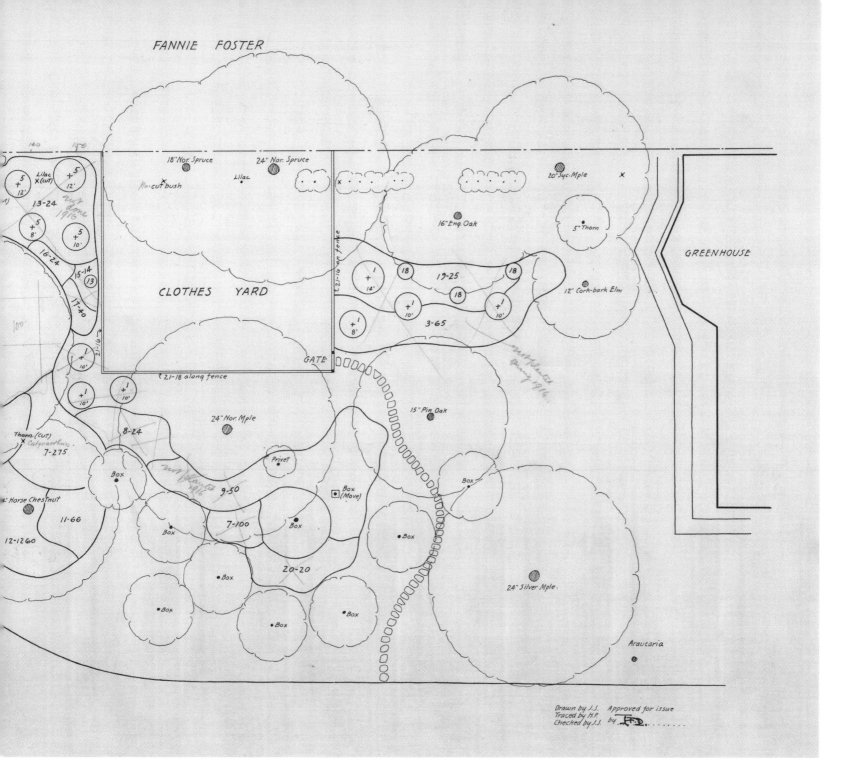

FANNIE FOSTER

18"Nor. Spruce   24"Nor. Spruce   20"Syc.Mple

Lilac   ×(cut)   12'

Haircut bush   Lilac

13-24   Aug. June 1916

16"Eng. Oak   5"Thorn

16-24   15-14   13

19-25   18

11-40   18

12"Cork-bark Elm

CLOTHES YARD

21-18 on fence   1 14'   18

1 10'   3-65

GATE   1 8'   1 10'

21-18 along fence

not planted Spring 1916

GREENHOUSE

24"Nor. Mple   15"Pin Oak

8-24   Box

Thorn (cut)   Calycanthus   7-275

Privet

Box

Box (Move)

Box

Horse Chestnut   11-66   9-50

12-1260   Box   7-100   Box   Box

20-20

24"Silver Mple.

Box   Box   Box

Araucaria

Drawn by J.S.   Approved for issue
Traced by H.P.   Checked by J.S.   by F.D.........

William, and violets.[69] From the lawns of William Shepard Wetmore to his son's weeping beeches and his grand-daughter's flower beds, Chateau-sur-Mer became a landscape of many layers in time, a picturesque composition of varied textures and tones—a perfect picture painted with nature's materials.

Newport and its houses and gardens featured often in articles and photographs in the burgeoning popular press. George Champlin Mason's *Newport and Its Cottages* (1875) was a fully illustrated volume presenting a myriad of villas in the prevailing picturesque styles. Their trellised porches and towers covered in woodbine, honeysuckle, and climbing roses, the lawns marked by beds of begonias and geraniums, and masses of hydrangea are examples of the manicured landscapes of the mid-nineteenth century. Each plant, tree, and urn is set with precision among lawns maintained as rich green carpets, canvases for the painterly showcasing of colorful flowers, ferns, and palms arranged in the gardenesque style promoted by Downing, who would have been most pleased. Gravel Court (1860) is a demonstration of the nursery owner's art, with potted plants placed on steps and balustrades as if on a stage set (Fig. 60). Downing warned that such lavish adornments were a sign of "too great a desire for display—too many vases, temples, and seats—and too little purity and simplicity of general effect."[70] The vagaries of

Fig. 60 (opposite)
Gravel Court, from *Newport and Its Cottages* (1875), photograph
Redwood Library and Athenaeum

Fig. 61 (above)
John Foster House, from *Newport and Its Cottages* (1875), photograph
Redwood Library and Athenaeum

taste and fashion often intruded upon philosophical principles. Newport was, after all, a resort designed for pleasure and show. Individual idiosyncrasies of owner and gardener often imposed themselves on a property, adding plants that might not have been approved by Downing or other landscape gardeners and critics. One generally accepted feature of any villa or cottage was the lawn, as green turf served as an essential canvas for horticultural display. The newly available lawnmower allowed for grass as smooth as a carpet, as noted by Mason on the Ochre Point estate of John Foster (Fig. 61):

Go where we may, we find nowhere a greensward equal to that on the southern portion of this island; and we wonder not that so much attention is paid to this feature of a Newport lawn. It is a thick, velvety pile, close bodied and fine, and of an exquisite color. It is always fresh, always dewy in the morning, always luxuriant in its growth; and it holds its own even down to the rocky edge of the cliff, everywhere short of where the salt sea-spray falls when the sea runs high.[71]

Fig. 62 (opposite)
Belair, ca. 1880, photograph
Newport Historical Society,
P8951
The estate of Mr. and Mrs.
George Norman, Belair
consisted of serpentine walks
and an elaborate greenhouse.

Fig. 63 (above)
Plan of Belair, from G. M.
Hopkins, *City Atlas of Newport,
Rhode Island* (1876)
Newport Historical Society
Photograph courtesy of
the Preservation Society of
Newport County

Fig. 64 (left)
Rustic garden furniture, Belair,
ca. 1880, photograph
Newport Historical Society,
P8969

Fig. 65
Rustic cottage, Belair, ca. 1880,
photograph
Newport Historical Society,
P8958

Newport's exceptional lawns are the ultimate expression of its landscape, pampered and polished as much as any interior space, a combination of the refined and the romantic that appealed to Victorian sentiments. The leisured pursuits of Newport's ladies and gentlemen embraced both of these qualities (Figs. 62–65). Leaving the manicured turf and potted flowers of elegant cottages and hotels, genteel tourists in Newport sought out the more rustic environments of wave-engulfed coves, jagged cliffs, and pebble-strewn beaches (Fig. 66). Young ladies collected seaweed, referred to as "marine flora," and pressed it in albums just as they did flowers and plants (Fig. 67).[72] The literati of Newport's summer colony also engaged in their own enlightened activities in nature. Julia Ward Howe, author of the *Battle Hymn of the Republic*, and Thomas Wentworth Higginson, novelist and mentor to Emily Dickinson, founded the Town and Country Club (1871), a group with the stated intention of "quiet enjoyment of nature and the culture their world offered them . . . in sharp contrast to the blatant and extravagant entertainments of Newport's society colonists."[73] Another organization, the Newport Natural History Society, promoted "the study of natural science with a focus on the flora, fauna, and geological formations of the area."[74] Among its members were leaders in the fields of geology, marine biology, the natural sciences, cartography, and gardening. Raphael Pumpelly, a geologist who served the U.S. Geological Survey, was its first president. Members included Alexander Agassiz, marine biologist and curator of Harvard University's Museum of Comparative Biology; Charles Hammett Jr., a landmark cartographer and author of a handbook on Newport's

Fig. 66
Sight-seers at Purgatory, ca. 1860, photograph
Newport Historical Society, 2003.9.119
"Beyond the bathing beach . . . rise the precipitous rocks, with the
deep and sharp lined fissure, known as 'The Purgatory.' How it ever
came to be called by this singular name, tradition does not inform us.
A little beyond this chasm, there is a pleasant spot, shaded by trees,
and commanding a beautiful view, which is known as 'Paradise,'—
so that, when a stranger in that region asks the way, he is likely to
be told he must pass by Purgatory to Paradise." George Champlin
Mason, *Newport and Its Cottages* (1875).

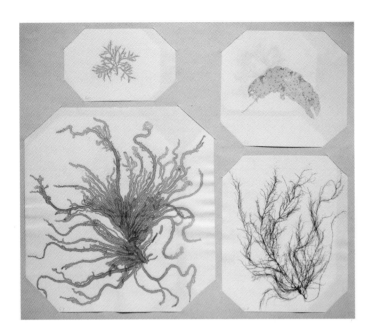 

Fig. 67 (above left)
Mrs. Alfred L. Carry, Book of
pressed marine flora,
ca. 1896–97
Newport Historical Society,
57.009

Fig. 68 (above right)
C. A. Thiebout, *Spouting Cave*,
ca. 1875, print
Private Collection

natural sites; and Lucius D. Davis, the editor and contributing writer for *Gardens and Gardening*.[75] In an address to the members, George Gordon King, whose family was central in developing large tracts of Newport, declared, "summer rest ought not to mean complete idleness."[76] The organization advocated for the Newport Park Commission to buy insect sprayers for the city's Elm trees and established the Natural History Collecting Contest Prizes for the collecting of leaves from specimen trees by the city's elementary and secondary students.[77]

The geology and scenery of Newport became the realm of that new breed of person in the nineteenth century, the sight-seer. Images both popular and poetic celebrated the natural wonders of Newport and other sites, from the White Mountains to Niagara Falls (Fig. 68). Magazines such as *Harper's New Monthly* featured articles and illustrations of these places of interest and proclaimed Newport the "Queen of Aquidneck."[78] William Cullen Bryant, renowned poet, champion of New York's Central Park, and editor of the New York *Evening Post*, authored the multivolume *Picturesque America* between 1872 and 1874, including Newport in his commentary. The artist John Collins capitalized on the general fascination for nature with his watercolors, including scenes of the rugged landscapes of Purgatory Chasm and Spouting Rock, which were sold to a wide audience.

Of a more sublime quality are the works of artists drawn by Newport's coastal atmosphere—"a chastened light under a glistening sea," according to Henry James.[79] Painters such as John Frederick Kensett, Worthington Whittredge, and Edward Mitchell Bannister found Aquidneck Island and its environs a source of inspiration, interpreting its light, color, and forms in their own artistic productions. They transformed the cliffs, orchards, and trees from physical features on the land to cultural icons of a mythic place. A leader of the luminist movement in American painting, Kensett came to Newport to experience the mercurial sun and haze on the Rhode Island coast. His nuanced rendering of Newport harbor's prominent rocky outcropping in *Beacon Rock* (1857) is a subtle study in atmosphere infused with light

Fig. 69
John Frederick Kensett, *Beacon Rock, Newport Harbor* (detail), 1857,
oil on canvas
National Gallery of Art, Gift of Frederick Sturges, Jr., 1953.1.1

Fig. 70
Worthington Whittredge,
Second Beach, 1878–80,
oil on canvas
National Gallery of Art,
Paul Mellon Fund and Gift of
Juliana Terian in memory of
Peter G. Terian, 2004.58.1

and color on both stone and water (Fig. 69). Whittredge took as his subject Second Beach and Hanging Rock in nearby Middletown (Fig. 70). This prominent geological formation was, for many, charged with historical meaning since the renowned metaphysician Dean George Berkeley had lived at a nearby farm in the early eighteenth century. The painter juxtaposes rock with sea in his exploration of sky, stone, sand, and water. Edward Mitchell Banister painted the adjacent landscape known as "Paradise," rendering through his rich brushwork the pastoral scene with sheep, rock outcroppings, and lush greenery (Fig. 71).

Just as many painters immersed themselves in landscape during the mid-nineteenth century, so too did writers, specifically Harriet Beecher Stowe, whose novel *The Minister's Wooing* (1859) is set in Newport, its natural environs the stage sets and symbols for both the purity and pain of her heroine's journey. Stowe's pen mirrored the painters' brushwork:

> *The sun was just setting, and the whole air and sea seemed flooded with rosy rays. Over the crags and rocks of the sea-shore took purple and lilac tints, and savins and junipers, had a painter been required to represent them, would have been found not without a suffusion of the same tints and through the tremulous rosy sea of the upper air, the silver full-moon looked out like some calm superior presence which waits only for the flush of a temporary excitement to die away, to makes its tranquilizing influence felt.*[80]

Fig. 71
Edward Mitchell Bannister, *Paradise*, 1895, oil on canvas
Newport Historical Society, 77.2

Fig. 72 (above)
William Trost Richards,
The Dumplings, ca. 1870,
oil on canvas
Private Collection
Picturesque scenery, a luminous
atmosphere, and a historic
fort in Narragansett Bay were
combined by the artist to
create a mythic landscape.

Fig. 73 (opposite)
William Trost Richards, *Old
Orchard at Newport* (detail),
ca. 1875, oil on canvas
Brooklyn Museum, Bequest
of Mrs. William T. Brewster
through the National Academy
of Design

The writer's use of landscape as a character, reinforcing both the plot and the qualities of her human subjects, exemplifies the regional focus that was a feature of American literature in the first half of the nineteenth century. Cultural expression found a vehicle in the natural environment, which was used to convey human traits of good and evil, and every condition in between. The power of the sea, the pastoral beauty of meadow and field, and the urban and urbane qualities of Newport's summer villas provide color and contrast between the natural and artificial in backdrops and behaviors, as in the following scene featuring Stowe's young heroine:

There was a little path through the orchard out to a small elevation in the pasture lot behind, where the sea was distinctly visible, and Mary . . . walked thoughtfully wondering if her true sailor love would ever return from his voyage.[81]

In addition to her hopes and desires, Mary is the object of temptation, one of the key features of the biblical story of the Garden of Eden, where the sacred and profane live close at hand: "she lives with her mother, a little walk out toward the seaside, in a cottage quite prettily sequestered among blossoming apple-trees, and the great hierarch of modern theology, Dr. Hopkins, keeps guard over them. No chance here for indiscretions, you see."[82] Mary daydreams of James, her true love away at sea, feeling closest to him when gazing out in solitude on rocky outcroppings overlooking a vast ocean. "James Marvyn," wrote Stowe, "as truly and heartily a

creature of this material world as Mary was of the invisible and heavenly,"[83] is a hero that shares the characteristics of the sea, storm-tossed, weathered, and powerful; Mary, the heroine, is reflected in the pastoral landscape, gentle, pure, and serene. With many suitors from town, Mary is drawn away from the peace of her rural setting to the profane pleasures of fashionable summer houses as "Newport at present day blooms like a flower garden with young ladies of the best *ton.*"[84] Stowe uses the orchard as a metaphor for temptation and as a temporal marker as the seasons change during Mary's adventures: "she looked out into the fragrant orchard, whose perfumes steamed in at her window, and listened to the first chirping of birds among the old apple-trees."[85]

Landscape and literature combine in Stowe's novel to evoke the eternal Eden, encompassing both virtue and vice. Nearly twenty years after Kensett and Stowe immortalized Newport's rocks and orchards in paint and pen, a new generation reinterpreted these same features for their own time. William Trost Richards's *Old Orchard at Newport* (1875) is suffused with a light similar to that of Kensett, but the spirit of the work is somewhat different. Whereas Kensett records a natural feature, Richards depicts a pastoral scene crafted by human hands. He painted in the nascent period of the Colonial Revival, as the nation approached its centennial (Figs. 72 and 73). Artists and writers seeking locations redolent with colonial-era associations could find them in Newport, whether real or imagined. As Richards captured old orchards with the oils on his canvas, the architect Charles Follen McKim did so with a camera. In 1874, he commissioned the photographer William James Stillman to undertake a study of Newport's buildings, places, and objects of historical interest. Among this portfolio of images is an apple orchard (Fig. 74). The scale of the trees suggests that they are at least a century old, harkening back to the colonial period. McKim viewed the site as a repository of historical and cultural meaning. How appropriate for Newport, proclaimed as America's Eden, to have an ancient apple orchard.

Stillman's photograph may have captured an apple orchard as a symbol of a bygone age. However, time did not stand still in Newport, which continued to expand with attendant changes to the landscape, as expressed by George Champlin Mason:

> *How time has changed the whole southern portion of this island! [H]ow the reality has surpassed the dreams of the most sanguine. . . . Where there was a wavy field a year ago, now there is a beautiful lawn, perfectly graded, and liberally stocked with trees that have numbered more than a score of years. Who that sees them in their budding freshness can realize this, or believes that so much could have been accomplished in so short a time?*[86]

The summer resort first developed in the 1840s and 1850s on the relatively flat terrain of Bellevue Avenue, where gardeners easily shaped and formed the earth to suit the taste for delicate flowers and rare trees. In terms of the topography, little stood in their way. Only the high winds off the ocean offered resistance, tempered by the planting of protective stands of

Fig. 74
William James Stillman,
Orchard, 1874, photograph
McKim Portfolio, Newport
Historical Society, P403

evergreens. With wealth and a cadre of nursery owners, horticulturists, and gardeners at their service, and guided by the principles of picturesque design, the great Victorians transformed an open meadowland into a summer paradise. Their achievement was duly recorded:

> *miles of barren pasture have been converted into lawns and gardens and verdant groves; millions have been expended in the erection of beautiful villas and stately palaces; the tide of population has set in like a flood; and such are the peculiar advantages which Nature has bestowed upon this lovely spot, that no caprice of fashion can ever turn back or arrest the flow of its prosperity. . . . the summer population will spread out over the southern portion of the island, from east to west, and then crowd back into the interior, until the whole area from south to north is made a garden of beauty.*[87]

While gardeners transformed the soil and arranged trees and flowers, artists were contributing to the creation of a mythic vision of the land with pen, paint, and photograph. As the decades progressed, a new version of the picturesque would evolve from the genteel, gardenesque landscapes of the mid-nineteenth century to a more rustic version embracing rough-hewn rock and churning waves.

TOURO PARK

Public Green Spaces in the Genteel Landscape

History, mystery, and strolling paths make up the romance and reality of Touro Park. With land gifted to the city by Judah Touro, a park was established in 1854 by the philanthropists, business owners, real estate investors, and cottage builders who were directing the future of the summer resort. Named after its benefactor, Touro Park is located between Pelham and Mill Streets, on a piece of land that had been owned during the colonial period by the Arnold family, its narrow rectangular shape a remnant of the original plots of land laid out by the first European settlers in the seventeenth century.

At the center of the park stands the Stone Tower, a source of mystery even today, since no documentation pertaining to its construction or original use has been found (Figs. 75–78). Emerging as an iconic image in engravings, illustrations, and photographs, the historic structure became an early sightseeing attraction, when the legend arose that it was built by Viking explorers, Newport's version of Stonehenge. Though these epic origins were not proven, they were entertained nonetheless. With its manicured lawn, flowering trees, serpentine paths, and centrally placed gazebo for concerts, the park served as place to promenade in the shadow of a grand historic monument. Over time, sculptures memorializing Newport figures were added: William Ellery Channing, the founder of Unitarianism, and Commodore Matthew Perry, who opened the ports of Japan to Western trade, each have their spot.

The motivations behind the creation of this open green space lie in Newport's emergence as a summer resort and in the nascent park movement in the United States. The public park as a designed space for the aesthetic appreciation of nature is a nineteenth-century development. Boston's Public Garden (1839) is one of the earliest botanical gardens in this mode. Touro Park falls within this model of urban spaces, with its emphasis on public access and enjoyment. Grander visions were soon realized. In the late 1850s, Frederick Law Olmsted and Calvert Vaux began work on Central Park in New York City, a major moment in the evolution of picturesque landscapes as primary feature of the geography of American cities. Olmsted came to Newport in 1894 to design Morton Park, and his sons, as the Olmsted Brothers firm, would advocate for the creation of Miantonomi Park in the early 1900s, which became a reality in 1923.

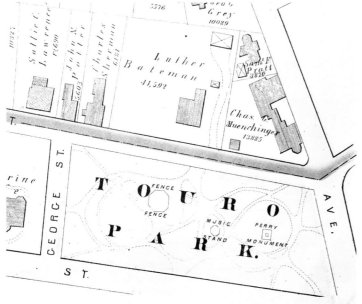

Fig. 75 (above)
H. S. Newcomb, *View of Newport Harbor*, 1823, watercolor
New-York Historical Society, Gift of Issac Cozzens

Fig. 76 (left)
Plan of Touro Park, from G. M. Hopkins, *City Atlas of Newport, Rhode Island* (1876)
Newport Historical Society
Photograph courtesy of the Preservation Society of Newport County

011392. OLD STONE MILL, NEWPORT, R.I.

Fig. 77 (opposite)
Stone Tower, Touro Park, ca. 1890, photograph
Library of Congress

Fig. 78 (above)
View of Touro Park, ca. 1880, photograph
Library of Congress

CASE STUDY

THE HORTICULTURISTS

Jennifer Robinson

Historic Preservation Specialist

I n the mid-nineteenth century, America's preeminent voice in the emerging field of American horticulture and landscape architecture was Andrew Jackson Downing, a New York pomologist, writer, and tastemaker. In 1846, Downing launched a periodical called the *Horticulturist*, offering advice to professional and amateur gardeners throughout the country. In its 1851 issue, Newport is highlighted as having "the mildest climate in the United States," and as such, is viewed as an ideal location for planting and gardening.[1]

The fact that Newport was singled out in Downing's journal certainly lent it high esteem; no doubt, Newport's garden enthusiasts would have had access to publications like Downing's and would have looked towards them for the latest fashionable advice. Newport's earliest summer cottages were emerging simultaneously with an explosion of horticultural guidance from new print material. Their owners relied on knowledge from these sources, as well as the local expertise of suppliers and experienced gardeners—a significant portion of whom originated from England, Scotland, and Ireland—to make decisions about their landscapes.

At the time of Downing's article, Newport had very few professional nurseries; Newport's earliest city directory, from 1856-7, indicates only three in existence.[2] Despite this, a local contributor to the *Horticulturist*, Alfred Smith, claimed that "250,000 ornamental trees," from both American nurseries and abroad, "have been planted in private grounds in and about Newport."[3] Although boastful, this statement suggests that during this early period plant material appears to have been sourced from a variety of locations, both professional and ad hoc.

From a professional perspective, perhaps no other nursery had the longevity or esteem of Thomas Galvin, one of Newport's earliest garden suppliers and professional "landscape gardeners." Galvin, an Irish immigrant who moved to Newport in 1845, began to cultivate and import plants to his nursery at the corner of Spring and Dearborn Streets in the mid-1800s. Upon his death in 1864, his son inherited the business and continued a tradition of horticultural excellence, adding multiple greenhouses and an ever-changing variety of so-called exotic plants.[4] However, city directories indicate that the Galvins were not alone in their business model. Newport's network of plant suppliers steadily grew throughout the nineteenth century—for example, to approximately twenty-two florists and nurseries in 1888—and provided residents with an increasing range of choices for their gardens and landscapes.[5]

Alternatively, there were other options available to estate owners and gardeners curious about improving their land. One of the most revealing primary sources related to this early era is the reminiscences of Mary Edith Powel, who lived on Bowery Street as a young girl beginning in 1853. Powel recalls an improvised network of local enthusiasts who shared both knowledge and plant material. She notes that her father, John Hare Powel, had a great deal of interest in designing and planting the family's garden; at her own house, cuttings and seeds were brought in from the family home in Philadelphia, including periwinkle, laburnum, and maple trees.[6] Other plants were exchanged or purchased among neighbors, including a fir tree from Edward King's house.[7] For these Newporters, horticulture was both a scholarly and genteel pursuit, a respectable pastime indicative of nineteenth-century preoccupations with the natural sciences.

Like John Powel, other Newport intellectuals and professionals took on gardening as a secondary, but nonetheless intense, avocation. Alfred Smith, a local real estate developer better-known today for his shrewd expansion of Bellevue Avenue, was an accomplished gardener in his own right. He wrote to the *Horticulturist* with suggestions for growing melons, and his personal garden at Mount Vernon Street was described as "the sylvan museum of the island."[8]

George Bancroft, a historian and diplomat, adopted a keen interest in horticulture, particularly in roses, at his summer home—aptly named Rose Cliff. From the 1850s until his death in 1891, Bancroft cultivated hundreds of varieties of roses, making his garden a known point of interest along the Cliff Walk.[9] In her reminiscences, Mary Edith Powel recalls visiting the Bancroft estate early in its conception with her family, remarking on rows of *Weigelia rosea* that had begun to populate the grounds. Powel remembers Bancroft visiting her family's home on Bowery Street, alluding to social exchanges that encouraged an emerging gardening community. There, according to Powel, he "would walk round our lot, and had a quizical [sic] way of turning his head on one side like a bird as he examined our trees about two feet high—well staked and mulched."[10]

In the end, Bancroft's name became associated with roses in the late nineteenth century; popular horticultural magazines even promoted "Bancroft roses" as a particular varietal.[11] His Washington, D.C., garden gained prominence in the 1880s, when many attributed the American Beauty rose to the site. However, vigorous debate ensued in periodicals, which argued that the American Beauty may have in fact originated in France, and that its ultimate lineage in the United States could not be determined.[12] Despite this, Bancroft still remains a horticulturist entwined with this cultivar, and with the history of rose culture in America.

The intense horticultural fascination exhibited at Bancroft's Newport garden was mirrored at the Gibbs Avenue home of Harvard chemist Oliver Walcott Gibbs, who built Hillside in 1887 and established a private laboratory there. He also assembled a wide variety of plants and trees and maintained a garden.[13] With apparent access to botanical expertise via his colleague Charles Sprague Sargent at the Arnold Arboretum in Boston, Gibbs also contributed to articles in Sargent's periodical *Garden and Forest*.[14] Mary Edith Powel recalled the Gibbs property, and Dr. Gibbs's circle of fellow Newport gardeners:

> *Mr [George] Bancroft . . . halted frequently his great horse at the [Hillside] gate, and long were the cogitations of the historian and the chemist over seeds, plants and roses . . . The garden in Gibbs Avenue, for a quarter of a century, has been a foremost in wealth of novelties, and Dr Gibbs' chief happiness lay in first proving the worth of his specimens and then bestowing the plants on some friends, enriching them and making space for new importations. No one in Newport grew such Spanish, German, and above all, Japanese Iris, such single paeonys [sic], such varieties or such stalwart stalks of gladioli. He revived the helebores [sic] of old gardens; mid-winter blooms—out of a frame, buried in snow and cautioned 'that the stalks must be slit for blossoming in the vases.' He set wake-robin in the shade of magnolias, and flowering shrubs too many to describe in a border about the grounds. Nursed a flowering cherry of his own planting and a giant hickory, that the British has forgotten to cut down in the Revolution, with equal solicitude, until both gave way to a single blizzard storm in [19]18.[15]*

It is important to note that this elaborate scheme was not produced and maintained solely by Dr. Gibbs. Powel mentions the assistance of both Neil Belton, Gibbs's nephew, and a skilful Black gardener named only as "Matthew," who had once also worked for Dr. David King of Bellevue Avenue.[16]

Nearby on Gibbs Avenue, Dr. Gibbs's cousin-in-law, Virginia Gibbs, was overseeing horticultural experiments at her home, Bethshan. Virginia had equal ambitions with her landscape, collaborating with Sargent in particular choices—including species sourced from China and beyond. She even purchased land in Middletown on Forest Avenue (then named Bethshan-in-the-Woods) to expand her ever-growing tree collection. In 1905, author Mariana Griswold Van Rensselaer praised Virginia as "a noted botanist and naturalist, having made some original researches that are very remarkable."[17]

This type of mania for botany, collection, and planting extended throughout the nineteenth and into the early twentieth century, as Bellevue Avenue continued to develop southward and Ocean Drive began to take shape. For many, access to renowned national firms and increasingly sophisticated networks resulted in highly developed and designed landscapes. However, most work and decision making was left to landscape architects' and gardeners' discretion. These professionals had considerable knowledge, evident in print publications that show local gardeners' broad regional and national participation in horticulture, through the exchange of ideas, contests, and advice on planting and related endeavors.

Notes

1 "The Horticultural Advertiser," *Gardeners' Monthly and Horticulturist* 24, no. 279 (March 1882): 8.

2 *Boyd's Newport City Directory*, compiled by William H. Boyd (Newport, RI: William H. Boyd, 1856–57).

3 Andrew Jackson Downing, "Domestic Notices: The Mildest Climate in the Northern States," *Horticulturist* 6, no. 12 (December 1851): 574–75.

4 Leonard J. Panaggio, "Thomas Galvin, An Early Professional Gardener," *Newport History Journal* 130 (Spring 1968): 85–89; Richard M. Bayles, ed., *History of Newport County* (New York: L. E. Preston, 1888), 596–97.

5 *Boyd's Newport City Directory*; Newport Directory (Providence, RI: Sampson, Murdock and Co., 1888).

6 Mary Edith Powel Diaries, vol. 1B, undated, pp. 25–26, 35, Box 150A, Newport Historical Society.

7 Mary Edith Powel Diaries, vol. 1B, undated, p. 33, Box 150A, Newport Historical Society.

8 A. Gerald Hull, "Melons and Their Culture," *Horticulturist* 6, no. 11 (November 1851): 513; Andrew Jackson Downing, "Domestic Notices: The Mildest Climate in the United States," *Horticulturist* 6, no. 7 (December 1851): 574–75.

9 M. A. DeWolfe Howe, *The Life and Letters of George Bancroft*, vol. 2 (New York: Charles Scribner's Sons, 1908), 99–100, 284 ; L. D. Davis, "The Gardens of Newport—I," *American Garden: An Illustrated Journal of Horticulture* 12, no. 6, (June 1891): 322.

10 Mary Edith Powel Diaries, "Bowery Street Volume 2," undated, p. 36, Box 150A, Newport Historical Society.

11 "The Horticultural Advertiser," *Gardener's Monthly and Horticulturist* 24, no. 279 (March 1882): 8.

12 John L. H. Frank, "The American Beauty," *Gardener's Monthly and Horticulturist* 29, no. 344 (August 1887): 232–33; "An Interesting Problem," *American Gardening* 18, no. 116 (March 1897): 206; L. H. Bailey, *Cyclopedia of American Horticulture* (New York: Macmillan Company, 1900), 131.

13 Maud Howe Elliot, *This Was My Newport* (1944; reprint, Salem, NH: Ayer Company, 1990), 106–7.

14 Richard Champlin, "Newport Estates and Their Flora," *Journal of Newport History* 53, part 2, no. 178 (Spring 1980): 52–55; "Plant Notes," *Garden and Forest* 7 (August 1, 1894): 304; Walcott Gibbs, "Wanted—A Hand-book of Horticulture," *Garden and Forest* 1 (April 4, 1888): 65–66.

15 Mary Edith Powel Journal, "The Gibbs Family of Rhode Island and Newport (to be kept with 'The Parade')," undated, Box 27, Newport Historical Society.

16 The full identity of the gardener referred to as "Matthew" remains unknown. U.S. Census records from 1870 to 1900 do not include him as part of the Gibbs household staff at the time of recording, and other census identifiers proved insufficient for a verified match. Mary Edith Powel's journal provides some details about Matthew's ties to Florida that may prove helpful in further research: "The chief gardeners were, of course, Dr Gibbs and his nephew Neil Belton, but the 'army' consisted of clever old Matthew." An African-American brought from Florida to Newport, Matthew worked for a Mrs. Belton and for many years served Dr. David King. (Mary Edith Powel Journal, "The Gibbs Family of Rhode Island and Newport (to be kept with 'The Parade')," undated, Box 27, Newport Historical Society).

17 Champlin, "Newport Estates and Their Flora," 49–55; Mrs. John King Van Rensselaer, *Newport: Our Social Capital* (Philadelphia: J. B. Lippincott, 1905), 65.

SUMMER HOUSE AT OCHRE POINT

The Art of Scenery

DESIGN IN THE AGE OF THE PICTURESQUE

We shall not attempt to describe the beautiful scenery which attracts the eye on every side . . . but as we have viewed the wide expanse of ocean on one side and the rugged, jutting rocks, and hills and valleys on the other, we were reminded of [Washington] Irving's saying that "never need an American look beyond his own country for the sublime and beautiful in nature's scenery.

—George Champlin Mason, "Local Matters: Ocean Avenue," 1867

Excitement and opportunity filled the air in the fall of 1867. Architects and landscape designers had a new canvas upon which to practice their art. Ocean Avenue officially opened to great acclaim, a much hoped for thoroughfare planned with an objective: the enjoyment of scenery. George Champlin Mason championed this grand undertaking with both his paint brush and his pen. He produced a painting suffused with ideal pastoral beauty and brimming with sublime light to sway and seduce both the public and potential investors (Fig. 79), and as early as the 1850s he was writing articles to promote the idea:

> *we venture to say that no more beautiful drive can be imagined than the one here projected. It has everything to make it attractive: the inequalities of the surface, the boldness of the rocky promontories, and the near approach to the sea, are charms that it will ever possess and fortunate will be the owner of one of the commanding sites along this line . . . and we look forward to the day when it will be studded with marine villas, rising from every commanding eminence.*[88]

Mason knew how to elicit temptation to further his cause. Property owners and real estate speculators, among them Kennedy, Bateman, Hazard, Bailey, and Smith, saw a combination of profit and civic improvement, commissioning the road and the necessary bridges along the coves.[89] This endeavor did not merely constitute a construction project, it signaled an aesthetic pivot point (Fig. 80). The undulating southern coastline of Newport appealed to picturesque tastes, already well established by the mid-1800s. It also provided a setting for landscape design less genteel, more in sync with rustic settings than the gardens of the mid-century with their delicate gardenesque beds of flowers. While celebrating nature, Andrew Jackson Downing endorsed its improvement, imposing a degree of civility on scenic

Summer house at Ochre Point, ca. 1885, photograph
Newport Historical Society, P9459

Fig. 79
George Champlin Mason, *Rocky Farm and Cherry Neck* (detail), 1857, oil on canvas
Redwood Library and Athenaeum
The artist depicts the south coast of Newport prior to construction of Ocean Avenue in the 1860s.

views and plant materials that might become unruly. In the hands of landscape designers in the 1880s and thereafter, and in the setting of Ocean Avenue in particular, nature reigned in its wilder form, still shaped and tempered by human effort but in a less rarefied form than in the cottages of Bellevue Avenue created between the 1840s and 1870s.

The terrain of Ocean Avenue offered opportunities to those with vision. It presented itself to some as a dramatic windswept series of hills and valleys, a blank canvas for creativity; to others, it appeared desolate. In either case, the taste of architects and landscape designers working in concert with topography guided its development (Fig. 81). Frederick Law Olmsted—a leader of the developing profession of landscape architecture, park maker, tree-lined-boulevard shaper, writer, and observer of the American scene—would exert an extraordinary influence upon the southern coast of Newport. Viewing landscape as the material for a work of art, he wrote,

> I shall venture to assume to myself the title of artist and to add that no sculptor, painter or architect can have anything like the difficulty in sketching and conveying a knowledge of his design to those who employ him which must attend upon an artist employed for such a kind of designing as is required of me. The design must be almost exclusively in my imagination . . . my picture is all alive—its very essence is life, human and vegetable.[90]

In 1885, the King, Glover, and Bradley families commissioned Olmsted to lay out their combined holdings of 361.5 acres in the Ocean Avenue district (Figs. 82–84). Here he combined his gifts as both visionary and pragmatist, devising a system of roads and house lots that capitalized on sight lines for distant views of terrain and ocean while requiring attention to every detail of the functional thoroughfares. Both topics were on his mind, as he wrote of his proposed scheme:

> The plan of the subdivision is to secure the largest advantages of scenery for each of a series of building sites . . . The eminences and seaward slopes are wind swept and now treeless, but bear an abundance of varied and very interesting forms of vegetation and owing to their

Fig. 80
Ocean Avenue (detail), from
Halt and Goy, *Newport 1878*
Library of Congress

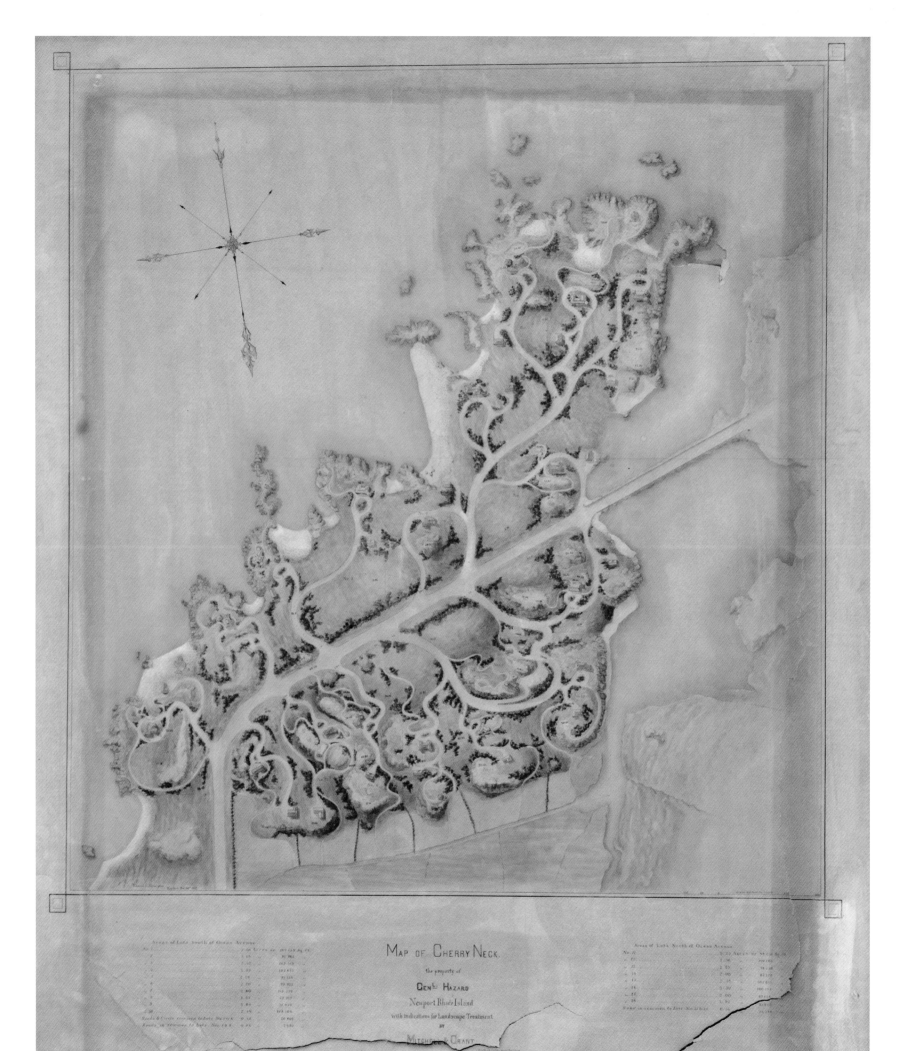

MAP OF CHERRY NECK.

the property of

Genl. Hazard

Newport Rhode Island

with indications for Landscape Treatment

BY

Mitchell & Grant.

abrupt craggy formation are of highest picturesque aspect. With buildings and gardens designed consistently with these natural circumstances, residences will be obtained of a more interesting and agreeable character, having great natural and permanent advantages over those of older villa districts of Newport for the enjoyment of sea breezes and of ocean and harbor scenery.[91]

The King-Glover-Bradley plat received accolades from the most prominent architectural and landscape critic of the era. Mariana Griswold Van Rensselaer, writing in *Garden and Forest*, praised Olmsted's work and offered a measure of censure to earlier landscapes.

Here the ground is hilly with bold and beautiful high rocks, offering building sites of a very desirable kind—with no sea fronts, it is true, but with the most superb distant views of land and water . . . It is to be hoped that those who may hereafter build here in this neighborhood will carefully and artistically preserve its character and not strive to subdue its rugged and individual charm to that neat prettiness which prevails in the level districts nearer town.[92]

The level districts Van Rensselaer refers to are the Bellevue Avenue and Kay-Catherine neighborhoods on the eastern side of Newport, the site of mid-nineteenth-century Gothic Revival, Italianate, and Second Empire French cottages surrounded by colorful flower beds and flat, manicured lawns. Changing tastes in landscape in general and topographical settings specific to Ocean Avenue dictated the ever more natural approach of the 1880s, defined in great measure by two masterful works by Frederick Law Olmsted: one set on the rocky shore, one sited high atop a rocky eminence, both displaying the sensitivity to site, soil, and scenery that are the hallmarks of his work.

The Reefs (1885), built for Theodore M. Davis, rested on the very southwestern tip of Newport on Brenton's Point, braced on one side by Rhode Island Sound and on the other by the entrance to Narragansett Bay. Olmsted welcomed the high winds and crashing waves. The house, built in granite and brownstone, had an unobstructed view of the ocean, an endless scene of blue or gray depending on the weather and the day (Figs. 85 and 86). Olmsted laid out a series of curving paths among open lawns, allowing the sea to play its central unrelenting part in the composition. To the northwest of the house, protected by the planting of a tree-lined walk, he installed rows of flowers and shrubs. Olmsted's plan offered a template for implementing a grounds scheme that worked with a panoramic scene and did not impose materials on the site but used the subtle contours of the land and protective elements, where appropriate, to create corridors of lush greenery.

Indian Spring (1887–92), originally designed for William Dorsheimer and later owned by J. R. Busk, surmounts a summit covered with rocky outcroppings. Olmsted's topographical plan consists of a drive that immediately confronts an enormous cliff face and closely follows the contour of the hill until arriving at the main house of rusticated granite and brownstone by

Fig. 81
Edward L. Hyde, *Map of Cherry Neck*, November 30, 1867
Newport Historical Society, FIC.2015.006
The map is inscribed as follows: "Map of Cherry Neck Property of Gen. L. Hazard Newport, Rhode Island with indications for Landscape Treatment by Mitchell and Grant, Bank Commerce Building." The serpentine roads contouring with natural topography to frame views of natural scenery inherent in this plan are evident in subsequent plans by Frederick Law Olmsted and his partners for the Ocean Avenue district.

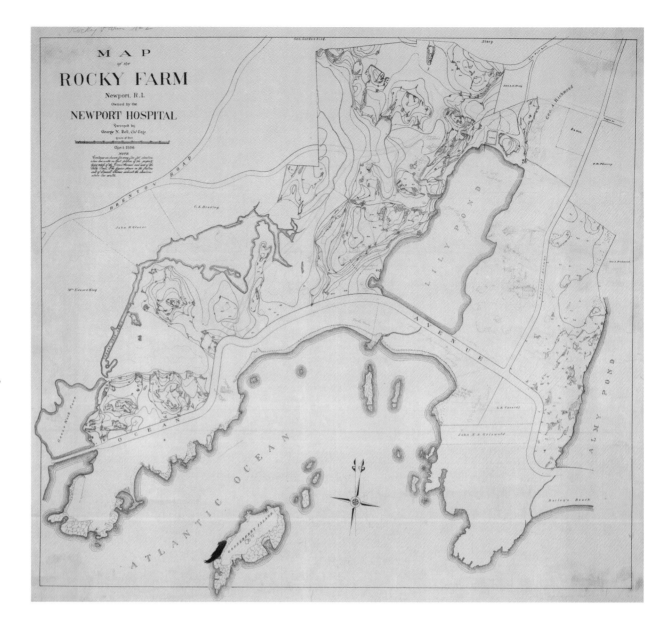

Fig. 82 (right)
Frederick and John Charles Olmsted, *Map of the Rocky Farm*, 1886
United States Department of the Interior, National Park Service, Frederick Law Olmsted National Historic Site

Fig. 83 (below)
Frederick and John Charles Olmsted, *Plan for the Subdivision of a Part of the Property of the Newport Hospital*, 1886
United States Department of the Interior, National Park Service, Frederick Law Olmsted National Historic Site

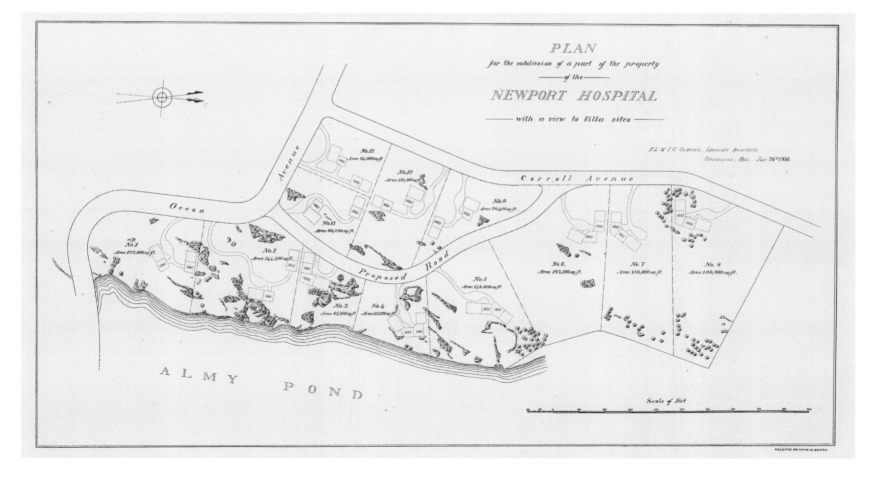

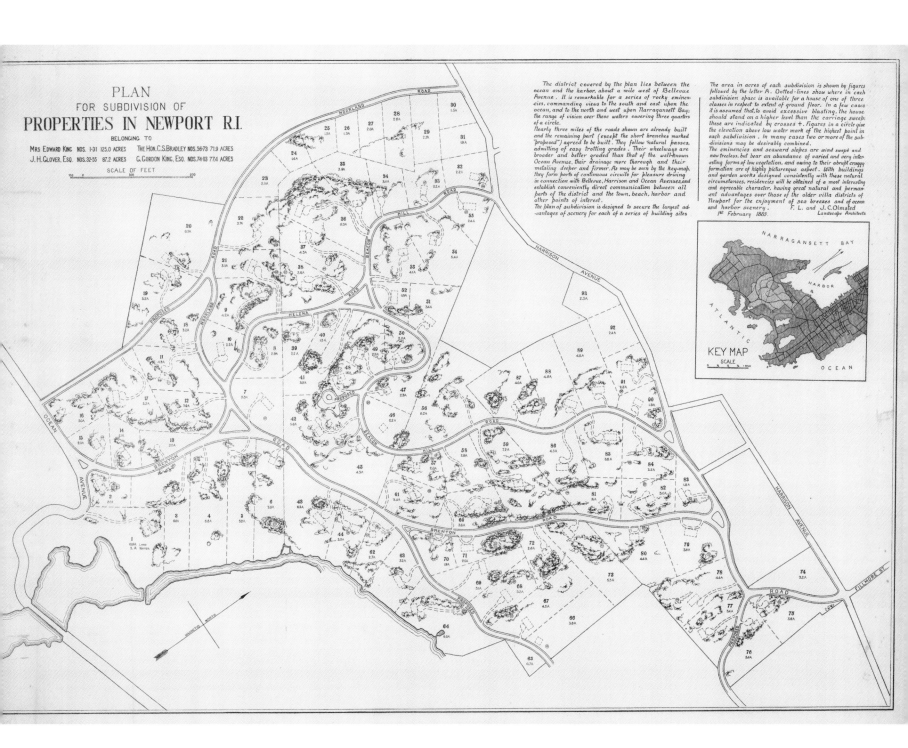

Fig. 84
Olmsted, Olmsted and Eliot, *Plan for Subdivision of Properties in Newport R.I.*, King-Glover-Bradley plat, 1886
United States Department of the Interior, National Park Service,
Frederick Law Olmsted National Historic Site

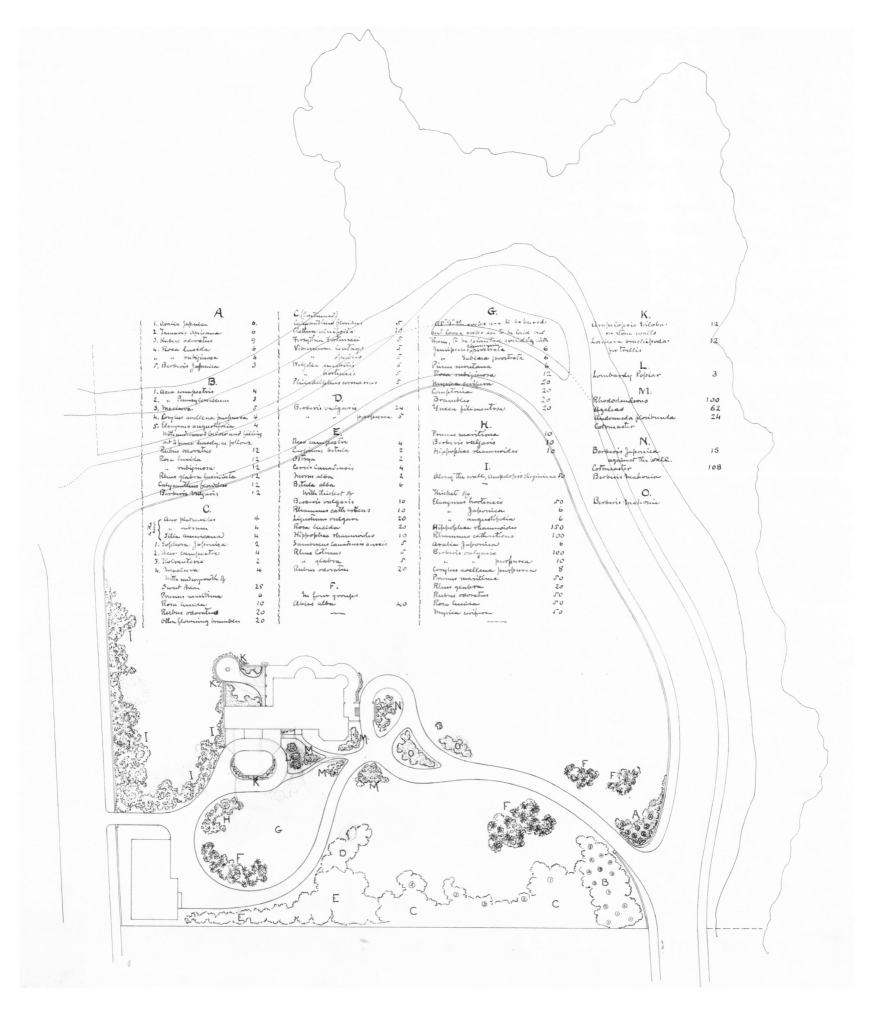

Richard Morris Hunt, who carefully inserted it among the ancient glacial remains (Figs. 87–90). The rough texture of stone, both natural and shaped by the artisan, is the dominant characteristic of the estate. This refined rusticity pervading the building and landscape of Indian Spring represented a novel approach in Newport. The ocean-facing side of the property is so laden with stone that a layer of topsoil was added and various succulents, such as sedum, planted in ground that was so arid as to be inhospitable to most plants. On the side of the hill facing the countryside, a protected valley fostered a microclimate, allowing for the propagation of woody plants, including viburnum and rhododendrons. Olmsted selected spruce and other fir trees, flowering shrubs, and plants that flourished naturally in this specific topography and soil, and perfected the art of scenery with sight lines that extended far beyond the confines of the estate itself. This integration of a designed landscape with distant views characterized his work in Central Park in the 1860s and would continue to be developed in both public and private landscape projects throughout his career.

Olmsted's work on The Reefs and Indian Spring provided a model for the development of succeeding houses and landscapes in the Ocean Avenue district.[93] His subdivision of the King-Glover-Bradley lands, which evolved into a harmonious series of estates extraordinary in their rustic manner and orientation towards panoramic views, is a case in point. Although Olmsted

Fig. 85 (opposite)
Frederick Law Olmsted, Site plan for The Reefs, 1886
United States Department of the Interior, National Park Service, Frederick Law Olmsted National Historic Site

Fig. 86 (above)
The Reefs, from *Gardens and Gardening* (1890), photograph
Redwood Library and Athenaeum

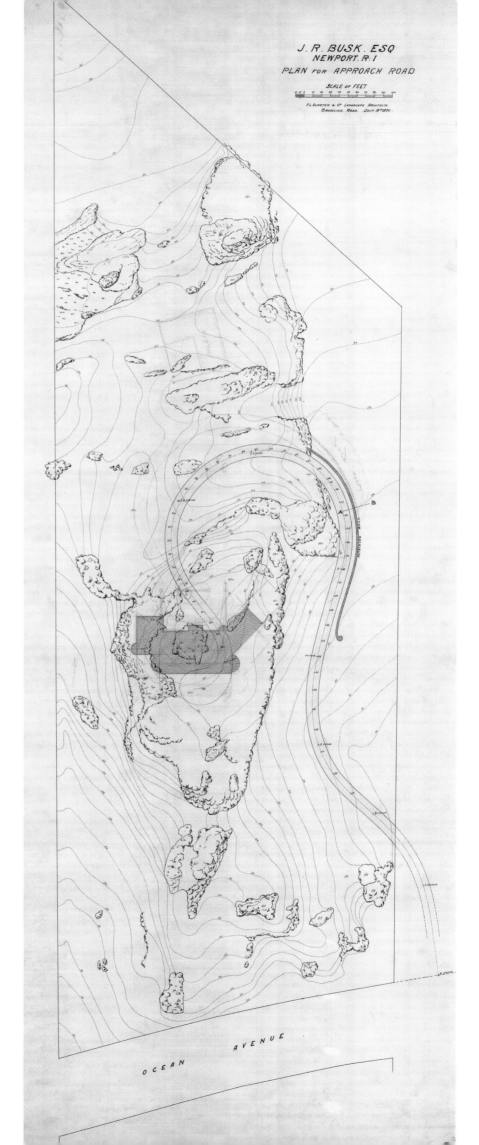

Fig. 87 (opposite, top)
Indian Spring, 1890,
photograph
Newport Historical Society,
P1790

Fig. 88 (opposite, bottom)
Richard Morris Hunt, William
Dorsheimer House, 1890,
elevation
Library of Congress

Fig. 89 (right)
Frederick Law Olmsted, *Plan
for Approach Road*, J. R. Busk
House, 1890
United States Department of
the Interior, National Park
Service, Frederick Law Olmsted
National Historic Site

Fig. 90
H.D. Perkins, Main drive, Indian
Spring, 1916, photograph
United States Department of
the Interior, National Park
Service, Frederick Law Olmsted
National Historic Site

determined the serpentine road system, he designed no estate landscapes in the subdivision. He did, however, assist in the siting of one of its first houses, Berry Hill (1886), now known as Wild Moor. McKim, Mead and White designed the house, with Samuel Parsons Jr. credited as advising on the plantings. Parsons partnered with Calvert Vaux in the late 1870s, working with the architect on New York City parks.[94] Fully trained in the picturesque art of shaping scenery and respecting the character of a site, Parsons had a superb location to work with in the geological formations and vistas of Berry Hill (Figs. 91–93). An entrance forecourt is created by a natural depression between two hills—one the foundation for the house, the other containing a collection of Asian specimen trees and shrubs. Olmsted's ideas for the positioning of the house and how people might move through the landscape are laid out in his proposal:

> *in each subdivision space is available for a house of one of three classes in respect to extent of ground floor. In a few cases it is assumed that to avoid excessive blasting, the house should stand on a higher level than the carriage sweep. . . . In many cases two or more of the subdivisions may be desirably combined.*[95]

Fig. 91
Berry Hill, ca. 1920, photograph
Newport Historical Society,
P5956

Walter and Mary Ann Bruce Howe acquired the nineteen-acre plot in 1887, giving them space to focus on their horticultural interests. For the next century, the family collected trees, shrubs, and flowers, combining a variety of natural textures and diverse plants. Walter Howe's essay in *The Garden* reveals his ideas about design and his plans for Berry Hill, writing that landscape

> *is indeed an art, demanding not merely refined taste, sound judgement, and a real love of nature, but thorough training and cultivation. . . . for those who own land the great pity is that they will not merely refrain from growing flowers, but they will plant no trees. If they care not for flowers, perhaps it may not be worthwhile to argue with them, but as to trees the case is different.*[96]

Committed to learning about landscape theory and practice, the Howes joined a circle of gardeners, both amateur and professional, who used their Newport estates as living experiments in horticulture. The Howes dedicated themselves to trees with vigor and discernment, adding East Asian specimens such as Japanese cypress and gingko along with many woodland shrubs popular at the time, including rhododendron, mountain laurel, and viburnum. Although Walter Howe died in 1890, Mary Ann Bruce remained at Berry Hill and carried on with the development of its grounds. She continued to maintain an interest in the landscape, studying botany at Columbia University. In 1893, she married Arnold Hague, a geologist with the U.S. Geological Survey and a dedicated botanist. Berry Hill became his ideal laboratory, with its rocky terrain and abundance of room for introducing new plants, some suited to the windswept meadows, others flourishing in the estate's protective groves of trees and small valleys. The Hagues laid out numerous trails

Fig. 92
Berry Hill, ca. 1920, photograph
Newport Historical Society, P9536

Fig. 93
Berry Hill, ca. 1920, photograph
Newport Historical Society, P9537

Fig. 94
Robert Yarnall Richie, Arthur
Curtiss James's Edgehill estate,
1932–34, photograph
Robert Yarnall Richie
Photograph Collection
DeGolyer Library, Southern
Methodist University
Also visible are Wyndham (top
left) and Roslyn (just below
Wyndham).

throughout the property and planted red maple, sweet gum, beech, and mugo pine along with ferns, yucca, autumn crocus, trout lilies, narcissus, and purple iris.[97] Mary Ann's son, Bruce Howe, and his Scottish gardener, Donald McKay Fraser, continued sourcing plants to add to the collection through the 1970s.[98] The diversity continued to become more complex with the planting of andromeda, hollies, lindens, dogwoods, flowering crabapples, white azaleas, pines, firs, yews, birches, and daffodils. By the time of a 1992 plant survey, over 350 varieties of trees and plants could still be found on the property.[99] As a result of continual collecting, the estate reads as an encyclopedia of horticultural specimens, both established and newly popular in the late nineteenth and twentieth centuries. It is the true creation of plant collectors extraordinaire.

Berry Hill (now called Wild Moor) crowns its rocky mount whereas Edgehill (1887–88), a short distance away, is true to its name, perched at the crest of a steep slope. McKim, Mead and White designed the stone and shingle house, and the Olmsted Brothers, the sons of Frederick Sr., devised a landscape along a narrow ridge with very little acreage for a garden. It was built for George Gordon King, whose father Edward and mother Mary Augusta Leroy were investors in the King-Glover-Bradley subdivision. With space limited, the Olmsteds focused on dramatic planning. The original drive climbed the hill at an unusually steep grade, revealing the view over the adjacent pastures as one came closer to the main house, which featured a small flower garden and an elaborate arbor and garden seat (Figs. 94–96). Evergreens framed the entrance, and the

Fig. 95 (left)
Olmsted Brothers,
*Planting Study
for Boundary
Plantations*,
Edgehill, 1906
United States
Department of the
Interior, National
Park Service,
Frederick Law
Olmsted National
Historic Site

Fig. 96 below)
Olmsted Brothers,
*Detail of Arbor to
be Built against
Existing Brick Wall*,
Edgehill, 1906
United States
Department of the
Interior, National
Park Service,
Frederick Law
Olmsted National
Historic Site

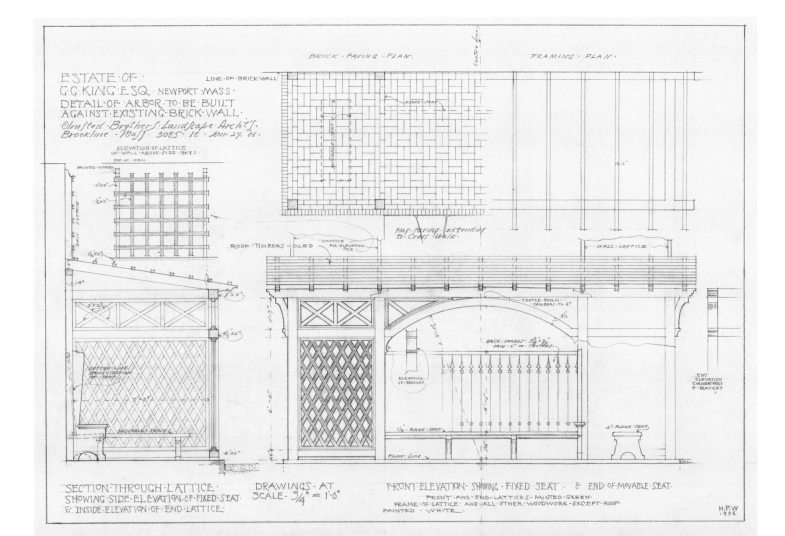

BLENDING an ESTATE
WITH the LANDSCAPE

hillside was graded to create an undulating platform for the building. The entire composition is an elegant series of sinuous lines on the land, an ingenious and theatrical adaptation of a demanding site.

Two properties across from Edgehill complete the picturesque ensemble on this high point of land: Wyndham for Rosa Anna Grosvenor and Roslyn for her brother, William Grosvenor, both built between 1890 and 1891 by architect William Ralph Emerson (Figs. 97–101). The American edition of *Country Life* expressed the essence of Wyndham, which occupied a sweeping hillside site of more than eleven acres, in an August 1923 article, describing the place as

a triumph of how an unpromising landscape can be used to best advantage. In developing Wyndham, Miss Grosvenor's main idea has been to maintain the note of rugged grandeur inherent in the site, but to soften it somewhat with careful planting. The blending of the house with the rocks, the relieving note of the foliage, and the introduction of the sheep into the picture, make it an ensemble worth of a Corot.[100]

The reference to the renowned mid-nineteenth-century French pastoral painter captures the spirit that permeates the estate and its neighbors. All features were directed towards an

artful effect of scene making, from the carefully staged series of walks to the composition of hills and hollows that directed the viewer's attention from a vista at one turn to a sheltered valley the next. Planned as a pastoral ideal, the grounds were planted with weeping beeches and a stately sawara falsecypress along the serpentine drive, while evergreens, notably juniper and weeping hemlocks, form an arcade of greenery along the steep stone steps leading from the highest promontory near the house into the sheltered sheep meadow below.

The extraordinary combination of view, geological interest points, and horticulture in the estates in the King-Glover-Bradley subdivision is an exceptional manifestation of the picturesque in a housing enclave. The unified design, both in architecture and in rolling landscapes, of the Ocean Avenue area had a counterpart on Ochre Point, where the civil engineer Ernest Bowditch worked with the architectural firm of Peabody and Stearns on two estates envisioned as a single garden with unobstructed views of the sea. At The Breakers (1877) and Vinland (1884), he stated, "the two places could be arranged to act as foils for each other."[101] Each house featured specimen trees, with several varieties of beech, and flowers set in beds on perimeter walkways (Figs. 102–4). Bowditch planned curving drives and interconnected paths to allow the occupants to freely stroll between the two properties.[102]

Fig. 100 (above)
Roselle McConnell, Garden house, Wyndham, 2020, photograph

Fig. 101 (right)
Robert Yarnall Richie, Rosa Grosvenor's Wyndham estate (center) and William Grosvenor's Roslyn estate (top left), 1932–34, photograph
Robert Yarnall Richie Photograph Collection, Negative Series: 0591, DeGolyer Library, Southern Methodist University

Fig. 102 (opposite, top)
The Breakers, ca. 1890, photograph
Newport Historical Society, P5608

Fig. 103 (opposite, bottom left)
Children's cottage, The Breakers, ca. 1890, photograph
Cornell University
The hollyhocks, clematis, and shrubs create a soft frame for the building.

Fig. 104 (below)
Ochre Point (detail), from G. M. Hopkins, *City Atlas of Newport, Rhode Island* (1883)
Newport Historical Society
Photograph courtesy of the Preservation Society of Newport County

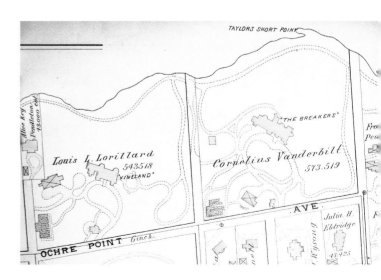

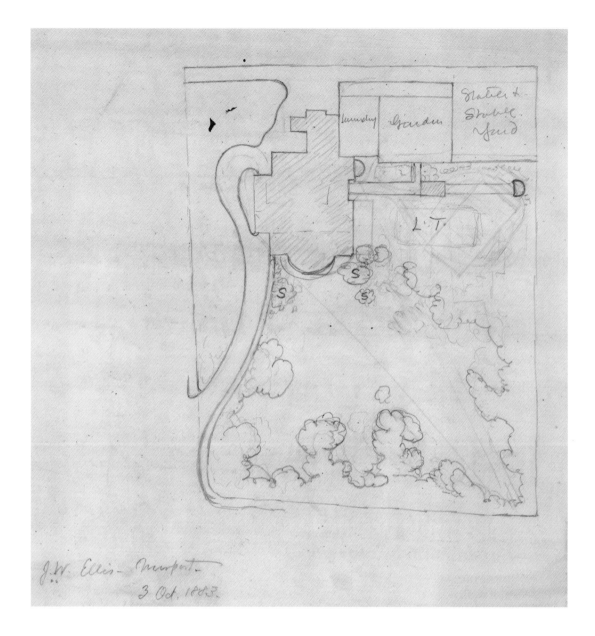

Fig. 105
Frederick Law Olmsted, Sketch
of John W. Ellis's Stoneacre
estate, 1883
United States Department of
the Interior, National Park
Service, Frederick Law Olmsted
National Historic Site
This preliminary drawing
illustrates Olmsted's process
for developing a serpentine
approach to the house.

With such energy and ingenuity being expended on Newport summer villas by the nation's leading, and emerging, architects and landscape designers, the art press turned its attention on the city to participate in what became a high-profile discourse on the present condition and future direction of American landscape design. The highly fashionable *Artistic Country Seats* (1886) expressed the transition in aesthetics from landscape gardening, with its lush use of flowers, to the more naturalistic work of the newly developing profession of landscape architecture:

> the artist who created the lawn, with its various embellishments, and a knowledge of the science of his business, and would have appreciated the emotions of the Andrew J. Downing, who said, "I love most of the soft turf which beneath the flickering shadows of scattered trees, is thrown like a smooth carpet over the swelling outline of the smiling earth. . . . Must we add flowers, exotic plants, fruits? Perhaps so; but they are all, in an ornamental light, secondary to trees and grass, where these can be had in perfection.[103]

Fig. 106
Stoneacre, 1885, photograph
Newport Historical Society,
P4096
Elms line this newly planted
landscape by Frederick Law
Olmsted.

In the pantheon of figures who shaped the landscapes of nineteenth-century America, a few in particular loom large. Andrew Jackson Downing began as a nurseryman who embraced the picturesque as an art form, championing its practice until his death in 1852. Frederick Law Olmsted rose as the leading light in landscape theory and practice in the 1860s, building on Downing's ideas and infusing them with a new spirit, redefining landscape gardening as the art of landscape architecture (Figs. 105 and 106). Olmsted wished to be known as an artist with a disciplined approach to his subject. He did not see himself only as a purchaser, propagator, and planter of trees, shrubs, and flowers, stating, "I have raised my calling from the rank of a trade, even of a handicraft, to that of a liberal profession, an art, an art of design."[104]

Mariana Griswold Van Rensselaer had already praised Olmsted's work on the King-Glover-Bradley subdivision and would continue to support his vision for the art and discipline of landscape architecture. Already established as an art and architecture critic, Mrs. Van Rensselaer, as she referred to herself, turned to writing about landscape in 1887 for *Garden and Forest*, the journal founded by horticulturist Charles Sprague Sargent, director of Boston's Arnold Arboretum. Her keen eye and nuanced sensibility for composition and color found its subject in Newport.

The best part of Newport is the beautiful Cliff Walk . . . passing villa after villa set back beyond verdant lawns . . . the appearance of brotherly concord between neighbor and neighbor and generosity towards the public, which it seems to reveal, added to its intrinsic charms, has made it a frequent theme for praise with foreign writers on landscape gardening and the arrangement of country towns.[105]

With their grand vistas and the artful placement of trees, the designs for the Lorillard estates on Ochre Point conformed to Van Rensselaer's ideal. However, she strongly disapproved in general of the type of elaborate flower beds deployed by Bowditch: "As a rule, their colors are crude and inharmonious, and they are multiplied out of all reason and placed where they do the greatest possible harm to the effect of the grounds as a whole."[106] Bowditch engaged in practices both fashionable and popular at the time, combining curving drives and paths with the bright colors of flowers (see Fig. 102). As a critic, Van Rensselaer firmly believed "the scheme is the main point. . . . do not be tempted by the beauty of individual things into frittering away or confusing its effect."[107] She believed that those creating landscapes should be not only trained practitioners but artists, enriched by a liberal education and intellectual and aesthetic discipline.[108] In a piece for *Garden and Forest*, she declared that the form, texture, and color of foliage were essential aspects to consider in the use of trees, just as a painter devises the composition, details, and hues of a work of art.[109]

The design principles articulated by Mrs. Van Rensselaer were championed by Frederick Law Olmsted at Rough Point, an estate at the juncture of Bellevue Avenue and Ocean Drive—a site where landscape architect and critic would prompt a national debate about the merits, and the future course, of the picturesque. Frederick William Vanderbilt, one of the heirs of the mighty New York Central Railroad, commissioned a house from Peabody and Stearns in rough-hewn granite and brownstone, much like so many along Ocean Avenue. Olmsted envisioned a "rugged moorland character" for the seaward side of the house, with the grass kept down by sheep and the ground between and above the rocks kept half arid, planted with low wild bushes.[110] There was nothing truly shocking about this. Sheep were kept at Olmsted's parks and at the Newport estate, Wyndham, but in the manicured world of Bellevue Avenue, the very idea caused consternation. At this point, the story became part of a drama played out in the press. Olmsted thought the Vanderbilts preferred a lawn rather than a meadow-like treatment, speculating, "it really seems as if [the blue turf] would be an abuse upon public taste."[111] Mrs. Van Rensselaer took up Olmsted's cause, declaring,

I am told that the owners are considering whether it will not be well to adopt a scheme for treating their grounds which will be an entire novelty in this part of Newport. This scheme would confine the lawns and garden shrubberies to the entrance side of the house, and treat the entire seaward slope in the most natural way possible. This portion is largely composed of visible rocks in varied shapes of the most interesting and picturesque character, and it certainly seems as though to plant it with low native shrubs and creepers and wildflowers, simulating, as far as possible, a spot which has not been planted at all, would be the best device.[112]

The Vanderbilts did not opt for a natural meadow tended by sheep, but they also did not choose to have elaborate flower beds. Instead, grass untroubled by any plantings rolled down to the sea. Olmsted's design, simple at first glance, is based on a careful consideration of the land mass of Rough Point (Figs. 107–9). Its simplicity was achieved through the complex study and shaping of the topography, retaining the stone outcroppings and emphasizing the major sight line to the waves that forcefully surged into an inlet with a stone bridge. Here the power of nature, the presence of geological features, and the vast expanse of sea were given their proper due. The transition from flower-filled genteel landscape gardening to a more natural mode of the picturesque was now firmly evident (Figs. 110 and 111).

Fig. 107
Frederick Law and John Charles Olmsted, *Study of Plan for Laying Out Rough Point*, 1888
United States Department of the Interior, National Park Service, Frederick Law Olmsted National Historic Site
The rock formations are integral to the Olmsted plan.

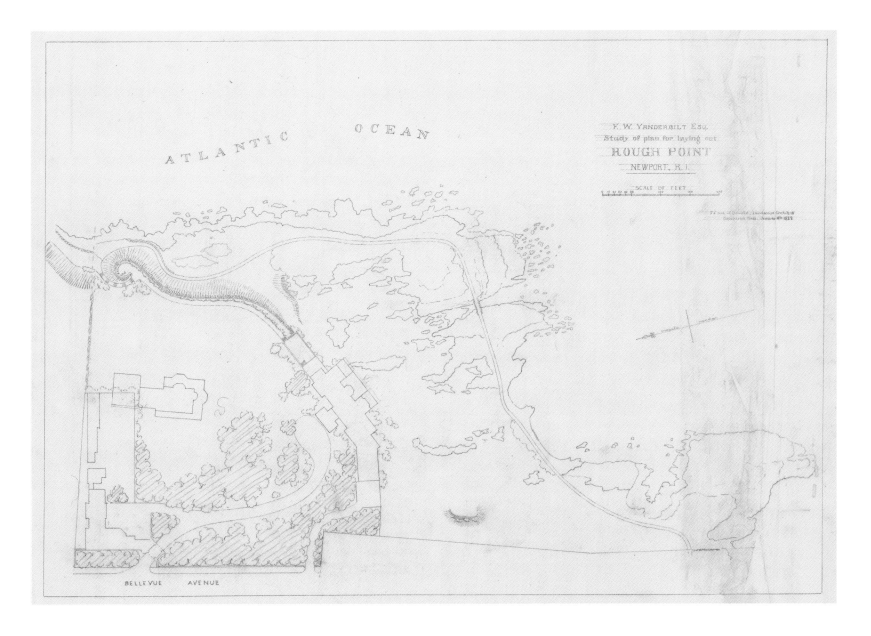

Fig. 108 (above)
H. D. Perkins, Rough Point,
1916, photograph
United States Department of
the Interior, National Park
Service, Frederick Law Olmsted
National Historic Site

Fig. 109 (left)
Stone Bridge, Rough Point,
ca. 1895, photograph
Newport Historical Society,
2009.3.60

Olmsted's achievement at Rough Point would be mirrored in his son's work at Wildacre (1902), set along a rock-strewn cove on Ocean Avenue. The California architect Irving Gill planned the Arts and Crafts house, while John Charles Olmsted advised Albert Olmsted, his father's half brother, on the grounds (Figs. 112–15).[113] The sheltered cove protected the gardens from high winds, allowing for the propagation of a rich collection of plants for the relatively small property. Green tones predominated, complimenting the weathered shingled surfaces and sweeping gables of the main house, which became enmeshed in a grove of pines and spruce.

In 1927, Olmsted Brothers advised on plantings for one of Newport's most elaborate Arts and Crafts gardens at The Waves, a house that lives up to its name, rising out of a pale pink-and rust-toned granite promontory almost continually awash in the sea. John Russell Pope designed the house for himself and his family in a Medieval English half-timbered style with a walled courtyard. Pope's skill in defying nature while integrating a building into it is in fine form at The Waves. Subject to gale-force winds, the location was not naturally suited to trees or fragile vegetation. Pope created a walled courtyard, sketching out his general ideas for the plan, which the Olmsteds implemented, focusing on four beds centered upon a sundial (Figs. 116–19). Within this sheltered setting, Pope requested layered borders of flowers, such as iris, peonies, and roses for the walled court and wisteria and honeysuckle for the entrance porch.[114]

Fig. 110
H. D. Perkins, Morton Park, 1916, photograph
United States Department of the Interior, National Park Service, Frederick Law Olmsted National Historic Site
Olmsted, Olmsted and Eliot employed similar approaches in public parks and private gardens. The designs for Morton Park and Rough Point (Fig. 107) preserve their respective topographies. Originally, the open space to the south of Morton Park afforded a view to Almy's Pond and the sea beyond, an example of Olmsted's use of distant views as part of his designed landscapes. In time, the land was developed, foreshortening the view.

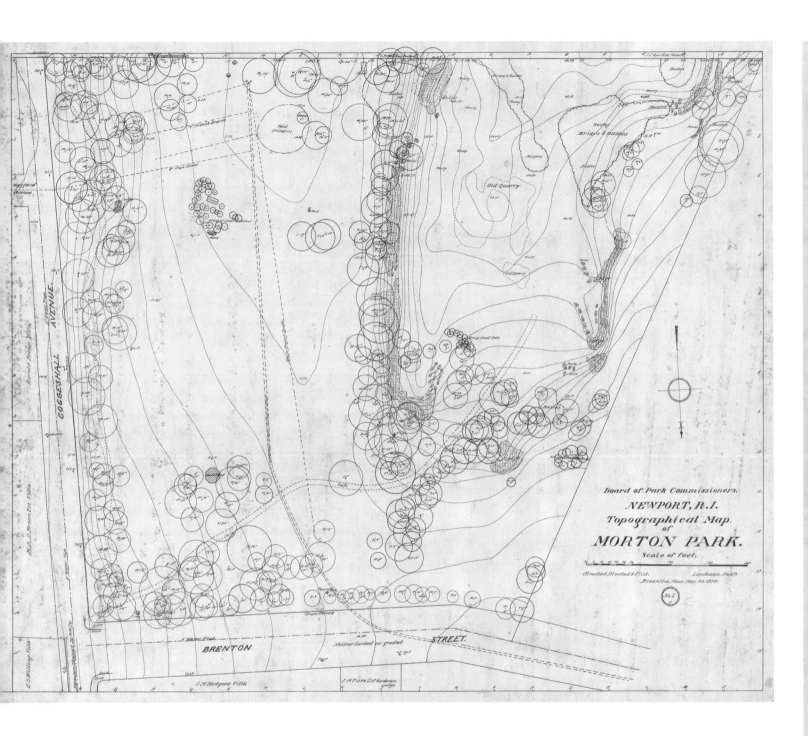

Fig. 111 (above)
Olmsted, Olmsted and Eliot, *Topographical Map of Morton Park*, 1894
United States Department of the Interior, National Park Service, Frederick Law Olmsted National Historic Site
The design has a large section of open lawn in the center of the park bordered by asymmetrically placed trees, including maple, elm, European and weeping beech, tulip, ash, and linden.

Fig. 112 (right)
John Charles Olmsted, *A.H. Olmsted, Esq. Planting Plan*, Wildacre, 1899
United States Department of the Interior, National Park Service, Frederick Law Olmsted National Historic Site

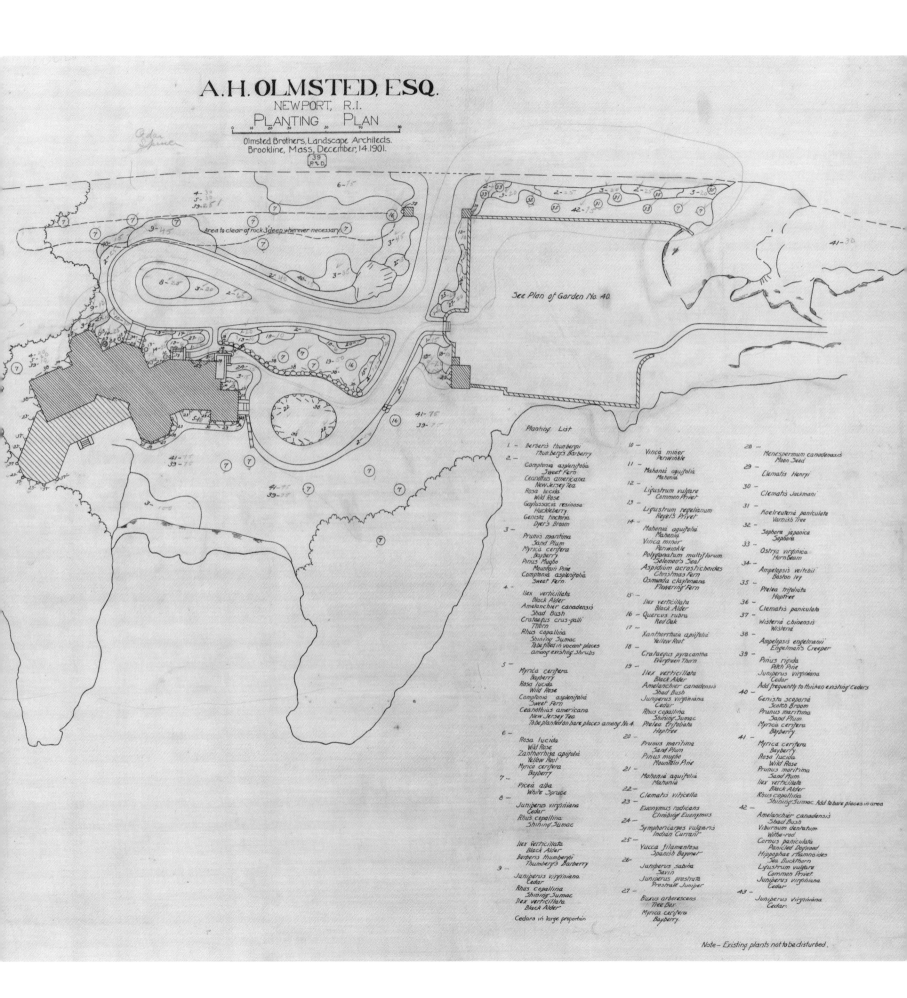

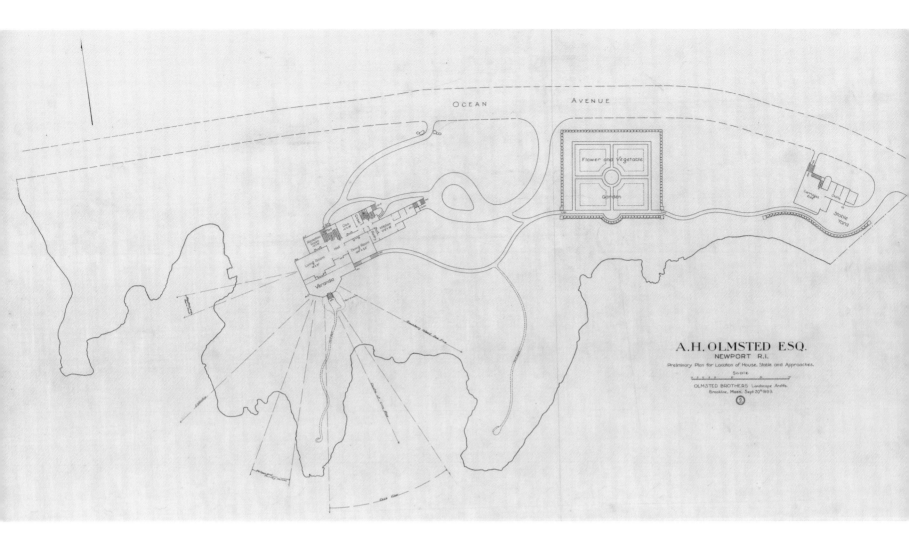

Fig. 113 (above)
John Charles Olmsted, *A.H. Olmsted, Esq. Preliminary Plan for Location of House, Stable and Approachess*, Wildacre, ca. 1899
United States Department of the Interior, National Park Service, Frederick Law Olmsted National Historic Site
This plan with sight lines marked and the scheme for the nearby Jelke house (Fig. 115), over twenty years later, illustrate the significant role of shaping views in picturesque landscape design.

Fig. 114 (below left)
Grass umbrella, Wildacre, ca. 1900, photograph
United States Department of the Interior, National Park Service, Frederick Law Olmsted National Historic Site

Fig. 115 (below right)
Olmsted Brothers, *Sketch Plan for Development in Vicinity of House*, Ferdinand Frazier Jelke House, ca. 1922
United States Department of the Interior, National Park Service, Frederick Law Olmsted National Historic Site

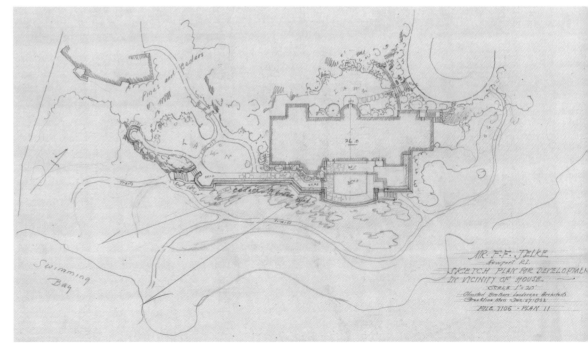

Fig. 116 (above)
The Waves, 1934, photograph
Gottscho-Schleisner Collection,
Library of Congress

Fig. 117 (left)
John Russell Pope's Studio, The
Waves, 1934, photograph
Gottscho-Schleisner Collection,
Library of Congress

135

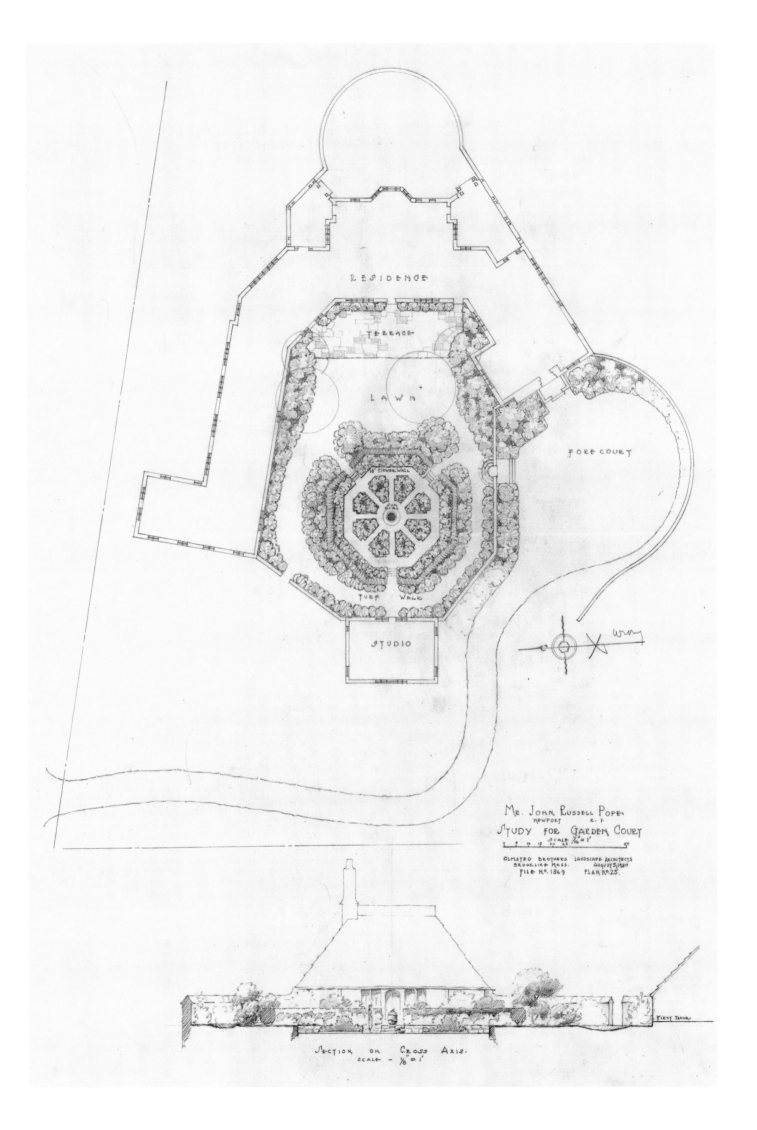

RESIDENCE

TERRACE

LAWN

FORE COURT

18" FLOWER WALL

TURF WALK

STUDIO

Mr. John Russell Pope
Newport R. I.
Study for Garden Court
Scale 1/16" = 1'

Olmsted Brothers Landscape Architects
Brookline Mass.   August 5, 1920
File No. 1869   Plan No. 25.

FIRST FLOOR

Section on Cross Axis.
Scale - 1/8" = 1'

The Reefs, The Breakers, Edgehill, Rough Point, Indian Spring, Wildacre, The Waves: these are the names of some of Newport's picturesque landscapes derived from the natural features of their sites. As landscape architects were working out design solutions for Newport's private estates, they were doing the same for the public green spaces across the nation. For example, Olmsted and his sons created plans for private estates and suburban subdivisions, metropolitan parkways, and parks from New York to California.[115] Ernest Bowditch devised Rockefeller and Lakeshore Parks and the Euclid Heights subdivision in Cleveland, Ohio, and Tuxedo Park in Orange County, New York. In each case, these designers worked with topography and sight lines, producing landscapes that were highly complex in planning, but appeared so effortlessly natural, the very foundations of the art of scenery.

Fig. 118 (opposite)
John Russell Pope, *Study for Garden Court*, The Waves, 1930
United States Department of the Interior, National Park Service, Frederick Law Olmsted National Historic Site

Fig. 119 (above)
Courtyard garden at The Waves, ca. 1934, photograph
United States Department of the Interior, National Park Service, Frederick Law Olmsted National Historic Site
The flower beds feature the soft lines of the Arts and Crafts-style garden.

The Gilded Age
ESTATE GARDENS AND URBAN FORESTS

The scenery of Newport is of two kinds . . . The larger kind of scenery of distant views and of the shores of open water. This scenery is a natural asset due to the topography of the island . . . The other kind of scenery is that to be found throughout the city. It is the scenery which the people of the city have made in adapting their environment to their own uses. It is the scenery of the streets and of the houses and gardens.
—Frederick Law Olmsted Jr., *Proposed Improvements for Newport, Rhode Island*, 1913

The Gilded Age was a dance between illusion and reality, especially in Newport where a taste for private opulence and the call for public improvements in the city's landscapes made their appearance at the same time. Reveling in the high noon of the American Renaissance, the nation's leading architects and landscape designers revived the classical architecture and gardens of Italy, France, and England, replete with a parterre here, a temple there (Fig. 120). History provided the inspiration for this fantasy, an illusory world of long-lost royal and aristocratic imagery in the form of clipped hedges, statues of Venus, and scrolled flower beds worthy of Versailles or a Medici villa (Figs. 121–27). This was an age of empire building, and the United States was to be a new incarnation of ancient Rome and Renaissance Florence, the heir to the glory of the classical heritage, something its captains of industry kept in mind when creating buildings and gardens, assembling art collections, and sitting for portraits. Imperial splendor exercised itself in domestic dream houses, while more democratic enhancements in the civic sphere occupied the Olmsted Brothers firm, which was engaged to study the urban forest and scenic vistas to address the very real challenges of preserving Newport's character in the face of modern development. The Olmsteds explored all aspects of the city: modest tree-lined streets, grand leafy avenues, and panoramic parks. Whether a French terraced garden on a glittering Bellevue Avenue estate or tree plantings around workers' houses on Broadway, these manifestations of nature in the city tell two sides of a Gilded Age tale, illustrating the aesthetics, theory, and practice of landscape architecture in the private and public realms in the period between 1890 and 1914.

Detroit Publishing Company, Beacon Rock, 1901, photograph Designed by McKim, Mead and White in 1890, Beacon Rock heralded the arrival of a Classical Revival aesthetic in Newport houses. Its siting on a rocky outcropping planted with pine, spruce, and hemlock is in the established picturesque fashion. The Greco-Roman-style porticos framing the centrally placed formal garden of clipped laurel trees demonstrates the emergence of classical landscape features in the 1890s. Locally, the estate was referred to as "The Acropolis."

Fig. 120
Masque of the Blue Garden, Beacon Hill, 1913, photograph
Redwood Library and Athenaeum

Fig. 121
Marble House, ca. 1900, photograph
Library of Congress
Alva Vanderbilt referred to Marble House (1892) as her "temple to
the arts." Inspired by the Parthenon, as a temple on a cliff, and the
Petit Trianon, a pavilion in a garden, Marble House was designed by
architect Richard Morris Hunt, who introduced an opulent French
classicism to the landscape of Newport.

RESIDENCE

Wᵐ K. VANDERBILT. ESQᴱ.
NEWPORT.R.I.

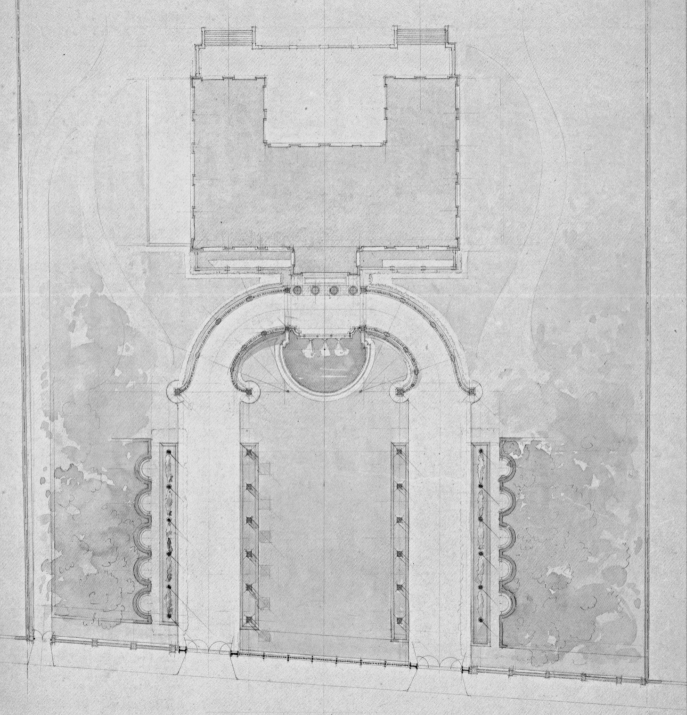

BELLEVUE   AVENUE

SCALE 20 FEET TO AN INCH.

Fig. 122 (opposite)
Richard Morris Hunt,
Residence, Wm K. Vanderbilt,
Esqe., plan for the main drive of
Marble House, ca. 1890
Library of Congress
The straight, formal lines of
the drives are evidence of the
classical aesthetic that emerged
in the 1890s. This approach
served as a stage set for a
monumental architecture of
classical proportions.

Fig. 123 (above)
Marble House, ca. 1900,
photograph
Library of Congress
In its final form, the drives were
lined with hydrangea. Hunt's
proposal for clipped hedges did
not, in the end, prevail.

Fig. 124 (left)
E. C. W., Girl on Farewell
Street, 1913, photograph
United States Department
of the Interior, National
Park Service, Frederick
Law Olmsted National
Historic Site
The image offers a
counterpoint to the
opulence of Gilded Age
houses on Bellevue
Avenue. Taken as part
of the Olmsted Brothers'
study of Newport's urban
landscape in 1913, the
young girl stands among
ancient trees on Farewell
Street, one of the oldest
thoroughfares, dating to
the colonial period.

Fig. 125
The Petit Trianon and the Jeu de Bague, from *Views and Plans of the Petit Trianon at Versailles* (1786), watercolor
Courtesy of Vartanian and Sons
The spirit of eighteenth-century garden pavilions informed Mrs. Belmont's choice of a Chinese-inspired teahouse at Marble House (Figs. 125 and 126), just as Marie Antoinette used a Chinoiserie carousel on the grounds of the Petit Trianon.

Fig. 126 (above)
Richard Howland Hunt, Hunt and Hunt, architects,
Tea House at Newport, Rhode Island, for Mrs. O. H. P.
Belmont, 1914, watercolor on graphite paper
Library of Congress
The architects modeled the tea house after 12th
century Sung dynasty temples.

Fig. 127 (right)
Roselle McConnell, Chinese teahouse with Marble
House in the background, 2020, photograph

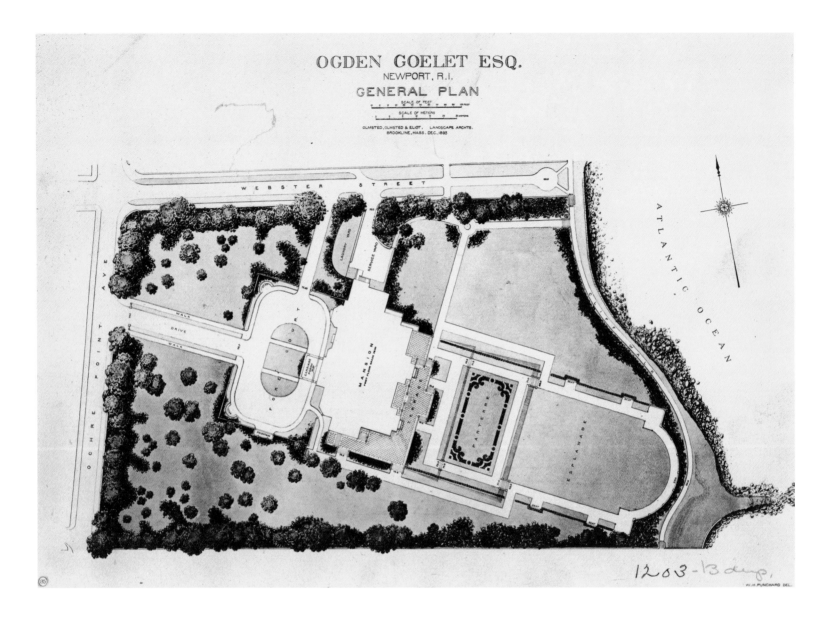

Fig. 128
Olmsted, Olmsted and Eliot,
General Plan, Ochre Court,
1893
United States Department of
the Interior, National Park
Service, Frederick Law Olmsted
National Historic Site

When Mr. and Mrs. Ogden Goelet stepped onto their new lawn, they entered upon the stage of a new era, furnished with gardens of terraces and tapestry-like turf inspired by a courtly past. Their estate, Ochre Court (1888–91), represented a pivotal moment in Newport's landscape, introducing a monumental scale and symmetrical order derived from the classical principles set forth at the École des Beaux-Arts in Paris. Richard Morris Hunt, the first American to train at the École, designed the house in the French Renaissance style. Frederick Law Olmsted Jr., John Charles Olmsted, and Charles Eliot planned the landscape.[116] All three men had worked for Olmsted Sr. and were imbued with his principles and practices in the picturesque. They also adapted to the emerging interest in classical design. Eliot's studies of the colonial landscapes of New England, his travels in Europe, and his writings on these subjects reflected his interest in the past as well as the picturesque. Indeed, he is credited as one of the earliest writers of landscape history in the United States.[117] Olmsted Sr. placed the timeless beauty and power of nature at the center of his design methodology. Charles Eliot followed in that practice while bringing a knowledge of period gardens to the occasion.

Ochre Court presents history as theater, in which the designers introduced the French Renaissance to the jagged New England shoreline. Located on the even terrain of Ochre Point, the flat, linear, sculpted grounds were perfectly precise and clipped in the formal French manner. The planning process of Olmsted, Olmsted and Eliot reveals not a complete break with the picturesque tradition but an evolution, a move toward adapting to a classical aesthetic (Figs. 128–32). They experimented with several approaches to the building, offering a varied number of sight lines. First, they conceived of a serpentine drive in the picturesque style practiced for decades in Newport and beyond. During the process of review, they eventually settled upon a straight drive entering a forecourt, which gave the visitor a singularly focused, axial view of the grand château. This ordered scheme is repeated on the ocean side of the house with a *tapis vert*, a green carpet of lawn, extending in a rectangle from a series of terraces lined with balustrades and urns inspired by Renaissance and Baroque models. Classicism, with its emphasis on symmetrical order, had arrived in the landscape as Beaux Arts gardening plans extended the formal lines of architecture into nature, imposing geometries upon the land.

Fig. 129
Robert Yarnall Richie, Ochre Court, ca. 1940, photograph Robert Yarnall Richie Photograph Collection, DeGolyer Library, Southern Methodist University

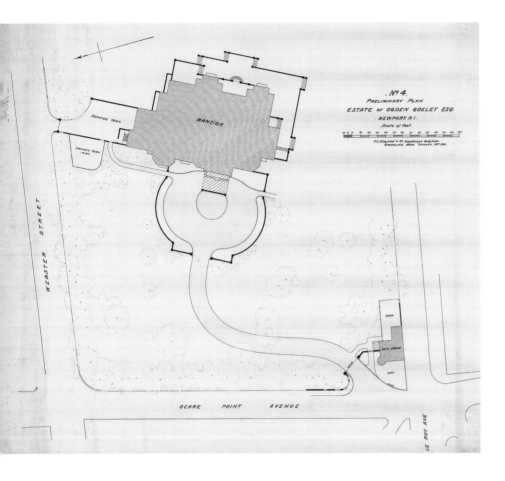

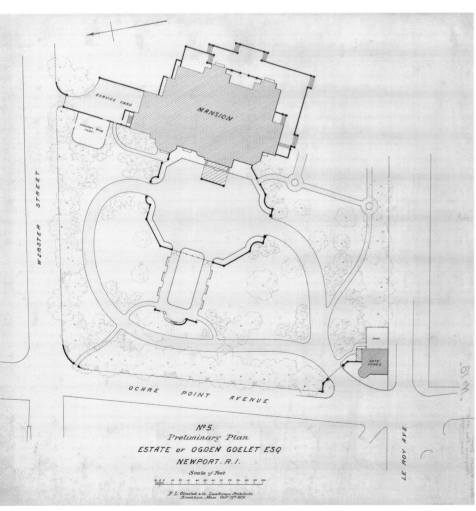

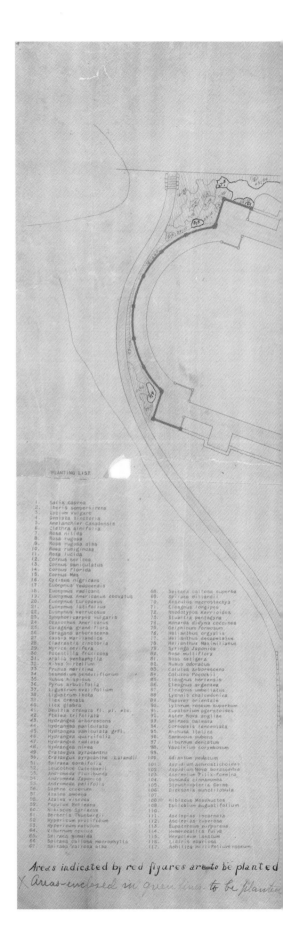

Fig. 130 (left, top)
Olmsted, Olmsted
and Eliot, *No. 4
Preliminary Plan*,
proposed serpentine
entrance drive for
Ochre Court,
ca. 1891
United States
Department of the
Interior, National
Park Service,
Frederick Law
Olmsted National
Historic Site

Fig. 131
(left, bottom)
Olmsted, Olmsted
and Eliot, *No. 5
Preliminary Plan*,
proposed entrance
drive with forecourt
for Ochre Court,
ca. 1891
United States
Department of the
Interior, National
Park Service,
Frederick Law
Olmsted National
Historic Site

Fig. 132 (right)
Olmsted, Olmsted
and Eliot, *Planting
Plan*, Ochre Court,
1894
United States
Department of the
Interior, National
Park Service,
Frederick Law
Olmsted National
Historic Site

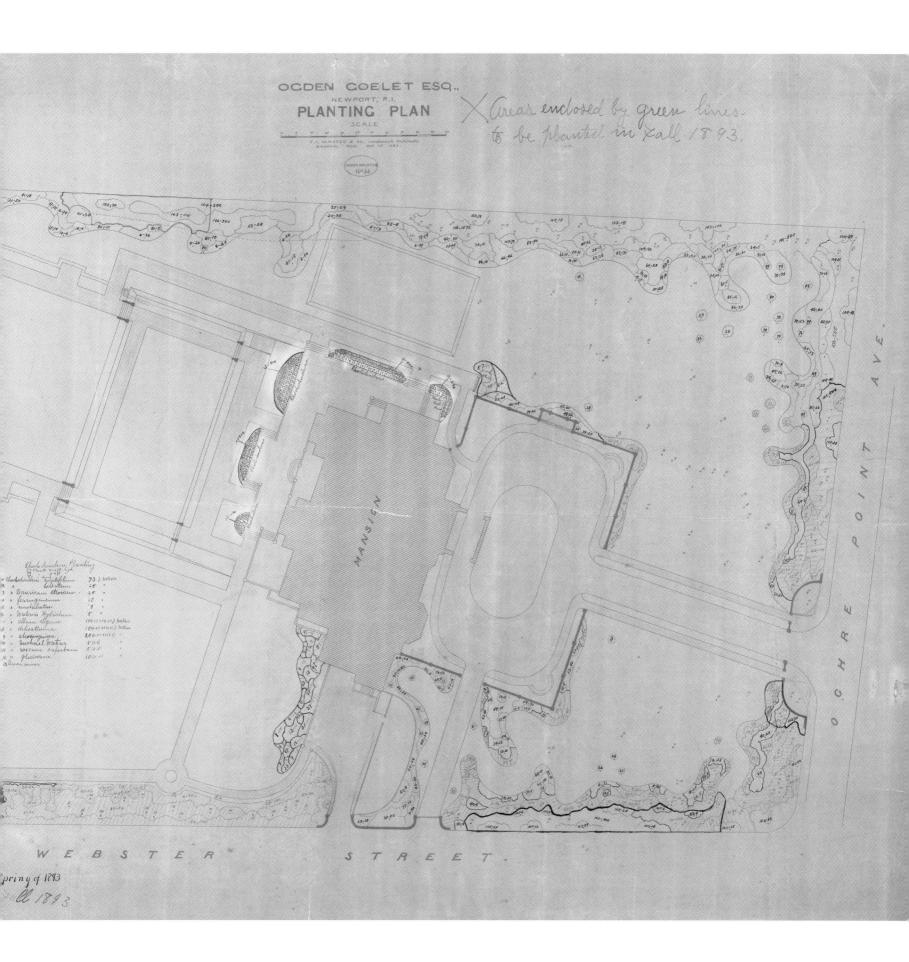

To label landscapes as Beaux Arts can seem vague, because the term is generally associated with architecture. The methods and aesthetics of Beaux Arts design fit into a larger classical revival in the arts during the aptly named American Renaissance. In buildings, the formal axis became paramount, relegating the undulating line of the picturesque to a supporting role. In landscapes, the emphasis was on developing plans to integrate grand Beaux Arts houses into their natural settings, combining both classical and picturesque elements.[118] These gardens appealed to reason and structure through clipped hedges and marble-lined paths, not to romance derived from weeping trees laid out to evoke mystery and wanderings in a shadowed landscape (Fig. 133). If the picturesque garden was intended to draw out emotions, to evoke nature's drama from high cliffs and crashing waves, the Beaux Arts landscape spoke of control and order, albeit in historical styles that conjured up romantic images of fairy-tale castles with towers where princesses might be found by their princes—or Gilded Age heiresses might be courted by fortune-seeking European aristocrats.

The herculean scale and classical proportions of a Beaux Arts house required a different kind of union with its landscape than earlier picturesque buildings with their asymmetrical profiles and rough-hewn materials. The picturesque, however, was not entirely exiled from these Beaux Arts landscapes. At Ochre Court, asymmetrical groupings of trees, remnants from the Second Empire French estate that had previously occupied the site, remained on the perimeter. Such fusion of the classical with the picturesque would define a significant mode of landscape design from the 1890s through the 1930s. The Olmsted Brothers combined both idioms. Frederick Law Olmsted Sr. did so as well, collaborating with Richard Morris Hunt on Biltmore in Asheville, North Carolina, the estate of George Washington Vanderbilt, composed of a French Renaissance château surrounded by formal gardens looking out upon tens of thousands of acres of forest. Neither Olmsted Sr. nor Olmsted, Olmsted and Eliot utterly abandoned the picturesque idiom. Their respect for topography and desire to integrate a building with its landscape remained guiding principles, regardless of changing styles of architecture.

The Breakers (1895), an Italian Renaissance-style palazzo built by Richard Morris Hunt for Mr. and Mrs. Cornelius Vanderbilt, shares many formal planning features with nearby Ochre Court, including straight drives, terraces, and parterre gardens. The landscape of The Breakers was originally laid out in the picturesque manner in 1877 for Pierre Lorillard by Ernest Bowditch, who returned to oversee improvements in 1885 when the Vanderbilts purchased the estate. He was engaged again in 1892 when the original house burned to the ground and Hunt's monumental house rose on its foundations. The stage was set for the introduction of the classical revival. Ernest invited his brother James, a forester, to assist with this latest iteration of the grounds. Rows of pin oaks, aligned in stately rows along the formal drive, purchased from the Pennsylvania estate of J. P. Widener, served as a natural colonnade framing the view of the house.[119] Acorns and oak leaves were also selected as symbols of the Vanderbilt family, appearing throughout the exterior and interior of the building. The oligarchs of American industry collected fine trees just as they acquired fine art and fine wine. Hunt, significantly, determined

Fig. 134
Main drive with newly planted
pin oaks, The Breakers,
ca. 1896, photograph
Library of Congress

the placement of these stately trees by laying out the drive itself and its terminus in a walled forecourt. He was the master of his own architecture of spectacle, controlling the approach to the building (Figs. 134–37). During this period, professional tensions between architects and garden designers arose on occasion in response to changing roles, as many architects began to exert greater influence on landscapes. Hunt would have viewed it as essential that he determine the planning of forecourts and terraced gardens to act as transitional spaces between his grand houses and the adjacent grounds, just as in the Renaissance villas and Baroque palaces of the past. He saw himself as following in a classical tradition. Bowditch, however, had a differing point of view, freely expressed in his letters:

> *Architects, as a rule, are pretty selfish, and are apt to try to subordinate everything to their work, which perhaps may be natural enough though it is sometimes discouraging. This has been most noticeable during the last ten years than it was prior to that time, because almost every architect now presumes to attend to all collateral landscape work, though their knowledge of the work of grading, draining, planting and even landscape design is next to nothing.*[120]

In 1893, around the same time Hunt added parterres to The Breakers to serve as outdoor drawing rooms, Charles Adams Platt published two articles in *Harper's New Monthly Magazine*,

Fig. 135
Southwest parterre, The
Breakers, ca. 1896, photograph
Library of Congress

the result of an 1892 trip to Italy with his brother. His book *Italian Gardens* (1894) soon followed, with text and photographs illustrating the architectural framework of Renaissance and Baroque gardens, where greenery often had no business growing, clipped to work in sync with staircases, pergolas, and pavilions. Hunt's drawings for The Breakers depict several studies for a pergola, first on the ocean façade and eventually settling on the southwest façade as the central motif of the attendant parterre.[121] This formal garden, as well as a main terrace and another parterre with a rose garden on the northeastern façade, overlooked a panorama of the ocean and lawns arranged in a picturesque manner with specimen trees, among them beech, Blue Atlas cedar, and hinoki cypress, along a curving perimeter path retained from the 1877 plan. Hunt and the Bowditch brothers appeared to have served the Vanderbilts well, according to an article in *Gardens and Gardening*:

> *The dwelling is one of the most costly and magnificent private houses in America, if not the world, and the grounds are laid out and planted to meet the demands of the situation. As might be expected, the landscape architect had the opportunity to do his best work, irrespective of financial limitations . . . these grounds are planted as a garden with numerous and fitting combinations of color, both of foliage and blossom, which is the prevailing type in Newport.*[122]

Fig. 136
Frances Benjamin Johnston,
Pergola, The Breakers, 1914,
photograph
Library of Congress

The Breakers is a fusion of the classical and the natural. This type of landscape appealed to the desire for architectural and social pageantry that enhanced Newport's role as a fashionable summer resort. The opulence of building in Newport during the 1890s coincided with the economic supremacy of the United States, which surpassed Great Britain, Germany, and France in both industrial output and financial power. Palatial houses and gardens inspired by European models heralded the ascendancy of a new world power replacing the old, taking on its artistic, cultural, and social images. This spirit was proclaimed by Barr Ferree in 1904 in a rather bombastic tone:

> The architectural thought which lay behind the creation of Versailles is identical with the ideas that have brought the great houses of Newport into existence. . . . the palace of Versailles was a vast architectural background for court fetes and festivities of all sorts. Just so the palaces of Newport are architectural backgrounds for the pleasures and sports of its inhabitants. The scale is different, the place and the manners, but the architectural meaning of both is identical.[123]

Fig. 137
Garden path, The Breakers,
from *Annuaire of the Newport
Garden Club* (1914), photograph
Redwood Library and
Athenaeum

Ferree's celebratory language was reinforced, in more restrained wording, by the scholarly work of Pierre de Nolhac in *Versailles and the Trianons* (1906). In this folio illustrated with photographs of the gardens, statuary, and various fountains and pavilions, de Nolhac wrote, "The grand architectural lines of the Palace of Versailles are continued in its gardens."[124] Similar observations were made by Edith Wharton, who approached the subject not as a historian but in literary fashion, capturing the timeless mood and unity of landscapes from Rome to Florence and Genoa in *Italian Villas and Their Gardens* (1904). She wrote of water, greenery, and stone as the primary features of classical planning and examined how these created "garden magic."[125] This atmosphere was realized in the book's ethereal Maxfield Parrish watercolors of fountains, terraced walks, and rows of clipped trees. The images seduced, but Wharton warned readers of the discipline also required in classical gardens:

> *a marble sarcophagus and a dozen twisted columns will not make an Italian garden; but a piece of ground laid out and planted on the principles of the old garden-craft will be, not indeed an Italian garden in the literal sense, but, what is far better, a garden as well adapted to its surroundings as were the models which inspired it.*[126]

Fig. 138
Edward Van Altena, Rose
trellis, Vernon Court, ca. 1920,
photograph
Archives of American Gardens

Wharton sought clarity in the use of classical design, emphasizing the need to adhere to its harmonious proportions, not just the fashionable application of its ornamental details. She directed her most pointed criticism at the Vanderbilts and their houses, declaring them "entrenched in a sort of Thermopylae of bad taste, from which apparently no force on earth can dislodge them."[127] How cutting to have your classically inspired abode and gardens compared to one of the most disastrous battles in classical history. Classicism was an unforgiving art form, its ill-used features an unmitigated error in the eyes of critics such as Wharton, who was intent not merely on promoting it but on seeing it practiced with refinement and restraint. Her books and those of Platt and de Nolhac were intended both to inform and instruct the profession and potential patrons.

If Americans with cosmopolitan tastes and financial means were embracing the classical tradition and debating approaches to its application, the French were not to be left out of the discussion. They came to assess the interpretation of their horticultural heritage. Paul Bourget, novelist, poet, and member of the Académie Française, cast a critical eye upon a luxuriant Newport. A man of refined sensibilities, at home in the intellectual and artistic circles of Paris, he was a colleague of the de Goncourt brothers, who had published *French Eighteenth Century Painters* (1875) and were central in the revival of interest in the intimate scale and delicacy of the Rococo and Neoclassical periods, which inspired so many Newport houses and gardens in the 1890s. Arriving in Newport in the summer of 1894, Bourget met Edith Wharton, beginning a lifelong friendship between these two cultural soulmates.[128] Wharton fully embraced his aesthetic, which dovetailed with her own interests in the fine points of classical art and design. While Wharton provided the subtlety he appreciated, Bourget was immediately struck by a lack of moderation as he engaged in the rest of Newport's social whirl.

This excess has a prototype in the rose so justly called the "American Beauty," enormous bunches of which crown their tables. It has so long a stem, it is so intensely red, so wide open, and so strangely perfumed that it does not seem like a natural flower. It requires the greenhouse, the exposition, a public display.[129]

Offend as it might Bourget's preference for delicacy, the American Beauty rose was a telling symbol for Gilded Age Newport. Bold, lush, and made for show like the houses and their occupants, the flower adorned Newport's most lavish parties and often the hats of its leading ladies (Fig. 138). In defense of America, if not the American Beauty itself, Mark Twain offered a counterpoint in an article titled "What Paul Bourget Thinks of Us":

I wish I could think what he is going to teach us. Can it be Deportment? But he experimented in that at Newport and failed to give satisfaction, except to a few . . . Newport is a disastrous place for the unacclimated observer, evidently . . . I think Mr. Bourget meant to suggest that he expected to find the great "American soul" secreted behind the ostentations of Newport; and that he was going to get it out and examine it, and generalize it, and psychologize it, and make it reveal to him its hidden vast mystery, "the nature of the people of the United States."[130]

Twain concluded that America was too vast to generalize for it was an empire of differences, of too many contrasts. This is the key to understanding Newport's landscapes: their many layers do reveal aspects of American culture at the time of their making. Newport, and the nation at large, was a booming, eclectic place. If Bourget pronounced that excess was the order of the day, and if Twain countered that to try to make sense of it was futile, an extravaganza of flowers in Newport would have certainly confounded the former and amused the latter.

On September 7, 1899, Alva Belmont hosted a Flower Car Parade, beginning on the grounds of her Bellevue Avenue estate, Belcourt. Electric cars, a newly introduced technology taken up by Alva and her social cohort, were festooned with flowers, exhibiting the skills of their head gardeners and Newport's horticultural masters (Figs. 139–41).

On the front lawn of Newport's most fashionable florist [Hodgson's Flower Shop on Bellevue Avenue] stood a dense crowd watching a small army of footmen and white aproned maids put the last finishing touches on Mrs. Astor's automobile carriage . . . In the meanwhile, all of Mrs. Belmont's household was busily engaged in transforming the smooth green lawn of Belcourt into an "obstacle park."[131]

After demonstrating their driving skills within the very private realm of Belcourt, grande dames and grand gentlemen steered their floral displays on wheels down Belleuve Avenue to public acclaim, delight, and, for some, dismay at the display. A creative way to promote a new invention, or an exercise in conspicuous consumption? The Flower Car Parade offered both. Emerging technology adorned by flowers and the accompanying social theater made for good press in an age of immense fortunes and industrial might. Readers were fascinated by such extravagance, but flowers were also used in satire masking social critique, according to one reporter:

Fig. 139 (above left)
Mr. Harry Lehr and Mrs.
Stuyvesant Fish at Mrs.
Belmont's Flower Car Parade,
1899, photograph
William K. Vanderbilt Museum

Fig. 140 (above right)
Car with hydrangea and
lanterns at Mrs. Belmont's
Flower Car Parade, 1899,
photograph
William K. Vanderbilt Museum

Everything in Newport is measured by the scale of millions. Even the flowers preach the gospel of wealth. Nature made it the most beautiful summer resort in the world; man has made it a monument to his colossal vanity. But it has the merit of being a beautiful and magnificent monument.[132]

Bourget's critiques, Twain's witticisms, and the barbs of the press made some gaze more critically on the follies of the age, but they did not appear to diminish the passion for houses and gardens in the grand manner. Writers, especially Platt, de Nolhac, and Wharton, did affect the course of events and exert a restraining hand, at times. The collective influence of their works is apparent in The Elms (1901), a combination of classical Italian and French models in architecture and nature created for Mr. and Mrs. Edward Julius Berwind by architect Horace Trumbauer. Modeled after the château of the Marquis d'Argenson at Asnières-sur-Seine (1750), The Elms rests upon a terrace lined with urns and sculpture, including white marble statues of Venus and Demeter copied after those at the Marquise de Pompadour's Château de Menars in the Loire Valley and two bronzes of lions cast after originals in the gardens of the Tuileries in Paris (Figs. 142–45). Inspired by aristocratic sources, its raison d'etre was realized in 1907 when Mr. Berwind, the Pennsylvania coal baron, and Mrs. Berwind, daughter of a former consul to Italy and a noted collector, received Prince Wilhelm of Sweden on August 22 at The Elms, its main hall decorated with blue hydrangea and yellow allamanda in honor of the colors of the Swedish flag. The house and gardens functioned in the manner of an eighteenth-century French château, with terraces acting as outdoor drawing rooms and the lawns illuminated like a theater set.

On the upper terrace. . . . the paths were covered with rugs and red carpets . . . being outlined with fairy lamps. Red ball lanterns were festooned the length of both marble walls separating the two terraces, and the marble urns on these terraces were filled with rare plants and lighted with French flowering cups of roses, tulips and lilies . . . The clusters of bay trees and the flower beds in the sunken garden were bright with variegated lights.[133]

Fig. 141
Alva and O. H. P. Belmont at
Mrs. Belmont's Flower Car
Parade, 1899, photograph
William K. Vanderbilt Museum

Between 1901 and 1907, the park of copper, weeping, and fernleaf beeches formed an asymmetrical composition originally leading the eye toward a lily pond with a rustic wooden bridge, the one remaining feature of the picturesque grounds of the original wooden Victorian cottage demolished for the construction of The Elms. In 1907, at a moment when the writings of de Nolhac and Wharton were highly popular, the Berwinds initiated a seven-year project directed by Horace Trumbauer to transform the lower part of the grounds into a formal allée with Italian Baroque fountains and French Neoclassical pavilions, a sunken garden to replace the lily pond, and a garage, stable, and carriage house masked to appear as a French château (Figs. 146–52). While classical features predominated in the stonework and in the formality of the terraces adjacent to the house and the lower garden, the great lawn in between these two ensembles adhered to a picturesque silhouette. Weeping beeches partly concealed views of the fountains and pavilions in the lower garden, tempting the viewer to venture forth. It was a compelling concoction of the classical and the natural.

Fig. 142 (above)
Garden elevation, The Elms,
ca. 1905, photograph

Fig. 143 (right)
Edward Van Altena, Bronze
lion with cubs, The Elms, 1914,
photograph
Archives of American Gardens

Fig. 144 (opposite, top)
Frances Benjamin Johnston,
Boxwood garden, The Elms,
1914, photograph
Library of Congress

Fig. 145 (opposite, bottom)
Lily pond, The Elms, ca. 1905,
photograph
Newport Historical Society,
P5918
The serpentine lily pond gave
way to the linear, classical
lines of the new allée design by
Horace Trumbauer (Fig. 146).

overleaf:

Fig. 146 (left)
Horace Trumbauer, *Treatment of Lower Garden Terrace*, The Elms, 1914
The Preservation Society of Newport County
Trumbauer's plan superimposes a classical scheme over the picturesque pond

Fig. 147 (right, top)
Edward Van Altena, Allée in the lower garden, The Elms, ca. 1920, photograph
Archives of American Gardens

Fig. 148 (right, bottom)
Edward Van Altena, Sunken garden, The Elms, ca. 1920, photograph
Archives of American Gardens

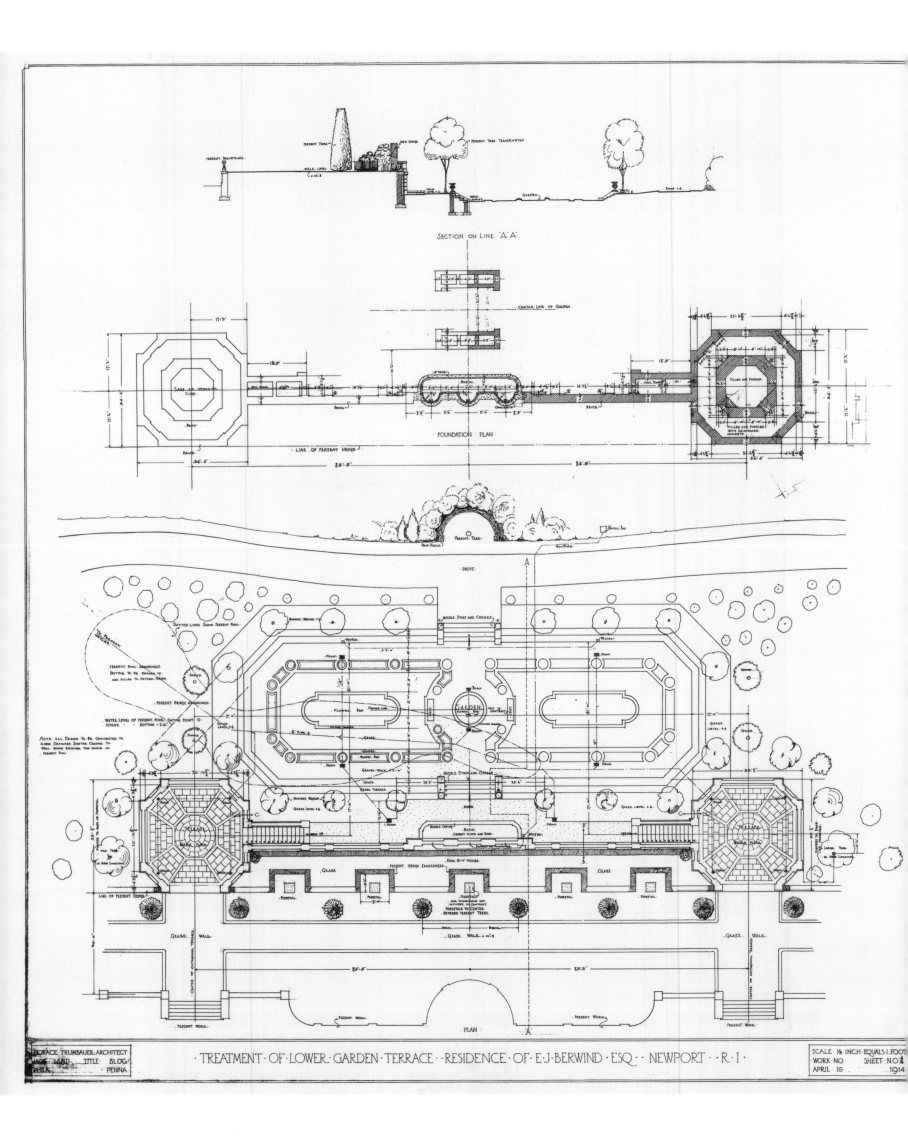

SECTION ON LINE "A·A"

FOUNDATION PLAN

PLAN

HORACE TRUMBAUER ARCHITECT
JACK LAND TITLE BLDG
PHILA PENNA

TREATMENT·OF·LOWER·GARDEN·TERRACE·RESIDENCE·OF·E·J·BERWIND·ESQ·NEWPORT·R·I

SCALE ⅛ INCH EQUALS 1 FOOT
WORK NO   SHEET NO 2
APRIL 16   1914

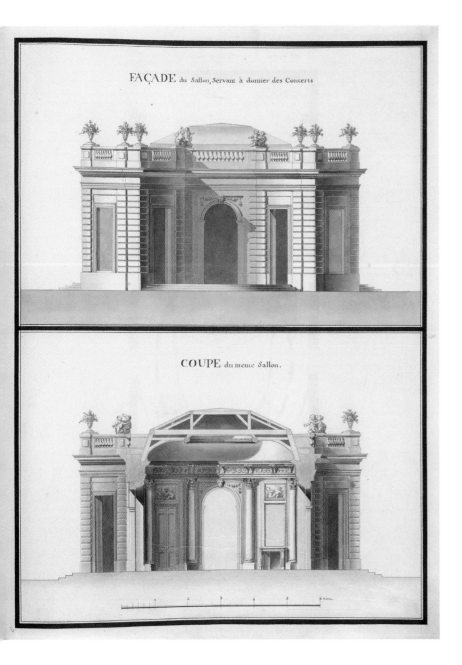

FAÇADE du Sallon, Servant à donner des Concerts

COUPE du meme Sallon.

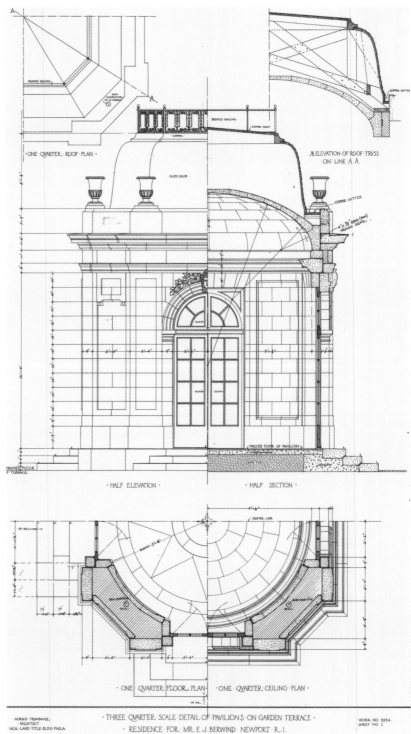

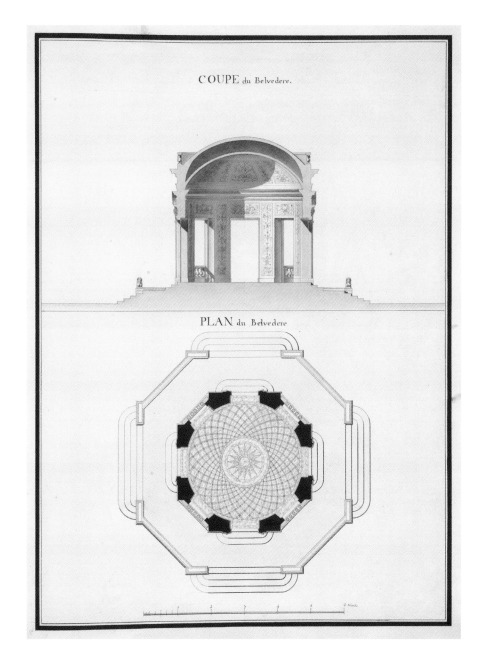

COUPE du Belvedere.

PLAN du Belvedere

Fig. 149 (opposite, left)
Façade and section of the pavilion at the Petit Trianon, from *Views and Plans of the Petit Trianon at Versailles* (1786)
Courtesy of Vartanian and Sons

Fig. 150 (opposite, right)
Horace Trumbauer, *Detail of Pavilions on Garden Terrace*, The Elms, 1914
The Preservation Society of Newport County
Trumbauer combined the decorative details of the French Pavilion (Fig. 149) and the octagonal plan of the Belvedere (Fig. 151) at the Petit Trianon.

Fig. 151 (right, top)
Section and plan of the Belvedere, from *Views and Plans of the Petit Trianon at Versailles* (1786)
Courtesy of Vartanian and Sons

Fig. 152 (right, bottom)
Frances Benjamin Johnston, Fountain at the southern terminus of the allée, The Elms, ca. 1920, photograph
Library of Congress
Clipped privet hedges and conical arborvitae frame the fountain with distant views to the elms and horse-chestnuts on the lawn.

Fig. 153 (right)
Roselle McConnell, Clipped lindens, Bellevue House, 2020, photograph
Bellevue House was originally known as "Berkeley Villa" when it was built by Martha Codman.

Fig. 154 (below left)
Roselle McConnell, Teahouse, Bellevue House, 2020, photograph

Fig. 155 (below right)
Roselle McConnell, Trellised Chinoiserie pavilion, Bellevue House, 2020, photograph

Historical fantasy of another sort prevailed in the work of Ogden Codman, decorator of Edith Wharton's Newport house, Land's End, and co-writer with her on *The Decoration of Houses* (1897). He practiced what he and Wharton preached in terms of refinement of forms and ornament in his house and garden for his cousin, Martha Codman, in 1910. The Colonial Revival house reads like an essay on eighteenth-century Georgian and Federal architectural details, with grounds devised as a series of garden rooms (Figs. 153–55). Terraces and lawns are treated as grass carpets, or *tapis vert*, in the French tradition.[134] Clipped linden trees frame the lawns and a Colonial Revival pavilion attests to Codman's design philosophy: rational spatial sequences, restrained use of historic sources, harmonious proportions (Figs. 156 and 157).

Fig. 156 (left, above)
Villa Rosa, ca. 1910, photograph
Newport Historical Society,
P9522
Ogden Codman designed the
Neoclassical house with the
attendant classical pergola
and terrace. The estate was
demolished in the early 1960s.

Fig. 157 (left, below)
Porch, *Villa Rosa*, ca. 1910,
photograph
Newport Historical Society,
P9520

Fig. 158 (above)
Robert Yarnall Richie, Miramar,
1932–34, photograph
Robert Yarnall Richie
Photograph Collection,
Negative Series: 0604, DeGolyer
Library, Southern Methodist
University

Fig. 159 (opposite, top)
Miramar, ca. 1914, pencil on
paper
Philadelphia Free Library

Fig. 160 (opposite, bottom)
Edward Van Altena, Parterre,
Miramar, ca. 1920, photograph
Archives of American Gardens
This was the most elaborate
parterre de broderie, or
embroidered parterre, in
Gilded Age Newport, composed
of boxwood swirls framing
marigolds, coleus, and
ageratum.

Newport's most ambitious classically inspired landscape appeared in the last years of the Gilded Age. Miramar (1914), by Horace Trumbauer for Eleanor Elkins Widener, is a swan song in the form of a seventeenth-century French *maison de plaisance*, or pleasure pavilion, created just as social and economic forces were set in play that would end an era. Inspired by the fantasy-based garden retreats of French kings, Miramar was an illusion perched at the edge of harsh truths. Mrs. Widener survived the sinking of the Titanic in 1912, the event that shook the confidence of the Gilded Age in the supremacy of its own technology. In 1913, the graduated personal income tax diminished the unlimited fortunes that funded the creation and maintenance of Newport's dream houses. The outbreak of World War I in 1914 destroyed the old social order of Europe and accelerated the pace of social change in the United States. Construction of Miramar continued, however, and its opening was celebrated in 1915. The grounds featured *parterres de broderie* of boldly colored flowers and plants with marble chips as ground cover (Figs. 158–60). The French landscape architect Jacques Henri Auguste Gréber based the parterres on seventeenth-century prototypes with sinuous boxwood scrolls reminiscent of elaborate embroidery. In its layout, however, the entire estate is singular and in no way followed a traditional French seventeenth-century plan, which would have placed the parterres behind the building. At Miramar, the viewer encounters the parterres first, at the very front of the house, protected from the high

winds on the back lawn facing the ocean. Miramar's plant materials, such as dwarf boxwood, caladium, coleus, santolina, blue ageratum, and dwarf marigolds, were selected for their ability to withstand the intensity of the summer sun and provide full color throughout the season.

Gréber attended the École des Beaux-Arts, graduating in 1909, and departed for the United States, where he was commissioned by Joseph Widener in 1913 to design a parterre for Lynnewood Hall, his country estate outside of Philadelphia. The connection led to his introduction to Horace Trumbauer and his assistant, Julian Abele, and their work on Miramar in Newport.[135] He became a major presence in the landscapes of the American Renaissance.

Gréber published *L'Architecture aux Etats-Unis* (1920), a two-volume work covering the influence and impact of French architecture and design principles in the United States, and including his work on Miramar and the Sunken Garden of The Elms.[136] Aside from commissions on private estates, Gréber became known for urban planning. In France he executed large-scale municipal work in Paris, Neuilly, and Marseilles. He was also a professor of town planning at the University of Paris and a master architect for the 1937 Paris International Exposition; in North America, he worked on the Benjamin Franklin Parkway in Philadelphia and on planting schemes for Ottawa, Canada.[137]

Versailles and the Grand Trianon reimagined for a New England cliff, Miramar was one of the last in a pageant of houses and landscapes intended for spectacle. Newport's Gilded Age gardens in stone and greenery sparked fascination, admiration, or disdain, or a combination of all of these, depending upon the viewer. Critics both celebrated and censured these sites, for they served as cultural touchstones. Henry James articulated his displeasure at the transformation of the city with classical allusions—features that may have initially caused creators of Newport's grand gardens to cheer, though James's biting criticism may have eventually led them to cringe.

Fig. 162
T. W. Sears, Summer House in the Vegetable Garden, Beacon Hill, March 3, 1914, photograph United States Department of the Interior, National Park Service, Frederick Law Olmsted National Historic Site
Mr. and Mrs. James created several arbors and pavilions from which to view their vegetable garden.

The place itself. . . . like some dim, simplified ghost of a small Greek island, where the clear walls of some pillared portico or pavilion, perched afar, looked like those of temples of the gods, and where Nature, deprived of that ease of merely massing herself on which "American scenery," as we lump it together, too apt to depend for its effect, might have shown a piping shepherd on a hillside or attached a mythic image to any point of rocks. What an idea, originally, to have seen this miniature spot of earth, where the sea-nymphs of the curved sands, at the worst, might have chanted back to the shepherds, as a mere breeding-ground for white elephants![138]

James evoked the image of a classical arcadia succumbing to excessive grandeur, and an apparition rose from the rocky outcroppings of Newport to prove his point. In August of 1913, an assembly of gods, goddesses, and nymphs materialized in the Blue Garden at the residence of Mr. and Mrs. Arthur Curtiss James. Set on Beacon Hill, the main house and grounds commanded the highest point in Newport—the city's own Mount Olympus, in a sense (Figs. 161 and 162). It certainly served that purpose on one legendary summer evening (Figs. 163 and 164). At the Masque of the Blue Garden, the Jameses and their gardeners turned landscape into pure theater:

The guests knew only that they were invited to witness the dedication of a garden: an addition to the Italian gardens which surrounded the James cottage. . . . Dimly outlined before them stretched the blue garden with a strip of lawn sloping towards a shallow lily pond, beyond which was a long lake reaching to a row of marble Grecian columns. When all was in readiness, Mrs. James, wearing a gown of dark blue brocade of fifteenth century Italy, was seen walking slowly through the shadowy garden . . . There, in a dim blue light, she faced her guests and said, "My dear friends, I am glad to have you with me tonight to witness the dedication of my blue garden." . . . Then, Mrs. James turned her back on her guests, and they became twentieth century spectators of a Greek play enacted before a fifteenth century hostess . . . The master of ceremonies announced the beginning of the dedication as he waved his electric wand. Harps played and two actors, dressed as minstrels, sang several old Italian songs. A shaft of blue light then illuminated the garden . . . The appearance of two grotesque little beings was in keeping with the mysteries of the scene. They played by the edge of the pool, and fled when Ceres . . . appeared between the marble columns. Ceres contemplated the surface of the lily pool.

Fig. 163
Edward Van Altena, Blue Garden, Beacon Hill, ca. 1920, photograph
Archives of American Gardens

Fig. 164
Masque of the Blue Garden, Beacon Hill, 1913, photograph
Redwood Library and Athenaeum

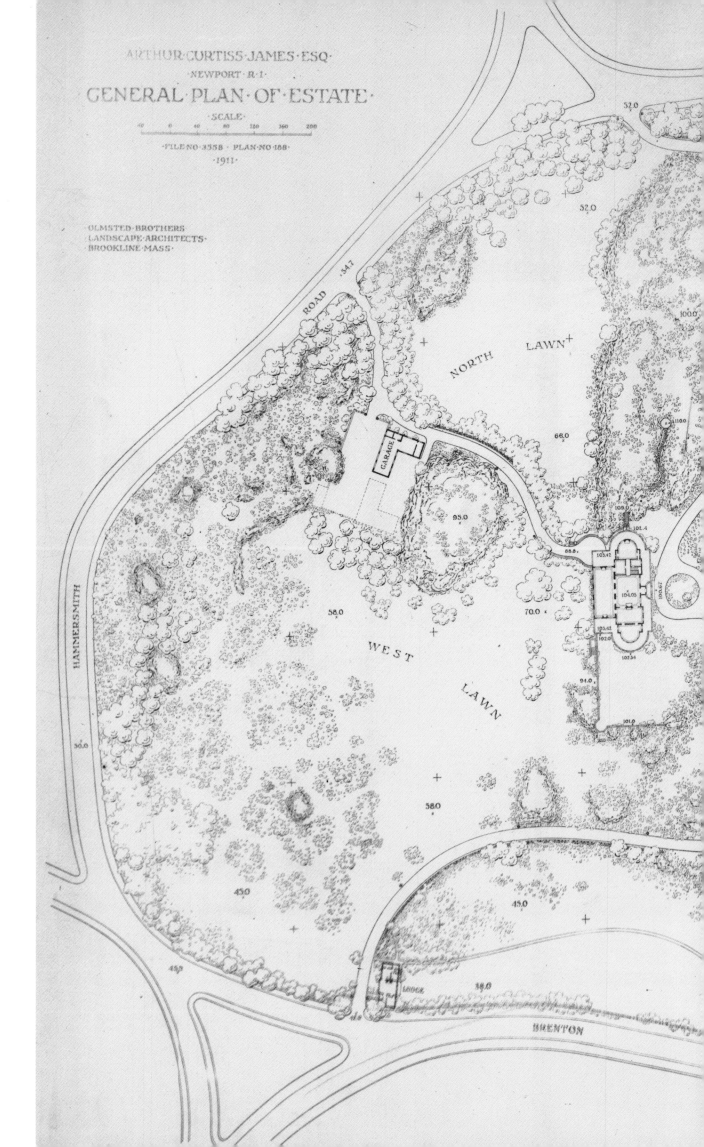

ARTHUR·CURTISS·JAMES·ESQ·
NEWPORT·R·I·
GENERAL·PLAN·OF·ESTATE·

·SCALE·

·FILE·NO·3338· PLAN·NO·188·
·1911·

OLMSTED·BROTHERS·
LANDSCAPE·ARCHITECTS·
·BROOKLINE·MASS·

Fig. 165
Olmsted Brothers, *General Plan of Estate*, Beacon Hill, ca. 1911
United States Department of the Interior, National Park Service, Frederick Law Olmsted National Historic Site

Fig. 166
Edward Van Altena, Rose
Garden, Beacon Hill, ca. 1920,
photograph
Archives of American Gardens

The water began to bubble, and from its disturbed surface, arose Water, a dripping figure with strands of lily pads upon her shoulders and arms. She danced across the lawn and was lost in the gloom. Pomona, Thymis and Cyria appearing to float across the moon-lit grass, joined Ceres . . . they stood in the bluish glow, until Ceres summoned Flora . . . found under a rosebush and, dragged to view and made to dance, garlands of roses flying behind her in the night breeze . . . Zephyrus joined her and danced until he fell exhausted by the pool's edge . . . Then darkness fell on the blue garden. Between the marble columns appeared Diana . . . She espied Endymion and flew to him. He carried her to the lily pool and they watched their reflections in the surface. Slowly they walked away and the gnomes had the garden again to themselves. At the far end they found two large seashells. Within these hid the water nymphs. The dwarves led them to the water's edge, where the nymphs tried to drag them under the surface. In terror, the gnomes fled . . . the nymphs turned and saw Aphrodite in the dim distance between the marble columns . . . she danced down the surface of the long lake . . . as she advanced to meet the nymphs. They joined in a wild bacchanale at the edge of the pool; and then, plunging in, sank among the lilies. Again, darkness fell over the blue garden. Suddenly, with a fanfare of trumpets, the whole

burst into electric bloom . . . Trumpeteers in fifteenth century livery led the way to the house . . . Reclining on a huge seashell, born by six Tritons, Florence Fleming Noyes was carried into the ballroom where, in the presence of society, she interpreted the Sea Goddess in a pageant. Neptune, following in her wake on a white horse . . . invited her to dance.[139]

Fig. 167
Edward Van Altena, Italian Garden, Beacon Hill, ca. 1920, photograph
Archives of American Gardens

Like the garden itself, the Jameses' masque was an exercise in historical whimsy, harking back to the lavish entertainments of the Medici spectacles in Florence, the Baroque masques of Modena, and the garden fetes of Louis XIV at Versailles.[140] The Blue Garden's pergolas and the reflecting pools arranged in a formal straight axis are essential elements of classical design. There are also references to Egyptian, Persian, Byzantine, and Chinese symbolism, among others, in this most cosmopolitan of landscape creations.[141] All of these features were coordinated into a unified whole by the Olmsted Brothers and the Jameses' gardener, John Greatorex.[142] This ensemble did not exist in splendid isolation; the estate, developed from 1908 through the 1930s, featured an Italian garden and extensive rose beds nestled among rock-strewn hills (Figs. 165–67).

Fig. 168 (above)
Frances Benjamin Johnston,
Surprise Valley Farm, 1917,
photograph
Library of Congress
Cows being brought into the
enclosure.

Fig. 169 (right)
Frances Benjamin Johnston,
Carpenter's shop, Surprise
Valley Farm, 1917, photograph
Library of Congress

Fig. 170
Frances Benjamin Johnston,
The Milk Toast mural, Surprise
Valley Farm, 1917, photograph
Library of Congress

In 1916, the Jameses commissioned the "Swiss Village," officially known as Surprise Valley Farm, in the same spirit of fantasy that prevailed in the Blue Garden (Figs. 168–70). Grosvenor Atterbury devised a farm complex inspired by the rural architecture of the Italian section of Switzerland, which the Jameses had admired on their travels. The architect arranged a carpenter shop, dairy, hen house, aviary, slaughterhouse, and workers' residences to produce a romantic scene that conjured up images of a fairy-tale village.[143] Joseph Lindon Smith, who had staged the Masque of the Blue Garden, created the Arts and Crafts–style murals that adorned the farm buildings.[144] Overlooking the central grass court, Atterbury placed a pergola, decorated by Smith with a mural of a master and mistress facing each other with steins, entitled *The Milk Toast*, where the Jameses and their guests watched the herding of cows from pasture to buildings. As one writer noted, "It is in this rustic retreat, before which the village panoramically unrolls, that Mrs. James entertains intimates a la Petit Trianon."[145] This complex is a successor to a long line of ornamental farms that combined function and fantasy, with models in Marie Antoinette's Petit Hameau (1783), a recreation of a rural French village at Versailles, and Blaise Hamlet (1811), near Bristol, England, a picturesque assembly of estate workers' houses with Medieval-inspired thatched roofs. Although intended to charm and enchant, the Swiss Village was no folly, for it had a utilitarian purpose in providing meat and poultry for the main house. Its outward appearance and arrangement, however, exist to amuse and delight, presenting rural pursuits in the most romanticized manner.

As some estate owners basked in the Augustan glow of their Neoclassical colonnades and Baroque fountains and others meandered among Arts and Crafts flower walks worthy of an English fairy tale, critics engaged in ongoing discussions about Newport's landscapes as expressions of either the desirable or the detestable in the art of shaping nature. Many patrons and practitioners,

Fig. 171 (above)
Peach arbor, Miss Ellen Mason
Estate, ca. 1920, photograph
United States Department of
the Interior, National Park
Service, Frederick Law Olmsted
National Historic Site

Fig. 172 (opposite)
Ernest Bowditch, *Plan for
Improving the Mason Estate*,
1882
United States Department of
the Interior, National Park
Service, Frederick Law Olmsted
National Historic Site

however, embraced varied approaches to the art of landscape. The estate of Miss Ellen Mason is a prime example. The site overlooking Easton's Pond, with views to the ocean, was originally laid out by Ernest Bowditch in the 1880s, then revised by Olmsted Brothers in the early 1900s, and also featured the work of Rose Standish Nichols (Figs. 171–75). Niece of the sculptor Augustus Saint-Gaudens, sister-in-law of the landscape architect Arthur Shurcliff, who would become the chief landscape architect of Colonial Williamsburg, and student of landscape architect and writer Charles Adams Platt, Nichols spent time in the art colony at Cornish, New Hampshire, and absorbed the lessons of both natural and formal landscape design from these prominent figures in their respective fields.[146] She also emerged as a writer of several books and articles on historic gardens in Britain, Europe, and Asia. The Mason estate presented a combination of a picturesque park of specimen trees with a series of formal gardens adjacent to the house (1902) in the Spanish Revival style by California architect Irving Gill. With the education and eye of a connoisseur, and with a noted preference for both English and Italian traditions, Nichols in 1904 devised the plantings for a series of enclosures, including a cutting garden, a fountain garden, and an ornamental "Spanish" garden within a classically inspired grid.[147] This landscape, with its views of the sea in the distance, the specimen trees, and series of formal garden rooms, integrated the softness of the English garden with the structure of the Italian.

In the dialogue about the merits of the ancient and classical versus the picturesque and natural, Mariana Griswold Van Rensselaer made her voice known, declaring the Mason estate in 1912 to be "literally perfect."[148] The great critic clearly sided with the naturalistic manner practiced by Frederick Law Olmsted, Jacob Weidenmann, Samuel Parsons Jr., and the Olmsted Brothers, whose work she promoted in her writings, rather than Charles Adams Platt's American revival of the classical Italian garden in the 1890s. One reviewer in *Garden and Forest* described

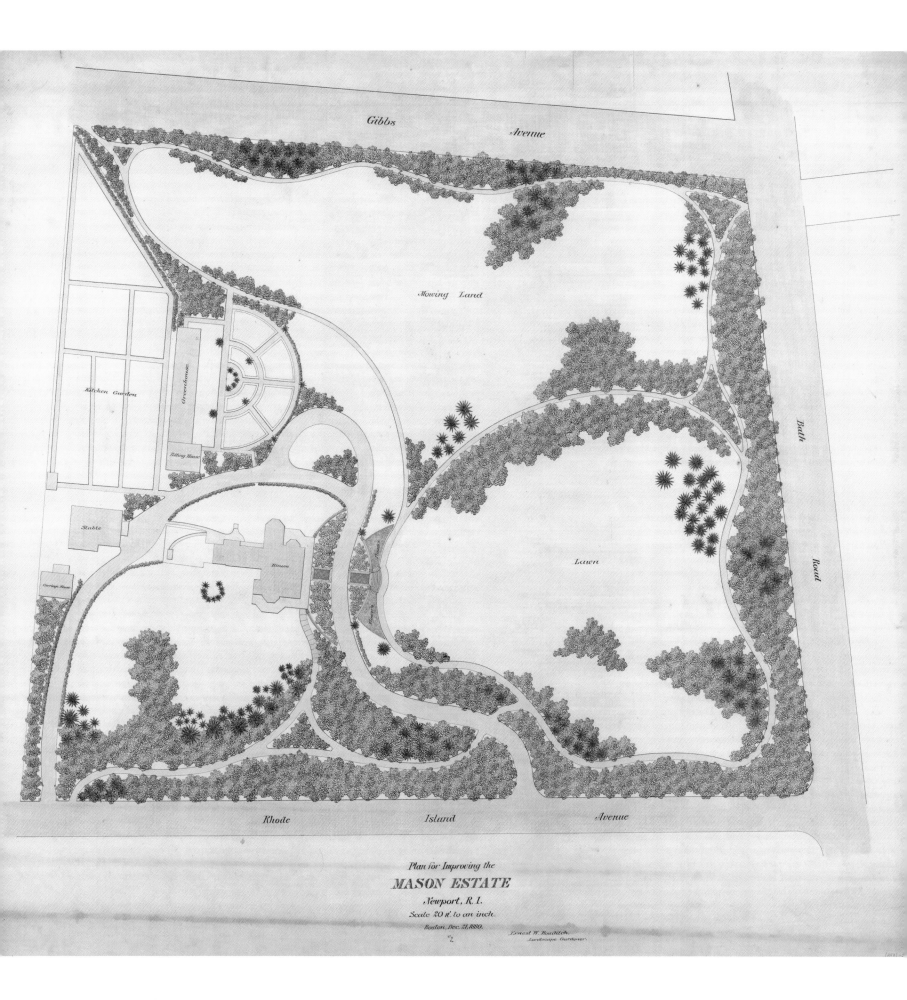

Plan for Improving the
MASON ESTATE
Newport, R.I.
Scale 20 ft. to an inch.
Boston, Dec. 21, 1880.

Ernest W. Bowditch.
Landscape Gardener.

Fig. 173 (above)
View of the grounds, Miss Ellen Mason Estate, ca. 1920, photograph
United States Department of the Interior, National Park Service,
Frederick Law Olmsted National Historic Site

Fig. 174 (below)
H. D. Perkins, Miss Ellen Mason House, 1916, photograph
United States Department of the Interior, National Park Service,
Frederick Law Olmsted National Historic Site

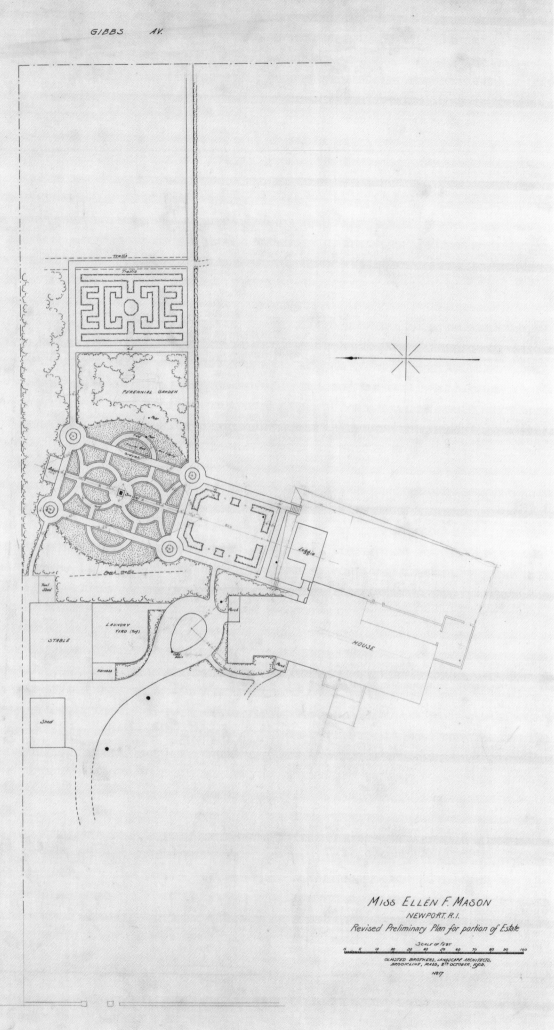

GIBBS AV.

RHODE ISLAND AV.

MISS ELLEN F. MASON
NEWPORT, R.I.
Revised Preliminary Plan for portion of Estate

SCALE OF FEET

OLMSTED BROTHERS, LANDSCAPE ARCHITECTS,
BROOKLINE, MASS, 2ⁿᵈ OCTOBER, 1902.

N°17

Fig. 175
Olmsted Brothers,
*Revised Preliminary
Plan*, Miss Ellen Mason
Estate, 1902
United States
Department of the
Interior, National Park
Service, Frederick
Law Olmsted National
Historic Site

Fig. 176
Rosecliff, ca. 1905, photograph
Library of Congress
McKim, Mead and White
created a version of Louis
XIV's Grand Trianon (1687), the
garden retreat that he referred
to as his "palace of flora."
Rosecliff has a centrally placed
parterre garden with classical
urns, sculpture, and clipped
laurel trees.

classical landscapes as having "no inner meaning; it does not address itself to the nobler part of our nature as simple natural scenery does."[149] Taking a balanced view, Van Rensselaer did not disparage the new interest in Renaissance and Baroque gardens, but insisted that a strong design determined a landscape of quality, whether it be natural or classical (Figs. 176–78). While embracing the art of scenery, Platt also emphasized the importance of the landscape as a complete design entity in his writing on Italian gardens:

> *The evident harmony of arrangement between the house and landscape is what first strikes one in Italian landscape architecture—the design as a whole, including gardens, terraces, groves, and their necessary surroundings and embellishments, it being clear that no one of these component parts was ever considered independently; the architect of the house also being the architect of the garden . . . so the garden was designed as another apartment, the terraces and groves still others, where one might walk about and find a place suitable to the hour.*[150]

Edith Wharton supported Platt's ideas, emphasizing that an effective design followed a disciplined sequence from house to landscape in stages beginning with the refined and progressing to the rustic, as she advised readers to

> *remember that the terraces and formal gardens adjoined the house, that the ilex or laurel walks beyond were clipped into shape to effect a transition between the straight lines of masonry and the untrimmed growth of woodland to which they led, and that each step away from architecture was a nearer approach to nature.*[151]

Advocates of either the natural or formal idiom tended to agree that landscape should be subject to coherent design, even if they differed in their preferred style and approach. The Olmsted Brothers ably applied both idioms in their landscapes. Their work at Ochre Court addressed the needs of a Beaux Arts château, while in projects for Mrs. Harold Brown, Mrs. John Nicholas Brown, and generations of the Auchincloss family they often merged the picturesque and the classical with an emphasis on a variety of flowers and plants appropriate to the character of the

Fig. 177
View of the gardens, Chetwode, ca. 1910, photograph
The Preservation Society of Newport County

Fig. 178
Residence of Mr. and Mrs. John Jacob Astor III, landscape plan for Chetwode, 1927, photograph
The Preservation Society of Newport County
Straight axes of clipped greenery define this classical landscape plan.

AVENUE

AVENUE

BELLEVUE

~ RESIDENCE OF ~
MR AND MRS · JOHN J · ASTOR III
NEWPORT R·I·

GORDON SYME

respective sites. These estates became horticultural showcases, and their owners had long-term relationships with the Olmsteds. As such, the landscapes are windows into the evolving tastes of patrons and the variety of plant material available in the late 1890s through the 1940s, an era when the country estate reached its peak of development.

Mr. and Mrs. Harold Brown engaged the Olmsted Brothers in 1894 to create a setting for their rough-hewn granite house by architect Dudley Newton. The landscape followed the established picturesque formula with weeping beeches, hemlocks, pine, oak, and maple as centerpieces of the main lawns, while a gardener's cottage, greenhouse, and flower garden occupied a corner of the estate. Mr. Brown died in 1900, and very little work was undertaken by his widow until 1912, when a flurry of activity commenced and continued through the 1930s. Percival Gallagher and Harold Hill Blossom served as the liaisons from the Olmsted Brothers office, dealing with volumes of correspondence with Mrs. Brown, who was meticulous in her further development and refinement of flower beds, a woodland, and fruit trees.[152] In a letter of November 1912, she stated her preference for an "Old English" atmosphere.[153] Set far from the ocean, the Bellevue Avenue estate had the ideal situation for the propagation of flowers and plants in a sheltered location. This became the guiding factor in extraordinarily detailed planting plans, which reflect the general influence of the lush flower beds, herbaceous borders, and woodland plantings of English Arts and Crafts designers such as Gertrude Jekyll and her contemporaries, whose work was internationally recognized at the time the Olmsteds began expanding the Harold Brown gardens. The Olmsteds did not slavishly copy the soft floral borders and woodlands of the English Arts and Crafts scenarios, but adapted them to the conditions of Newport and their own established pattern of using woodland plants. The flower beds featured 127 types, including phlox, iris, gladiolus, alyssum, aster, delphinium, dahlia, astilbe, poppy, lavender, moon daisy, and bugle flower planted in masses to create a broad palette of colors. (Figs. 179–85). Since Mrs. Brown used the estate as her primary residence, the plantings were planned for continual blooming from spring through late fall. The 109 trees and shrubs listed for the woodland are of the kind used in many Olmsted gardens. Fifteen types of rhododendron, viburnum, and forsythia lined the curved path through red oak, American beech, American mountain ash, and katsura. Euonymous, English ivy, and pachysandra formed ground cover around Japanese anemone, lily-of-the-valley, and Virginia cowslip, and a collection of maidenhair, evergreen wood, prickly shield, and chain ferns. On the perimeter of this wooded enclave, Tatarian and Morrow's honeysuckle grew in apparent wild abandon, though it was actually managed by the estate gardeners to maintain this effect. In the spirit of the Arts and Crafts movement, this composition evoked the carpets of flowers of a Medieval tapestry and the wooded groves in the pastoral poetry of Elizabethan England, albeit with plants from Europe, Asia, and America, typical of the eclecticism of the era. Mrs. Brown had her old English gardens to complement her rusticated stone villa, a scene that a wandering knight would have been pleased to come upon. Such was the intent the Olmsteds inferred from Mrs. Brown's letter, and they achieved it with attention to every detail.

Fig. 179 (opposite, top)
View of Harold Brown House, 1913, photograph
United States Department of the Interior, National Park Service, Frederick Law Olmsted National Historic Site

Fig. 180 (opposite, bottom)
Bosquet, Harold Brown House, 1913, photograph
United States Department of the Interior, National Park Service, Frederick Law Olmsted National Historic Site

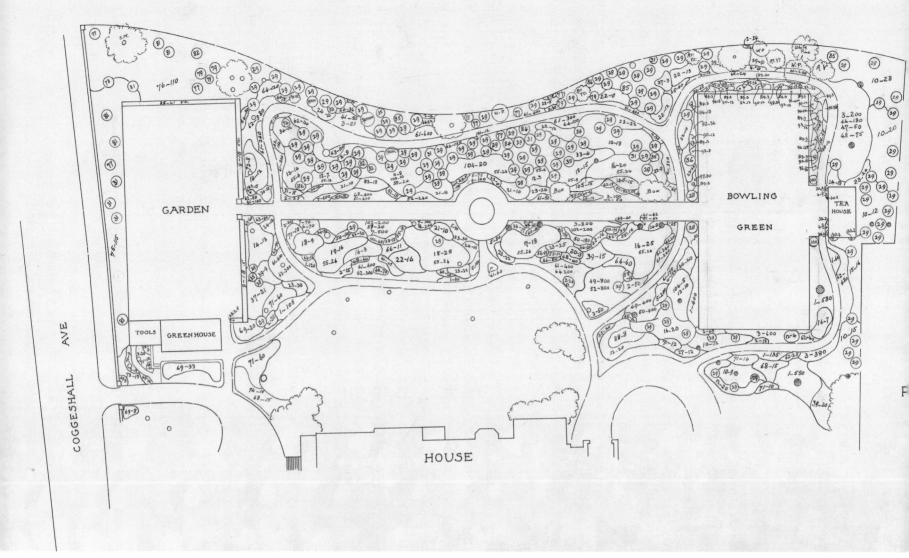

GARDEN

TOOLS · GREEN HOUSE

COGGESHALL AVE

BOWLING GREEN

TEA HOUSE

HOUSE

---

21. Andromeda floribunda, 44 plants, 3' apart,
Mountain Fetter Bush
22. Kalmia latifolia, 87 plants, 3' apart,
Mountain Laurel
23. Leucothoe catesbaei, 277 plants, 1½' apart,
Catesby's Leucothoe
24. Taxus canadensis, 100 plants, 2' apart,
American Yew
25. Tsuga canadensis, 24 plants, 3' apart,
Hemlock
26. Juniperus tamariscifolia, 12 plants, 2' apart,
Savin Juniper
27. Berberis aquifolia, 12 plants, 2' apart,
Mahonia
28. Buxus sempervirens, 2 plants,
Box Bush
29. Tsuga canadensis, 126 plants,
Hemlock
30. Ampelopsis engelmanni, 12 plants,
Englemann's Creeper
31. Betula papyrifera, 7 plants,
Paper Birch
32. Carpinus betulus, 3 plants,
Hornbeam
33. Hydrangea arborescens, 4 plants,
Hydrangea
34. Viburnum lantana, 12 plants, 3½' apart,
English Wayfaring Tree
35. Amelanchier canadensis, 3 plants,
Shad Bush
36. Cornus florida rubra, 1 plant,
Pink-Flowering Dogwood
37. Forsythia fortunei, 24 plants, 3½' apart,
Fortune's Golden Bell
38. Cornus florida, 1 plant,
White Flowering Dogwood
39. Forsythia suspensa, 70 plants, 3' apart,
Weeping Golden Bell
40. Mertensia virginica, 35 plants, 1' apart,
Virginia Cowslip
41. Convallaria majalis, 610 plants, 6" apart,
Lily of the Valley
42. Funkia subcordata, 15 plants,
Day Lily
43. Smilacina racemosa, 123 plants, 9" apart,
False Solomon's Seal
44. Ajuga reptans, 40 plants, 6" apart,
Bugle
45. Arabis albida, 60 plants, 6" apart,
Rock Cress
46. 3 beds, 330 plants, 6" apart,
Trillium grandiflorum, 200 plants, 6" apart,
Large-Flowered Wake Robin
Trillium erithrocarpum, 130 plants, 6" apart,
Painted Wake Robin
47. Trillium nivale, 50 plants, 6" apart,
Early Wake Robin
48. Tiarella cordifolia, 695 plants, 6" apart,
Foam Flower
49. Smilacina bifolia, 1200 plants, 6" apart,
False Solomon's Seal
50. Sanguinaria canadensis, 835 plants, 6" apart,
Bloodroot

51. Mitella diphylla, 442 plants, 6" apart,
Bishop's Cap
52. Mitchella repens, 1040 plants, 6" apart,
Partridge Berry
55. Digitalis purpurea, 261 plants, 15" apart,
Foxglove
56. Cimicifuga racemosa, 15 plants, 15" apart,
Black Snakeroot
58. Aster laevis, 27 plants, 1' apart,
Aster
59. Lilium pennsilvanicum, 20 plants, 1' apart,
Wild Orange Lily
61. 18 beds, 4416 plants, 6" apart,
Asplenium ebeneum, 1472 plants,
Ebony Spleenwort
Polypodium vulgare, 1472 plants,
Rock Fern
Woodsia obtusa, 1472 plants,
Woodsia
62. 14 beds, 1820 plants, 9" apart,
Aspidium acrostichoides, 607 plants,
Christmas Fern
Aspidium marginale, 607 plants,
Evergreen Wood Fern
Aspidium braunii, 707 plants,
Aspidium
63. Adiantum pedatum, 430 plants, 6" apart,
Maidenhair Fern
64. 10 beds, 684 plants, 1' apart,
Asplenium thelypteroides, 228 plants,
Free-veined Fern
Woodwardia virginica, 228 plants,
Chain Fern
Phegopteris hexagonoptera, 228 plants,
Beech Fern.
65. Xanthorrhiza apiifolia, 153 plants, 1' apart,
Yellow Root
66. Azalea viscosa, 11 plants, 3' apart,
Swamp Pink
68. Ligustrum regelianum, 32 plants, 3' apart,
Regel's Privet
69. Berberis thunbergii, 64 plants, 2½' apart,
Japanese Barberry
71. Symphoricarpos racemosus, 183 plants, 2' apart,
Snowberry
72. Ligustrum vulgaris, 11 plants, 3' apart,
Common Privet
73. Rhodotypos kerrioides, 13 plants, 2' apart,
White Kerria
74. Ligustrum ibota, 16 plants, 3' apart,
Japanese Privet
75. 1 bed, 115 plants, 3½' apart,
Ligustrum ibota, 23 plants,
Japanese Privet
Symphoricapos racemosus, 23 plants,
Snowberry
Forsythia suspensa, 23 plants,
Weeping Golden Bell
Lonicera morrowi, 23 plants,
Japanese Bush Honeysuckle
Cercis canadensis, 23 plants,
Red Bud.

76. 1 bed, 112 plants, 4½' apart,
Viburnum lentago, 16 plants,
Sheepberry
Viburnum cassinoides, 16 plants,
Witherod
Viburnum tomentosum, 16 plants,
Single Japanese Snowball
Halesia tetraptera, 16 plants,
Silver Bell
Sorbus americana, 16 plants,
Mountain Ash
Lonicera tatarica, rosa, 16 plants,
Tartarian Honeysuckle
Rhodotypos kerrioides, 16 plants,
White Kerria
77. Cercidiphyllum japonicum, 7 plants,
Kadsura Tree
78. Cladrastis tinctoria, 1 plant,
Yellow Wood
79. Chionanthus virginica, 5 plants,
Fringe Tree
81. Laburnum vulgare, 6 plants,
Golden Chain
82. Sophora japonica, 1 plant,
Japan Pagoda Tree.
83. Rhododendron wilsoniana, 18 plants, 2' apart,
Dwarf Rhododendron.
84. Quercus rubra, 5 plants,
Red Oak.
85. Fagus ferruginea, 4 plants,
American Beech
86. Magnolia conspicua,
White Chinese Magnolia
87. Cherry, May Duke, 1 plant,
Cherry
88. Rhododendron everestianum, 8 plant, 4½' apart,
Rhododendron.
89. Delphiniums, 39 plants, 18" apart,
Perennial Larkspur
90. Coreopsis grandiflora, 66 plants, 12" apart,
Yellow Coreopsis.
91. 1 bed, 400 plants, 8" apart,
Campanula carpatica, 200 plants,
Blue Carpathian Harebell
Campanula carpatica alba, 200 plants,
White Carpathian Harebell
92. Funkia subcordata grandiflora, 120 plants, 15" apart
93. Chrysanthemum maximum, 44 plants, 15" apart,
Hybrid Shasta Daisy
94. Veronica subsessilis, 108 plants, 12" apart,
Speedwell
95. Phlox divaricata alba grandiflora, 36 plants,
Dwarf Phlox
96. Phlox divaricata laphami, 48 plants,
Dwarf Phlox
97. Delphinium belladonna, 150 plants, 12" apart,
Pale Blue Dwarf Perennial Larkspur
98. Delphinium Lamartine, 94 plants, 12" apart,
Deep Blue Dwarf Perennial Larkspur
99. Potentilla, Miss Willomott, 80 plants, 12" apart,
Pink Cinquefoil.

100. Buxus sempervirens, (Globe Form) 2 plants,
Box Bush.
101. Digitalis ambigua, 45 plants, 1' apart,
Foxglove
102. Myosotis palustris grandiflora, 450 plants, 3" apart,
Forget-me-not.
103. Rhododendron kettledrum, 10 plants,
Hybrid Rhododendron
104. Rhododendron, Minnie, 25 plants,
Hybrid Rhododendron
105. Rhododendron punctatum, 30 plants, 2½' apart
Dwarf Rhododendron.

Note: First figures in beds indicate plants or mixture of plants to be used in each space. Second figures indicate number of plants or mixture of plants estimated as required to fill each space.

Drawn by E.C.W.   Approved for Issue
Traced by M.H.D.
Checked by H.S.   by E.C.W.

PLANTING LIST

1. Hedera helix, 2120 plants, 9" apart
   English Ivy
2. Euonymus radicans carrieri, 200 plants, 1' apart
   Evergreen Creeper
3. Vinca minor, 1636 plants, 5" apart
   Periwinkle
4. Daphne cneorum, 288 plants, 9" apart
   Garland Flower
5. Pachysandra terminalis, 625 plants, 6" apart
   Japanese Spurge
6. Asarum virginicum, 90 plants, 6" apart
   Snakeroot
7. Galax aphylla, 1120 plants, 6" apart
   Galax
8. Coptis trifoliata, 240 plants, 4" apart
   Goldthread
9. Tsuga canadensis, 36 plants, 3' apart
   Hemlock
10. Rhododendron maximum plants, 5' apart
    Great Laurel
11. Rhododendron atrosanguineum, 9 plants, 4½' apart.
12. Rhododendron, Boule de Niege, 73 plants, 2½' apart.
13. Rhododendron caracticus, 14 plants, 4½' apart
14. Rhododendron, Charles Dickens, 33 plants, 4½' apart
15. Rhododendron Parsons grandiflorus, 41 plants, 4½' apart.
16. Rhododendron everastianum, 72 plants, 4½' apart.
    (Rosy lilac)
17. Rhododendron Parsons Gloriosum, 18 plants, 4½' apart
    (Rose White)
18. Rhododendron elegans, 24 plants, 4½' apart
    (Lilac purple)
19. Rhododendron album elegans, 16 plants, 4½' apart
    (tall, pure white)
20. Rhododendron catawbiense album, 3 plants.
    (white)

MRS HAROLD BROWN
NEWPORT R.I.
~~ING PLAN FOR PORTION NORTH OF HOUSE
SCALE 20'=1"

10 0 10 20 30 40 50 60 70 80 90 100

OLMSTED BROTHERS LANDSCAPE ARCHITECTS
BROOKLINE MASS   MARCH 24 1913

FILE NO 1726
PLAN NO 59
REVISED APRIL 22, 1913.

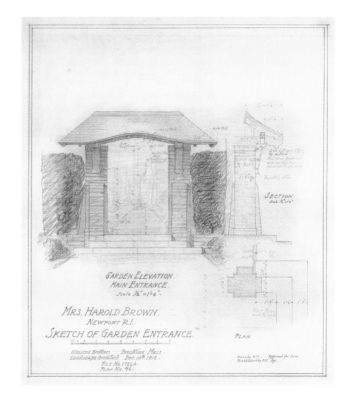

Fig. 181 (left and left below)
Olmsted Brothers,
*Planting Plan for Portion
North of House*, Harold
Brown Estate, 1913
United States Department
of the Interior, National
Park Service, Frederick
Law Olmsted National
Historic Site

Fig. 182 (right)
Harold Hill Blossom,
*Sketch of Garden
Entrance*, Harold Brown
Estate, 1912, drawing
United States Department
of the Interior, National
Park Service, Frederick
Law Olmsted National
Historic Site

Fig. 183 (below left)
Harold Hill Blossom, Lych
gate in the woodland
garden, Harold Brown
Estate, 1913, photograph
United States Department
of the Interior, National
Park Service, Frederick
Law Olmsted National
Historic Site

Fig. 184 (below right)
Edward Van Altena, Flower garden, Harold Brown
Estate, ca. 1920, photograph
Archives of American Gardens

Fig. 185 (overleaf)
Olmsted Brothers, *Planting Plan for Flower Garden*,
Harold Brown Estate, 1912
United States Department of the Interior, National
Park Service, Frederick Law Olmsted National
Historic Site

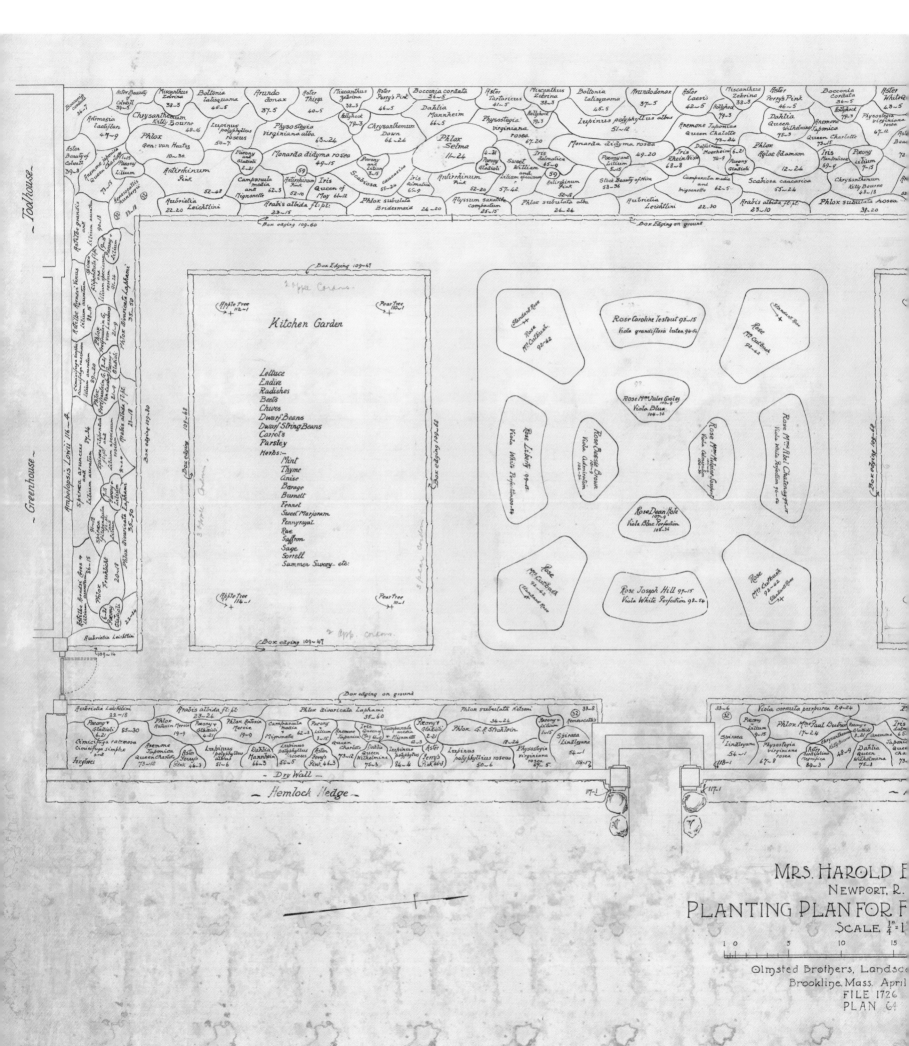

MRS. HAROLD B.
NEWPORT, R.
PLANTING PLAN FOR F
SCALE ¼" = 1
Olmsted Brothers, Landsca
Brookline, Mass. April
FILE 1726
PLAN 64

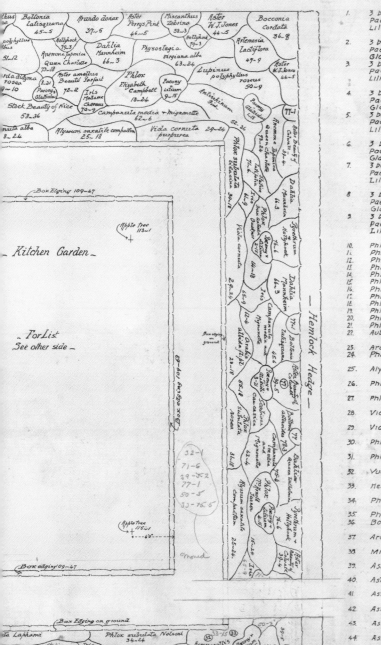

Kitchen Garden

For List
See other side —

— Hemlock Hedge —

Hedge —

ER GARDEN

chitects

1. 3 beds, 45 plants
   Paeony, Aldred de Musset, 9 plants, 18" apart
   Lilium speciosum roseum, 36 plants, 9" apart,
   Rose-spotted Lily
2. 3 beds, 63 plants:
   Paeony Cytheree, 9 plants, 18" apart
   Gladioli America, 54 plants, 6" apart
3. 3 beds, 45 plants,
   Paeony, Duchess de Nemours, 9 plants, 18" apart
   Lilium speciosum melpomene, 36 plants, 9" apart
   Crimson Spotted Lily
4. 3 beds, 63 plants:
   Paeony, Gloria Mundi, 9 plants, 18" apart
   Gladioli Ceres, 54 plants, 6" apart
5. 3 beds, 45 plants:
   Paeony Festiva maxima, 9 plants, 18" apart,
   Lilium speciosum roseum, 36 plants, 9" apart
   Rose Spotted Lily
6. 3 beds, 63 plants,
   Paeony, Lais, 9 plants, 18" apart
   Gladioli, Gil Blas, 54 plants, 6" apart,
7. 3 beds, 45 plants:
   Paeony Marie Lemoine, 9 plants, 18" apart
   Lilium speciosum magnificum, 36 plants, 9" apart
   Large spotted Lily
8. 3 beds, 63 plants
   Paeony, Mme. Calot, 9 plants, 18" apart
   Gladioli Rosella, 54 plants, 6" apart
9. 3 beds, 45 plants:
   Paeony, Zoe Calot, 9 plants, 18" apart
   Lilium speciosum rubrum, 36 plants, 9" apart
   Red Spotted Lily
10. Phlox, Gen. van Heutsz, 30 plants, 10" apart
11. Phlox, Selma, 24 plants, 10" apart
12. Phlox, Aglae Adamson, 24 plants, 10" apart
13. Phlox, Elizabeth Campbell, 24 plants, 10" apart
14. Phlox, Frau Antonin Buckner, 18 plants, 10" apart
15. Phlox, Mrs. Arnold Turner, 24 plants, 10" apart,
16. Phlox, Eugene Danzanvillier, 16 plants, 10" apart
17. Phlox, Mme. Paul Dutrie, 24 plants, 10" apart,
18. Phlox, G. A. Strohlein, 24 plants, 10" apart,
19. Phlox, Antonin Mercie, 18 plants, 10" apart
20. Phlox, Fruhlicht, 18 plants, 10" apart
21. Phlox, Freifraulein G. von Lassburg, 18 plants, 10" apart,
22. Aubrietia leichtlini, 92 plants, 8" apart
    Pink Rock Cress
23. Arabis albida fl. pl. 85 plants, 8" apart
24. Phlox subulata Bridesmaid, 20 plants, 8" apart
    Creeping Phlox
25. Alyssum Saxatile compactum, 57 plants, 8" apart
    Gold Dust
26. Phlox, subulata alba, 24 plants, 8" apart
    Creeping Phlox
27. Phlox subulata atropurpurea.
    NOT USED.
28. Viola cornuta alba, 24 plants, 6" apart
    White Horned Pansy.
29. Viola cornuta purpurea, 72 plants, 6" apart
    Purple Horned Pansy.
30. Phlox subulata lilacina, 18 plants, 8" apart
    Creeping Phlox
31. Phlox subulata rosea, 18 plants, 8" apart
    Creeping Phlox
32. Yucca filamentosa, 7 plants
    Adam's Needle
33. Hemerocallis thunbergii, 47 plants, 1' apart
    Day Lily
34. Phlox subulata nelsoni, 48 plants, 8" apart
    Creeping Phlox
35. Phlox divaricata Laphami, 220 plants, 9" apart
36. Bocconia cordata, 33 plants, 18" apart
    Plume Poppy
37. Arundo donax, 15 plants, 18" apart
    Giant Reed
38. Miscanthus japonica zebrina, 18 plants, 2' apart
    Eulalia
39. Aster Beauty of Colwall, 31 plants, 18" apart
    Double-Flowered Michaelmas Daisy
40. Aster Thirza, 5 plants, 18" apart
    Michaelmas Daisy
41. Aster tartaricus, 5 plants, 18" apart
    Michaelmas Daisy
42. Aster laevis, 5 plants, 18" apart
    Michaelmas Daisy
43. Aster White Queen, 5 plants, 18" apart
    Michaelmas Daisy
44. Aster W. T. Jones, 10 plants, 18" apart
    Michaelmas Daisy
45. Boltonia latisquama, 21 plants, 18" apart,
    False Starwort
46. Aster, Perry's Pink, 24 plants, 18" apart
    Michaelmas Daisy
47. Artemesia lactiflora, 26 plants, 18" apart,
    Artemesia
48. Chrysanthemum Kitty Bourne, 43 plants, 12" apart
    New English Semi-double.
49. Monarda didyma rosea, 45 plants, 12" apart
    Bergamot
50. Lupinus polyphyllus roseus, 32 plants, 18" apart
    Rose Lupine
51. Lupinus polyphyllus albus, 150 plants, 18" apart
    White Lupine
52. Antirrhinum Pink, 150 plants, 9" apart
    Snapdragon
54. Spiraea Lindleyana, 2 plants
    Shrubby Spiraea
55. Scabiosa caucasica, 66 plants, 12" apart
    Blue Scabius
57. 1 bed, 42 plants, 12" apart
    Sweet William, Pink Beauty, 18 plants
    Lilium speciosum roseum 24 plants
58. Stock Beauty of Nice, 72 plants, 10" apart
59. Gypsophila paniculata fl. pl. 3 plants
    Double Baby's Breath
61. Iris, Queen of May, 30 plants, 9" apart
62. 7 beds, 28 plants
    Campanula media pink, 28 plants.
    Canterbury Bells
    Mignonette (seed)
63. Physostegia virginiana alba, 48 plants, 12" apart
    False Dragon's Head
64. Chrysanthemum, Dawn, 24 plants, 12" apart
65. Iris pallida dalmatica, 45 plants, 9" apart
66. Dahlia Mannheim, 20 plants, 2' apart
67. Physostegia virginiana rosea, 45 plants, 12" apart
    Rose Dragon's Head
68. Iris Rhein Nixie, 16 plants, 9" apart
69. Iris mandraliscoe, 9 plants, 9" apart
70. Iris Madame Chereau, 9 plants, 9" apart
71. Statice latifolia, 12 plants, 12" apart
    Sea Lavender

72. Aster amellus Beauté Parfait, 24 plants, 9" apart
    Dwarf Michaelmas Daisy
73. Anemone japonica Queen Charlotte, 162 plants, 9" apart
    Japanese Anemone
74. Delphinum Moerheimi, 9 plants, 12" apart
    White Delphinium
75. Dahlia Queen Wilhelmina, 13 plants, 2' apart
76. 3 beds, 17 plants, 18" apart
    Pyrethrum uliginosum, 10 plants
    Moon Daisy
    Hollyhock, Single Pink, 7 plants.
77. Miscanthus japonica zebrina, 5 plants
    Eulalia
78. Boltonia asteroides, 3 plants, 18" apart.
    False Starwort
79. Hollyhock, double pink, 18 plants, 18" apart
80. Aster cordifolius magnificus, 12 plants, 15" apart
    Michaelmas Daisy
81. 2 beds, 44 plants, 15" apart
    Statice latifolia, 20 plants
    Sea Lavender
    Gladiolus america, 24 plants,
83. Pyrethrum uliginosum, 3 plants, 18" apart
    Moon Daisy
84. Lupinus polyphyllus, 4 plants
    Blue Lupine
85. 1 bed, 30 plants, 15" apart
    Cimicifuga racemosa, 10 plants
    Black Snake Root
    Cimicifuga simplex, 10 plants,
    Snake Root
    Foxglove, 10 plants
86. 1 bed, 15 plants, 18" apart
    Astilbe Arendsii Ceres, 6 plants
    Pink Spiraea
    Lilium auratum, 9 plants
    Gold-rayed Lily of Japan
87. 1 bed, 21 plants, 18" apart
    Spiraea aruncus, 10 plants, 18" apart
    Goat's Beard
    Lilium auratum, 24 plants,
    Gold-rayed Lily of Japan
88. 1 bed, 15 plants, 18" apart
    Astilbe Arendsii Venus, 6 plants
    Pink Spiraea
    Lilium auratum, 9 plants
    Gold-rayed Lily of Japan.
89. 1 bed, 20 plants, 15" apart
    Cimicifuga, simplex, 4 plants
    Snake Root
    Cimicifuga, racemosa, 4 plants
    Black Snake Root
    Lilium auratum, 12 plants
    Gold-rayed Lily of Japan
90. 1 bed, 18 plants, 18" apart
    Astilbe grandis, 6 plants
    White Spiraea
    Lilium auratum, 12 plants
    Gold-rayed Lily of Japan
91. 3 beds, 62 plants, 15" apart
    Spiraea filapendula, fl. pl. 28 plants
    Double Flowered Spiraea
    Lilium speciosum roseum, 34 plants
    Spotted Lily
92. 4 beds, 182 plants, 12" apart
    Rose Mrs. Cutbush, 78 plants
    Standard Rose Frau Karl Druschki, 4 plants
93. Rose Carolina Testout, 15 plants, 20" apart
94. Viola grandiflora lutea, 54 plants
95. Rose, Madame Abel Chatenay 15 plants, 20" apart
96. Viola White Perfection, 54 plants
97. Rose Joseph Hill, 15 plants, 20" apart
98. Viola White Perfection, 54 plants
99. Rose, Liberty, 15 plants, 20" apart
100. Viola White Perfection, 54 plants
101. Rose Bessie Brown, 9 plants, 20" apart
102. Viola Admiration, 36 plants
103. Rose Madame Jules Groley, 9 plants, 20" apart
104. Viola Blue Perfection, 36 plants
105. Rose Mme. Melaine Soupert, 9 plants, 20" apart
106. Viola Admiration, 36 plants
107. Rose Dean Hole, 9 plants, 20" apart
108. Viola Blue Perfection, 36 plants
109. Box Edging, 620 plants, 6" apart
110. Pear, Beurré d'Anjou, 2 plants.
111. Pear, Louise Bonne of Jersey, 2 plants.
112. Apple, Northern Spy, 1 plant
113. Apple, Jonathan, 1 plant
114. Apple, Farmeuse, 1 plant
115. Apple, Gravenstein, 1 plant
116. Ampelopsis Lowii, 4 plants
117. Lonicera Halleana, 2 plants
118. Ampelopsis Henryi, 2 plants

Note :- First figures in beds indicate the plants or mixture of
plants to be used in each space. Second figures indicate
number of plants or mixture of plants estimated as required to fill each space.
Plants not in list are omitted from plan.

Drawn by	H.S.	Approved for Issue.
Traced by	H.S.	by E.C.W.
Checked by		

Fig. 186 (above)
Robert Yarnall Richie, Harbour
Court, 1932–34, photograph
Robert Yarnall Richie
Photograph Collection,
Negative Series: 0596, DeGolyer
Library, Southern Methodist
University

Fig. 187 (right)
Edward Van Altena, Pool and
flower garden, Harbour Court,
ca. 1920, photograph
Archives of American Gardens

Fig. 188 (opposite)
Harold Hill Blossom, Proposed
Estate plan, Harbour Court,
1920
United States Department of
the Interior, National Park
Service, Frederick Law Olmsted
National Historic Site
Harbour Court combines the
picturesque arrangement
of specimen trees with the
classical revival forms of
the flower and rose gardens.
The central lawn, or *tapis
vert*, between the two flower
gardens was not implemented.

The Olmsteds devised an equally complex scheme for Mrs. John Nicholas Brown's French château Harbour Court. Designed and built by Cram, Goodhue and Ferguson between 1903 and 1905, the house sits atop a hill overlooking Newport harbor (Figs. 186–92). The initial landscape plan was augmented with a summer house and rock garden by 1913, followed by a formal garden in 1921. Percival Gallagher and Harold Hill Blossom, of Olmsted Brothers, located the formal flower and rose gardens in a natural depression protected from the high winds of the harbor.[154]

Fig. 189 (overleaf)
Harold Hill Blossom, *Planting Plan for Rose and Flower Gardens*, Harbour Court, 1920
United States Department of the Interior, National Park Service, Frederick Law Olmsted National Historic Site

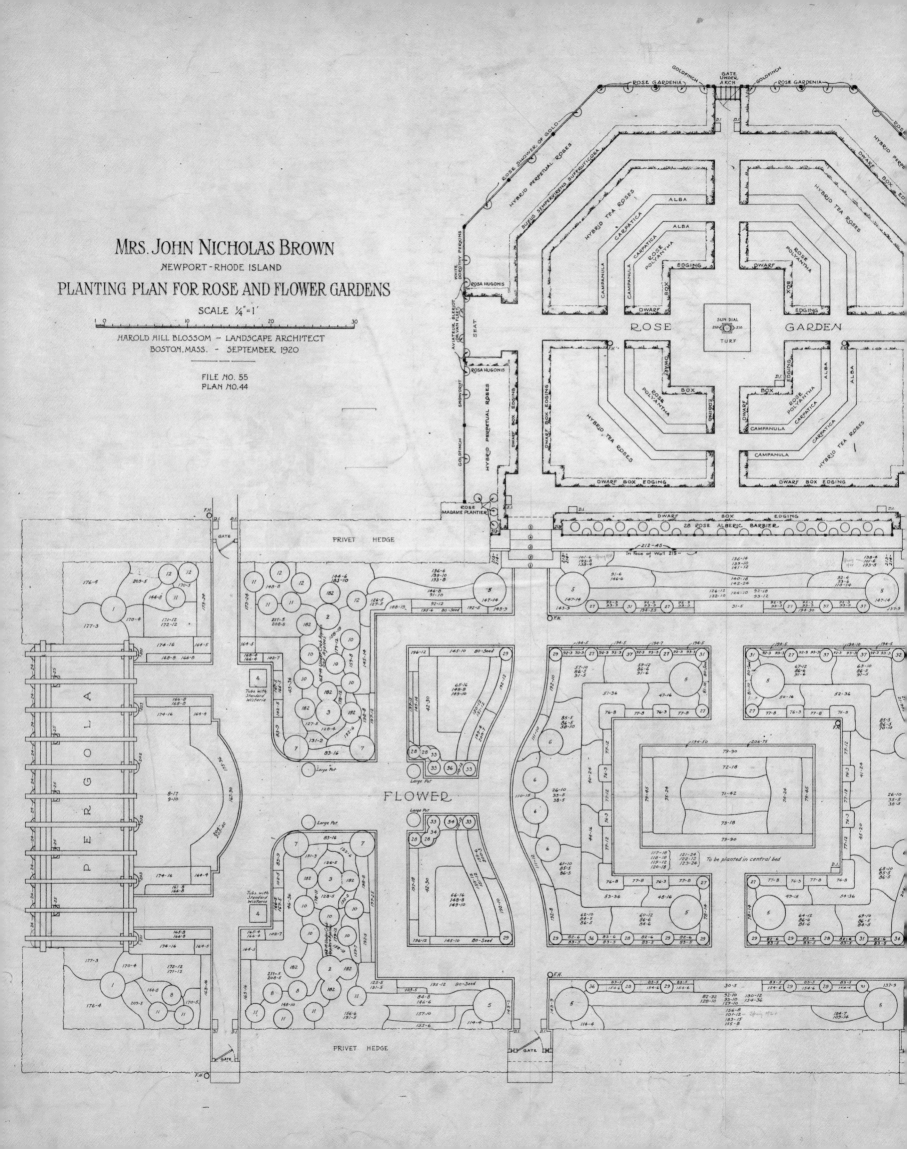

MRS. JOHN NICHOLAS BROWN
NEWPORT - RHODE ISLAND
PLANTING PLAN FOR ROSE AND FLOWER GARDENS
SCALE ¼" = 1'

HAROLD HILL BLOSSOM — LANDSCAPE ARCHITECT
BOSTON, MASS. - SEPTEMBER 1920

FILE NO. 55
PLAN NO. 44

ROSE GARDEN

FLOWER

PERGOLA

PRIVET HEDGE

PRIVET HEDGE

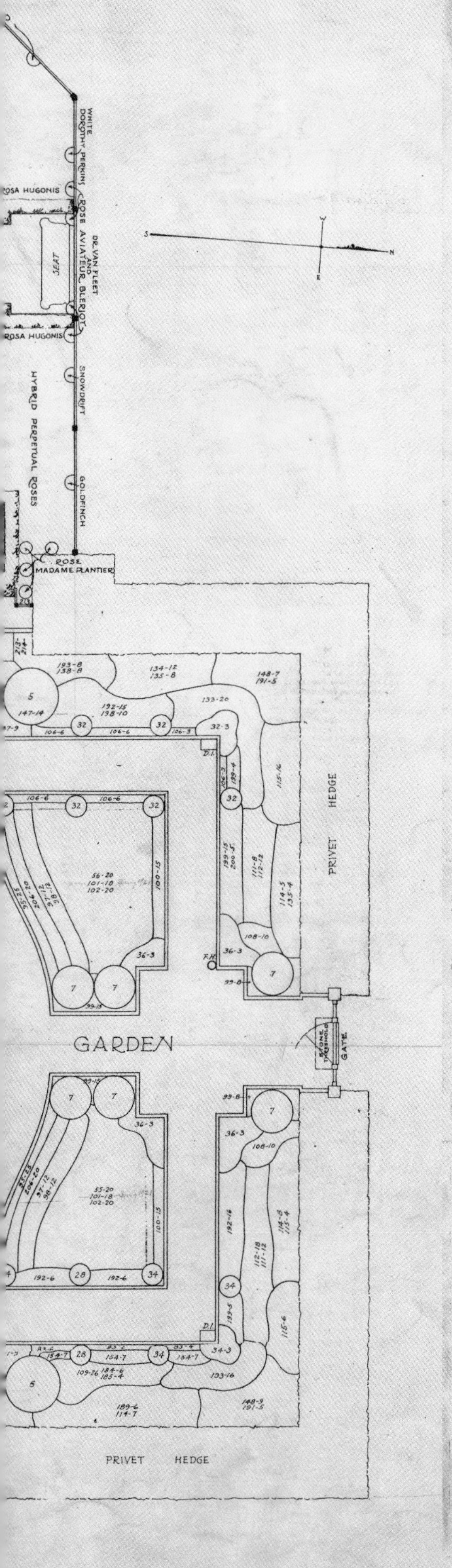

ROSA HUGONIS
SEAT
ROSA HUGONIS
HYBRID PERPETUAL ROSES
WHITE DOROTHY PERKINS
ROSE AVIATEUR BLERIOT
DR VAN FLEET
SNOWDRIFT
GOLDFINCH
ROSE MADAME PLANTIER
PRIVET HEDGE
GARDEN
GATE
PRIVET HEDGE

PLANTING LIST
for
Rose and Flower Gardens

Mrs. John Nicholas Brown — Plan No. 44
Newport, Rhode Island. — September, 1920

NOTE: First figure in the bed indicates the plant or mixture of plants to be used in that bed. Second figure indicates the number of plants estimated as required to fill the space.

No. as on plan	Scientific and Popular Name	Quantity
1	Cornus florida White Flowering Dogwood	2
2	Malus floribunda Japanese Flowering Crab Apple	2
3	Malus spectabilis Chinese Flowering Crab Apple	2
4	Wistaria chinensis Chinese Blue Wistaria	2
5	Syringa Marie Le Graye Single White Lilac	12
6	Syringa Negro Single Dark Crimson Lilac	8
7	Deutzia Lemoinei Lemoine's Deutzia	10
8	Azalea Hollandia Blush-yellow Azalea	20
9	Azalea Daviesii Cream-white Azalea	10
10	Azalea Nancy Waterer Yellow Azalea	10
11	Azalea Charles Dickens Creamy-white Azalea	10
12	Azalea Anthony Koster Golden-yellow Azalea	5
13	Rosa Hugonis Single clear-yellow Climbing Rose	6
14	Rosa Mme. Plantier Double-white Rose	8
15	Buxus suffruticosa Dwarf Box	800
16	Rosa Alberic Barbier Deep-cream Climbing Rose	28
17	Rosa Aviateur Bleriot Double Saffron-yellow Climbing Rose	6
18	Rosa Dr. Van Fleet Double Shell-pink Climbing Rose	4
19	Rosa Gardenia Bright-yellow Climbing Rose	8
20	Rosa Goldfinch English Rambling Yellow Rose	4
21	Rosa Shower of Gold Yellow Climbing Rose	6
22	Rosa Snowdrift Clear Snowy-white Climbing Rose	2
23	Rosa White Dorothy Double-white Climbing Rose	2
24	Vitis riparia Sweet-scented Flowering Grape	11
25	Euonymus vegetus Evergreen Bittersweet	5
26	Paeonia festiva maxima Waxy-white Peony	20
27	Paeonia Hermes Hydrangea-pink Peony	10
28	Paeonia La Fiancee White Peony	10
29	Paeonia Eduard Andre Crimson-maroon Peony	10
30	Paeonia Prince of Wales Dark-crimson Peony	5
31	Paeonia Venus Shell-pink Peony	10
32	Paeonia Felix Crousse Claret-red Peony	10
33	Paeonia Jules Calot Solferino-pink Peony	5
34	Paeonia Mme. Emile Gallee Shell-pink Peony	10
35	Paeonia Baroness Schroeder Flesh-colored Peony	10
36	Paeonia Therese Flesh-pink Peony	15
37	Paeonia M. Martin Cahuzac Dark-garnet Peony	5
38	Paeonia Mr. Manning Dark-crimson Peony	10
39	Not used	
40	Not used	
41	Iris Dawn Pale-yellow Fleur-de-lis	48
42	Iris florentina alba Pure-white Fleur-de-lis	60
43	Iris pallida dalmatica Clear Deep-lavender Fleur-de-lis	36
44	Iris lutescens statellae Early Pale-yellow Fleur-de-lis	16
45	Iris Penelope Amber-yellow Fleur-de-lis	20
46	Iris Albert Victor Light Hyssop-violet Fleur-de-lis	36
47	Iris Mrs. Horace Darwin White to violet Fleur-de-lis	16
48	Iris Victorine White and lavender Fleur-de-lis	16
49	Iris Innocenza Cream-white to Yellow-brown Fleur-de-lis	18
50	Iris Ingeborg White Fleur-de-lis	16
51	Iris Dr. Bernice Yellowish-brown Fleur-de-lis	36
52	Iris Her Majesty Pale Purplish-rose Fleur-de-lis	36
53	Iris Amas Deep-blue Fleur-de-lis	36
54	Iris Medallion Yellow Fleur-de-lis	36
55	Phlox General Von Heutz Brilliant Salmon-pink Phlox	20
56	Phlox Thor Deep Salmon-pink Phlox	20
57	Phlox Gefion Salmon-pink Phlox	10
58	Phlox Eugene Danzanvilliers Soft Lilac-blue Phlox	10
59	Phlox Antonin Mercie Whitish-lilac Phlox	12
60	Phlox Mme. Pape Carpentier White Phlox	12
61	Phlox Mme. Paul Dutrie Lilac-rose Phlox	10
62	Phlox Elizabeth Campbell Salmon-pink Phlox	10
63	Phlox Rynstroom Rose to White Phlox	10
64	Phlox Hermione Dwarf White Phlox	12
65	Phlox Czarina Late Tall White Phlox	16
66	Phlox Albion White to Pale-rose Phlox	16
67	Phlox ornament Clear Rose Phlox	12
68	Phlox F. G. Von Lassburg Large Pure-white Phlox	10
69	Phlox Coquelicot Pure Scarlet Phlox	10
70	Phlox Mrs. Arnold Turner White Crimson-eyed Phlox	10
71	Iris Kaempferi Koki-no-iro Reddish-purple Japanese Iris	42
72	Iris Kaempferi Bandai-no-ami White to Creamy-yellow Japanese Iris	18
73	Iris Kaempferi Shirataki Primrose white Japanese Iris	18
74	Iris Kaempferi Hana-aoi Gray to Bluish-lilac Japanese Iris	24
75	Iris Kaempferi Tora-odori Gray to Lavender-blue Japanese Iris	24
76	Anemone Queen Charlotte Semi-double Pink Japanese Windflower	36
77	14 Beds - 136 Plants Dianthus plumarius Scotch Pink Primula polyantha Clear-yellow Primrose Phlox Drummondii Dwarf Phlox	136
78	Aster alpinus Deep-blue Dwarf Aster	28
79	1 Bed - 270 Plants Callistephus China Asters Heliotropium Heliotrope Iberis sempervirens Evergreen Candytuft	270
79	Continued Dianthus Heddewigi Vary-colored Chinese Pinks Reseda odorata Mignonette Primula polyantha Clear-yellow Primrose	
80	Papaver, Shirley Finest Mixed Shirley Poppy	
81	Daphne cneorum Garland Flower	20
82	Dianthus barbatus Sweet William	80
83	Arabis albida Rock Cress	126
84	Lupinus polyphyllus, blue Blue Lupine	30
85	Lupinus polyphyllus, white White Lupine	20
86	Lilium testaceum Buff-colored Nankeen Lily	58
87	Iberis umbellata Annual Candytuft	
88	Delphinium - Annual Annual Larkspur	
89	Arctotis grandis African Daisy	15
90	Matthiola Annual Stock	
91	Lupinus polyphyllus, Moerheimi Pink Lupine	38
92	Digitalus pupurea Purple Foxglove	82
93	Digitalis alba White Foxglove	70
94	Escholtzia californica California Poppy	
95	Phlox divaricata Dwarf Pale-blue Phlox	50
96	Not used	
97	Campanula persicifolia, blue Blue Peach Bells	24
98	Campanula persicifolia, white White Peach Bells	24
99	Alyssum saxatile compactum Gold Dust	46
100	Trollius asiaticus Orange Globe Flower	30
101	Hyacinthus canidcans Giant Summer Hyacinth	60
102	Aquilegia long spurred hybrids Long-spurred Columbines	64
103	Antirrhinum majus Snapdragon	5
104	Calendula officinalis Pot Marigold	
105	Zinnia elegans Zinnia	
106	Iberis sempervirens Evergreen Candytuft	24
107	Salpiglossis Painted Tongue	
108	Anemone japonica Whirlwind Double-white Japanese Windflower	26
109	Dimorphatheca aurantiaca African Golden Daisy	10
110	Calliopsis Annual Tickseed	53
111	Daisy, Burbank's Shasta Snowy-white Shasta Daisy	42
112	Lillium tenuifolium Scarlet Siberian Coral Lily	30
113	Not used	
114	Boltonia latisquama False Chamomile	28
115	Aster, Novi-Belgii-Amos Perry Deep-pink Fall Aster	26
116	Dahlias Various Dahlias	
117	Gladiolus Baron Josef Hulot Dark-violet Gladioli	18
118	Gladiolus Canary Bird Canary-yellow Gladioli	18
119	Gladiolus Brenchleyensis Scarlet Gladioli	12
120	Gladiolus Hollandia Cream-pink and yellow Gladioli	18
121	Gladiolus Lily Lehman Creamy-white Gladioli	24
122	Gladiolus Mrs. Francis King Light-pink Gladioli	12
123	Gladiolus America Soft-pink Gladioli	24
124	Chrysanthemum Dawn Daybreak-pink Chrysanthemum	10
125	Chrysanthemum Seven Oaks Double-yellow Chrysanthemum	5
126	Chrysanthemum Roupal Beauty Deep-pink Chrysanthemum	22
127	Chrysanthemum Lillian Doty Lavender-pink Chrysanthemum	10
128	Chrysanthemum Mrs. Penry Pure White Chrysanthemum	19
129	Chrysanthemum Mrs. Porter Bright Bronze Chrysanthemum	10
130	Chrysanthemum Golden West Yellow Chrysanthemum	12
131	Chrysanthemum Inez Scarlet-bronze Chrysanthemum	10
132	Chrysanthemum James Boone Pure-white Chrysanthemum	24
133	Pyrethrum roseum Persian Daisy	36
134	Cosmos Vary-colored Cosmos	12
135	Baptisia australis False Indigo	12
136	Althea rosea (single) Hollyhocks	20
137	Funkia lancifolia Lavender Plantain Lily	36
138	Delphinium elatum Bee Larkspur	16
139	Delphinium King-of-the-Blues Deep-blue Larkspur	20
140	Delphinium hybrids Larkspurs	18
141	Campanula pyramidalis Chimney Bell-flower	18
142	Lilium candidum Madonna Lily	24
143	Dictamnus fraxinella alba White Gas Plant	36
144	Aster tataricus Tartarian Aster	22
145	Campanula medium Canterbury Bells	48
146	Chrysanthemum uglinosum Giant Daisy	20
147	Achillea ptarmica "Perry's White" Pure-white Yarrow	56
148	Aconitum acutum Monkshood	50
149	Lilium Parryi Yellow Parry's Lily	20
150	Platycodon grandiflorum Blue BalloonFlower	24
151	Platycodon grandiflorum album White BalloonFlower	24
152	Petunia Rosy Morn Single Light-pink Petunia	
153	Not used	
154	Lupinus, Pink Beauty Annual Pink Lupine	93
155	Aster Novae Angliae New England Aster	14
156	Helenium autumnale Sneezewort	14
157	Helianthus mollis Hairy Sun-flower	10
158	Lilium elegans, Alice Wilson Yellow Thunbergian Lily	36
159	Papaver orientale Mrs. Perry Salmon-rose orientale Poppy	16
160	Not used	
161	Not used	
162	Hypericum Moserianum St. John's Wort	32
163	Polymonium reptans Greek Valerian	32
164	Dicentra spectabilis Bleeding Heart	28
165	Primula polyantha Yellow Primrose	20
166	Papaver nudicaule Iceland Poppy	50
167	Viola cornuta lutea splendens Golden-yellow Tufted Pansy	100
168	Campanula carpatica Blue Carpathian Harebell	20
169	Not used	
170	Mertensia virginica Virginian Cowslip	18
171	Hemerocallis flava Lemon Lily	24
172	Hemerocallis Thunbergii Thunberg's Lily	24
173	Heuchera sanguinea Coral Bells	48
174	Anemone japonica alba Snowy-white Japanese Windflower	64
175	Iris pumila Dwarf Flag	36
176	Azalea arborescens Fragrant White Azalea	8
177	Azalea nudiflora Pink Native Azalea	6
178	Lilium speciosum album White Japanese Lily	23
179	Lilium speciosum rubrum Red Japanese Lily	24
180	Not used	
181	Not used	
182	Azalea Louisa Hunnewell Yellow Azalea	10
183	Delphinium moerheimi Pure-white Larkspur	25
184	Delphinium Mrs. J. S. Brunton Sky-blue Larkspur	13
185	Delphinium grandiflorum album Large White Larkspur	4
186	Not used	
187	Not used	
188	Oneothera youngi Evening Primrose	19
189	Aster Climax Light-blue Aster	6
190	Not used	
191	Helenium autumnale Hoopeau Orange-yellow Sneezewort	15
192	Coreopsis lanceolata grandiflora Large-flowering Tickseed	93
193	Gypsophila paniculata fl.pl. Double-flowering Baby's Breath	32
194	Myosotis palustris semperflorens Ever-flowering Forget-me-not	92
195	Campanula calycanthema Cup-and-Saucer Canterbury Bells	18
196	Verbena - pink Pink Verbena	24
197	Iberis gibraltica Gibralta Candytuft	70
198	Doronicum caucasicum Caucasian Leopard's Bane	26
199	Anthemis tinctoria Golden Chamomile	34
200	Anthemis tinctoria alba White Chamomile	15
201	Moore's Early Grape Early Black Grape	2
202	Niagara Grape White Grape	2
203	Worden Grape Large Black Grape	2
204	Campanula carpatica alba White carpathian Harebell	10
205	Viola gracilis yellow Dwarf yellow Tufted Pansy	40
206	Scabiosa caucasica Blue Bonnet	139
207	Scabiosa caucasicum alba White Blue Bonnet	24
208	Helenium Riverton Gem Lemon-yellow Sneezewort	10
209	Helianthus mollis cordatus Cordate-leaved Sunflower	10
210	Clematis montana rubens Rosy-red Clematis	2
211	Digitalis ambigua Yellow Foxglove	10
212	Arctostaphylos uva ursi Bearberry	45
213	Cotoneaster adpressa Cotoneaster	10
214	Cotoneaster perpusilla Cotoneaster	10
215	Planted in Stone Wall	
	Arabis alpina Alpine Rock Cress	15
	Alyssum saxatile compactum Golden Tuft	25
	Alyssum rostratum Beaked Madwort	10
	Campanula carpatica Carpathian Hare Bell	10
	Cerastium tomentosum Mouse ear Chickweed	10
	Dianthus deltoides Maiden Pink	5
	Draba aizoides Whitlow Grass	20
	Heuchera sanguinea Coral Bell	10
	Helianthemum vulgaris Rock Rose	5
	Lythospermum prostratum Gentian blue Gromwell	15
	Nepeta mussini Cat Mint	15
	Oenothera missouriensis Missouri Primrose	15
	Phlox subulata - white White Moss Pink	10
	Phlox subulata - lavender Lavender Moss Pink	10
	Portulaca - yellow Purslane	
	Potentilla tridenta Three-toothed Cinquefoil	30
	Saponaria ocymoides Soapwort	5
	Sedum acre Wall Pepper	35
	Stellaria Holstea Easter Bell	15
	Silene maritima Double Seaside Catchfly	20
	Veronica rupestris Rock Speedwell	20
	Viola cornuta-white White Horned Violet	10
	Viola cornuta-purple Purple Horned Violet	10
	Viola cornuta-yellow Yellow Horned Violet	10

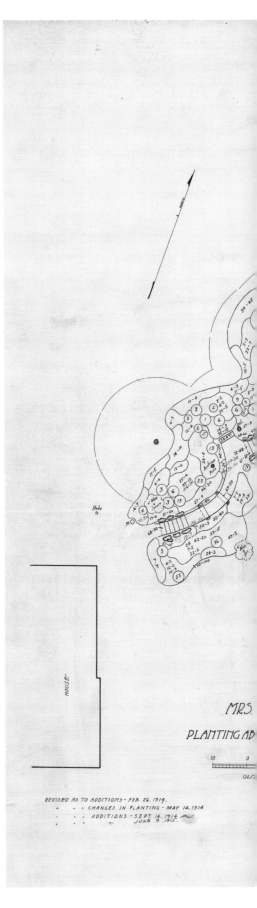

MRS.

PLANTING AB

10   0

OLF

REVISED AS TO ADDITIONS - FEB. 26, 1914.
" " " CHANGES IN PLANTING - MAY 14, 1914
" " " ADDITIONS - SEPT 14, 1914
JUNE 9, 1915.

PLANTING LIST

Note: First figures in beds indicate plants or mixture of plants to be used in each space. Second figures indicate number of plants or mixture of plants estimated as required to fill each space.

1. Picea alba, 3 plants, 7' apart
   White Spruce
2. Juniperus virginiana, 31 plants, 5' apart
   Red Cedar
3. Pinus montana, 18 plants, 3½' apart
   Swiss Mountain Pine
4. Pinus mugho, 23 plants, 2½' apart
   Dwarf Mountain Pine
5. Pinus austriaca, 1 plant
   Austrian Pine
6. Pinus cembra, 6 plants, 4' apart
   Swiss Stone Pine
7. Juniperus virginiana glauca, 4 plants, 5' apart
   Blue Cedar
8. Pinus divaricata, 8 plants, 3' apart
   Jack Pine
9. Pinus sylvestris, 7 plants, 5' apart
   Scotch Pine
10. 4 beds, 26 plants, 2' apart
    Juniperus sabina prostrata, 16 plants
    Prostrate Juniper
    Juniperus communis, 10 plants
    Common Juniper
11. Myrica carolinensis, 17 plants, 1½' apart
    Bayberry
12. Juniperus Kosteri, 3 plants 3' apart
    Koster's Cedar
13. Retinospora filifera, 4 plants
    Thread-like Japanese Cypress
14. Ilex crenata, 4 plants, 3½' apart
    Japanese Holly
15. Crataegus pyracantha, 2 plants
    Evergreen Thorn
16. Juniperus communis, 27 plants, 2' apart
    Common Juniper
17. Juniperus tamariscifolia, 29 plants, 2' apart
    Tamarisk-leaved Juniper
18. Juniperus sabina, 7 plants, 2' apart
    Savin Juniper
19. Carpinus caroliniana, 3 plants
    Hornbean
20. Amelanchier canadensis, 2 plants
    Shad Bush
21. Betula alba, 3 plants
    White Birch
22. Betula papyrifera, 7 plants
    Paper Birch
23. Crataegus cordata, 1 plant
    Washington Thorn
24. Juniperus tr. partita, 3 plants
    Juniper
25. 1 bed 4 plants, 5' apart
    Betula alba, 2 plants
    White Birch
    Juniperus virginiana, 2 plants
    Red Cedar
26. 2 beds, 20 plants, 2½' apart
    Aronia nigra, 10 plants
    Black Chokeberry
    Symphoricarpos vulgaris, 10 plants
    Indian Currant
27. 2 beds, 20 plants, 2' apart
    Andromeda japonica, 15 plants
    Jap. Lily-of-the-Valley Shrub
    Andromeda floribunda, 15 plants
    Lily-of-the-Valley Shrub
28. 1 bed, 7 plants 3' apart
    Amelanchier rotundifolia, 3 plants
    Round-leaved Juneberry
    Rhus copallina, 4 plants
    Dwarf Sumac
29. 3 beds, 38 plants, 1½' apart
    Myrica carolinensis, 18 plants
    Bayberry
    Rosa lucida, 20 plants
    Dwarf Wild Rose
30. Crataegus crus-galli, 1 plant
    Cockspur Thorn
31. Not used
32. Vinca minor, 220 plants, 3' apart
    Periwinkle
33. 5 beds, 116 plants, 1½' apart
    Ilex glabra, 30 plants
    Ink Berry
    Rosa carolina, 30 plants
    Carolina Rose
    Myrica carolinensis, 36 plants
    Bay Berry

34. 1 bed, 45 plants, 2½' apart
    Pinus mugho, 7 plants
    Dwarf Mountain Pine
    Juniperus sabina, 8 plants
    Savin Juniper
    Xanthorrhiza apiifolia, 30 plants
    Yellow-root
35. Arctostaphylos uva-ursi 220 plants, 3' apart
    Bearberry
36. Pyrus parkmanni, 1 plant
    Parkmann's Flowering Crab
37. Tamarix africana, 8 plants, 4' apart
    African Tamarisk
38. Prunus maritima, 2 plants
    Beach Plum
39. Prunus tomentosa, 3 plants
    Downy-leaf Plum
40. Lilium batemanni, 30 plants
    Bateman's Lily
41. Dendrium prostratum, 16 plants, 3' apart
    Prostrate Dendrium
42. 2 beds, 250 plants, 2' apart
    Galanthus elwesii, 50 plants
    Elwes' Snowdrop
    Muscari botryoides, Heavenly Blue, 100 plants
    Grape Hyacinth
    Chionodoxa gigantea, 100 plants
    Glory of the Snow
43. 1 bed, 300 plants, 2' apart
    Colchicum autumnale major, 150 plants
    Autumn Crocus
    Colchicum agrippinum, 150 plants
    Autumn Crocus
44. Azalea hinodegiri, 5 plants, 18" apart
    Chinese Azalea
45. Azalea indica alba, 3 plants, 18" apart
    White Indian Azalea
46. 2 beds, 40 plants, 1' apart
    Lilium myriophyllum 20 plants
    Lily
    Lilium speciosum melpomene, 20 plants
    Lily
47. 1 bed, 18 plants, 3' apart
    Aquilegia chrysantha, 6 plants
    Columbine
    Aquilegia nivea grandiflora, 8 plants
    Columbine
    Cimicifuga simplex, 4 plants
    Bugbane
48. Pachysandra terminalis, 340 plants, 4' apart
    Japanese Spurge
49. Retinospora obtusa nana, 4 plants, 3' apart
    Dwarf obtuse-leaved Japanese Cypress
50. Cotoneaster microphylla, 3 plants
    Evergreen Cotoneaster
51. Alyssum saxatile compactum, 35 plants, 6' apart
    Gold Dust
52. Fritillaria meleagris, 30 plants, 6' apart
    Guinea Hen Flower
53. Pyrus arnoldiana, 1 plant
    Arnold's Flowering Crab
54. Pyrus scheideckeri, 1 plant
    Scheidecker's Flowering Crab
55. Nepeta mussini, 15 plants, 3' apart
    Mussin's Catmint
56. Dianthus, Her Majesty, 15 plants, 6' apart
    Garden Pink
57. Aster alpinus, 40 plants, 6' apart
    Blue Alpine Aster
58. Daphne cneorum, 8 plants, 3' apart
    Garland Flower
59. Viola cornuta purpurea, 55 plants, 6' apart
    Tufted Pansy
60. Sedum acre, 55 plants, 4' apart
    Dwarf Stonecrop
61. Armeria maritima splendens, 20 plants, 6' apart
    Sea Thrift
62. Thymus serpyllum, 60 plants, 6' apart
    Thyme
63. Armeria maritima alba, 45 plants, 6' apart
    White Sea Thrift
64. Aubretia leichtlini, 35 plants, 6' apart
    Purple Rock Cress
65. Phlox subulata, lilacina, 15 plants, 6' apart
    Lilac Moss Pink
66. Arabis alpina flore pleno, 40 plants, 6' apart
    Double flowering Rock Cress
67. Dianthus plumarius, 18 plants, 6' apart
    Garden Pink
68. 1 bed, 30 plants, 6' apart
    Sedum acre, 10 plants
    Dwarf Stone Crop
    Adonis vernalis, 5 plants
    Adonis
    Aubretia moerheimi, 5 plants
    Purple Rock Cress
    Cerastium bierbersteini, 10 plants
    Snow in summer
69. Thymus lanuginosus, 20 plants, 6' apart
    Thyme, Woolly-leaved.

70. Thymus citriodorus, 30 plants, 6' apart
    Lemon-scented Thyme
71. 1 bed, 20 plants, 4' apart
    Dianthus deltoides, 10 plants
    Maiden Pink
    Campanula rotundifolia, 5 plants
    English Harebell
    Sedum acre, 5 plants
    Stone Crop
72. 1 bed, 40 plants, 4' apart
    Veronica repens, 10 plants
    Dwarf Speedwell
    Herniaria glabra, 10 plants
    Herniaria
    Saponaria ocymoides, 4 plants
    Soapwort
73. 1 bed, 14 plants, 6' apart
    Phlox subulata rosea, 10 plants
    Rose Moss Pink
    Alyssum saxitile compactum, 4 plants
    Gold dust
74. 1 bed, 20 plants, 6' apart
    Gypsophila repens, 5 plants
    Dwarf Baby's Breath
    Sedum album, 5 plants
    White Stone crop
    Tunica saxifraga, 10 plants
    Coat Flower
75. 1 bed, 30 plants, 4' apart
    Campanula carpatica, 10 plants
    Carpathian Harebell
    Pachystima conbeyi, 10 plants
    Pachystima
    Thymus serpyllum coccineus, 10 plants
    Scarlet Thyme
76. Lilium speciosum album, 10 plants
    Lily
77. Arenaria montana, 10 plants, 6' apart
    Sandwort
78. Picea nana compacta, 5 plants,
    Dwarf Spruce
79. Azalea amoena, 'Firefly', 5 plants, 3½' apart
    Brick-red Azalea
80. Azalea amoena, low type, 5 plants, 3' apart
    Evergreen Azalea
81. Lilium auratum, 20 plants
    Gold-banded Japanese Lily
82. Lilium superbum, 20 plants,
    Turk's Head Lily
83. Lilium krameri, 20 plants
    Pink Japanese Lily
84. Viola, White Perfection, 20 plants, 6' apart
    Tufted Pansy
85. Thymus serpyllum, coccinea, 8 plants
    Scarlet Thyme
86. Phlox subulata, alba, 30 plants, 6' apart
    White Phlox
87. Aquilegia coerulea alba, 30 plants, 6' apart
    White Columbine
88. Myosotis palustris sempervirens, 20 plants, 6' apart
    Forget-me-not
89. Thymus vulgaris, 20 plants, 6' apart
    Common Thyme
90. Veronica, Royal Blue, 50 plants, 6' apart
    Speedwell
91. Dianthus neglectus, 50 plants, 6' apart
    Glacier Pink
92. Sanvitalia procumbens fl. pl., 5 pkts. seed
    Sanvitalia
93. Trillium grandiflorum, 200 plants,
    Wood Lily
94. Colchicum autumnale album, 50 plants
    White Meadow Saffron
95. Colchicum cilicicus, 50 plants
    Pink Meadow Saffron
96. Crocus setivus, 200 plants
    Light blue autumn-flowering Crocus
97. Crocus speciosus, 400 plants
    Blue autumn-flowering Crocus
98. Crocus zonatus, 200 plants
    Lilac autumn-flowering Crocus

ADDITIONS FOR 1915

99. Primula veris superba, 20 plants, 3' apart
    Primrose
100. Campanula rotundifolia, 20 plants, 6' apart
     Harebell
101. Erysimum pulchellum, 20 plants, 6' apart
     Wall Flower
102. Thymus serpyllum album, 20 plants, 6' apart
     English Thyme
103. Mitella diphylla, 30 plants, 3' apart
     Bishops' Cap
104. Viola canina, 30 plants, 4' apart
     Dog Violet

DRAWN BY HHB   APPROVED FOR ISSUE
TRACED BY AES   BY *Percival Gallagher*
CHECKED BY SAHB.

NICHOLAS BROWN
NEWPORT, R.I.
STEPS AT CORNER OF TERRACE
SCALE 10'=1'

20   30   40   50

...ERS, LANDSCAPE ARCHITECTS
...MASS. JAN. 22, 1914.
FILE 1220
PLAN 15

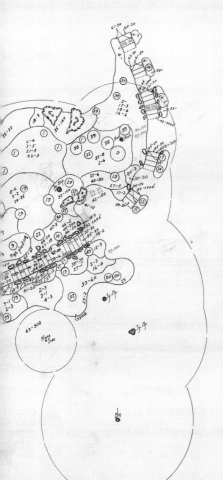

Fig. 190 (opposite, top)
Edward Van Altena, Pond, Harbour Court,
ca. 1920, photograph
Archives of American Gardens

Fig. 191 (opposite, bottom)
H. D. Perkins, Plantings near the terrace,
Harbour Court, 1914, photograph
United States Department of the Interior,
National Park Service, Frederick Law
Olmsted National Historic Site

Fig. 192 (above)
Olmsted Brothers, *Planting about Steps at
Corner of Terrace*, Harbour Court, 1914
United States Department of the Interior,
National Park Service, Frederick Law
Olmsted National Historic Site

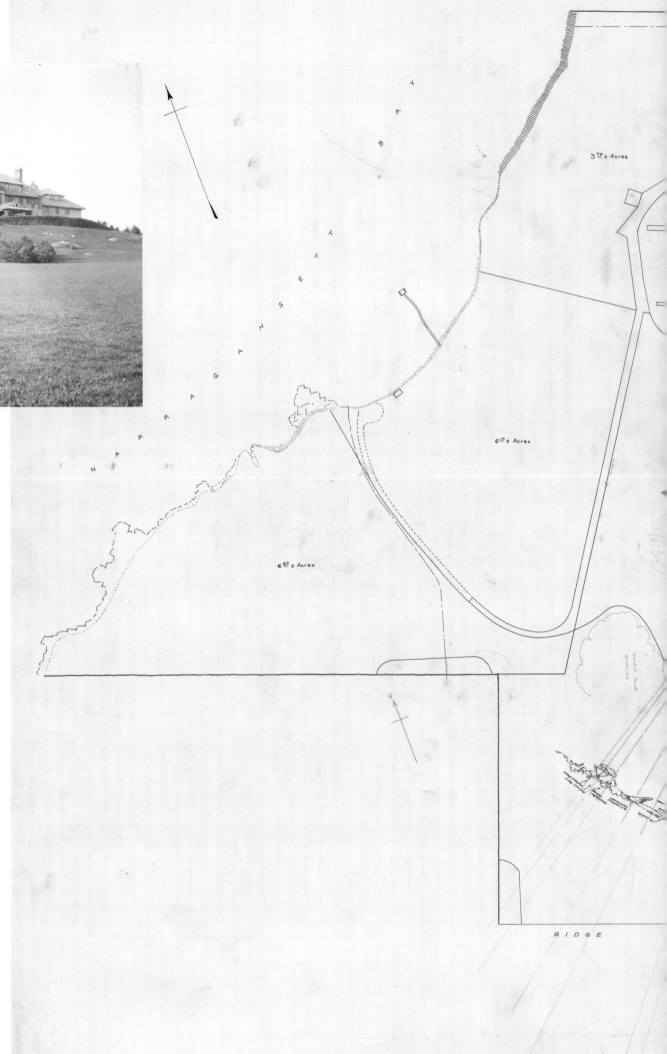

Fig. 193 (above)
View of the house,
Hammersmith Farm, 1916,
photograph
United States Department of
the Interior, National Park
Service, Frederick Law Olmsted
National Historic Site

Fig. 194 (right)
Olmsted Brothers, *Planting
Study*, Hammersmith Farm,
1909
United States Department of
the Interior, National Park
Service, Frederick Law Olmsted
National Historic Site
The plan unites the pastureland
of the working farm with the
picturesque assembly of trees
and the formal axis of garden
spaces, from the fern walk
leading from the house to the
flower and Italian gardens.
Views from the house and
grounds, indicated by lines
cutting across the landscape,
attest to the art of framing
scenic vistas.

H.D. AUCHINCLOSS, ESQ.

NEWPORT, R.I.

PLANTING STUDY

SCALE 50'=1"

FILE NO. 3794
PLAN NO. 2

Landscape Architects
Brookline Mass. Oct. 6th 1909
Revised Apr. 2, 1910.

Fig. 195 (right, top)
Edward Van Altena, Fern
walk, Hammersmith Farm,
ca. 1920, photograph
Archives of American
Gardens

Fig. 196 (right)
Edward Van Altena, Rock
garden, Hammersmith
Farm, ca. 1920,
photograph
Archives of American
Gardens

Fig. 197 (left)
Edward Van Altena,
Flower garden,
Hammersmith Farm,
ca. 1920, photograph
Archives of American
Gardens

Fig. 198 (below)
Edward Van Altena,
Italian garden,
Hammersmith Farm,
ca. 1920, photograph
Archives of American
Gardens

Fig. 199 (above)
Edward van Altena, Sunken
Garden, Hammersmith Farm,
ca. 1920, photograph
Archives of American Gardens

Fig. 200 (opposite)
Olmsted Brothers, *Study for
Garden Area*, Hammersmith
Farm, 1945
United States Department of
the Interior, National Park
Service, Frederick Law Olmsted
National Historic Site

If the gardens for the Brown family consisted of detailed planting schemes, the commission for Hammersmith Farm on a hill overlooking the east passage to Narragansett Bay afforded the Olmsted Brothers one of their most extensive projects. The firm engaged in a decades-long design and subsequent redesign of Hammersmith Farm. Mr and Mrs Hugh D. Auchincloss Sr. hired the firm after they bought the property in 1897. Olmsted Brothers developed a master plan composed of picturesque meadows and a sequence of landscape spaces extending from the house, beginning with a fern- and cryptomeria-lined walk leading to a rock garden and culminating in an Italian garden (Figs. 193–200). In one unified scheme, Hammersmith Farm offered picturesque, rustic, and classical landscape experiences in a seamless progression. After a meeting with the clients in 1910, Harold Hill Blossom reported, "Mr. and Mrs. Auchincloss are both very much pleased in the outlook across the lawn and pasture."[155] The overall character of Hammersmith Farm was pastoral, a scene of meadows, sheep pastures, groves of trees, a working farm, and pleasure grounds. Though hidden by walls of trees in order to preserve the rural atmosphere, the Italian Garden had strategically placed clearings to allow spectacular views of Narragansett Bay. Harold Blossom, however, recommended more plantings for the estate to shield the meadows from the street. He reported, "Together with Mr. Dow [the gardener] and Mr. Auchincloss, I went to local nurseries and sleuthed at Thomas Galvin's eight evergreens and at Wilson's twenty-one."[156] The gentlemen also acquired English yew, Siberian and North American arborvitae, and four red cedars; Hill commented, "Mr. Auchincloss agrees to take cheerfully the risk on the four cedars."[157] Mrs. Auchincloss was an active member of the Newport Garden Club, her gardens being the centerpiece of her interests in design and horticulture. In the early 1920s, she commissioned the noted photographer and colorist Edward Van Altena to produce hand-painted glass lantern slides of Newport's estates. Hammersmith functioned as both farm and floral extravaganza through the 1930s. Hugh D. Auchincloss Jr. inherited the estate in the 1940s and was confronted with the issues of maintaining such a large property in an age when labor was difficult to both find and fund. He asked the Olmsted Brothers to reduce flowers and increase farmland.

Although Mrs. Auchincloss and I would probably wish to restore the rose garden and also a cutting garden for flowers our main purpose will be to rearrange the place and plant trees and shrubs which will leave an attractive effort and which will require the minimum of labor and expense to maintain.[158]

The Olmsteds' redesign maintained the original character of the estate while making it more manageable for the mid-twentieth century. It retained a juxtaposition of intimately enclosed spaces with openings offering distant vistas, while streamlining the plant materials in the gardens. Flowers were valued by the Auchinclosses, who commissioned Boris Timchenko

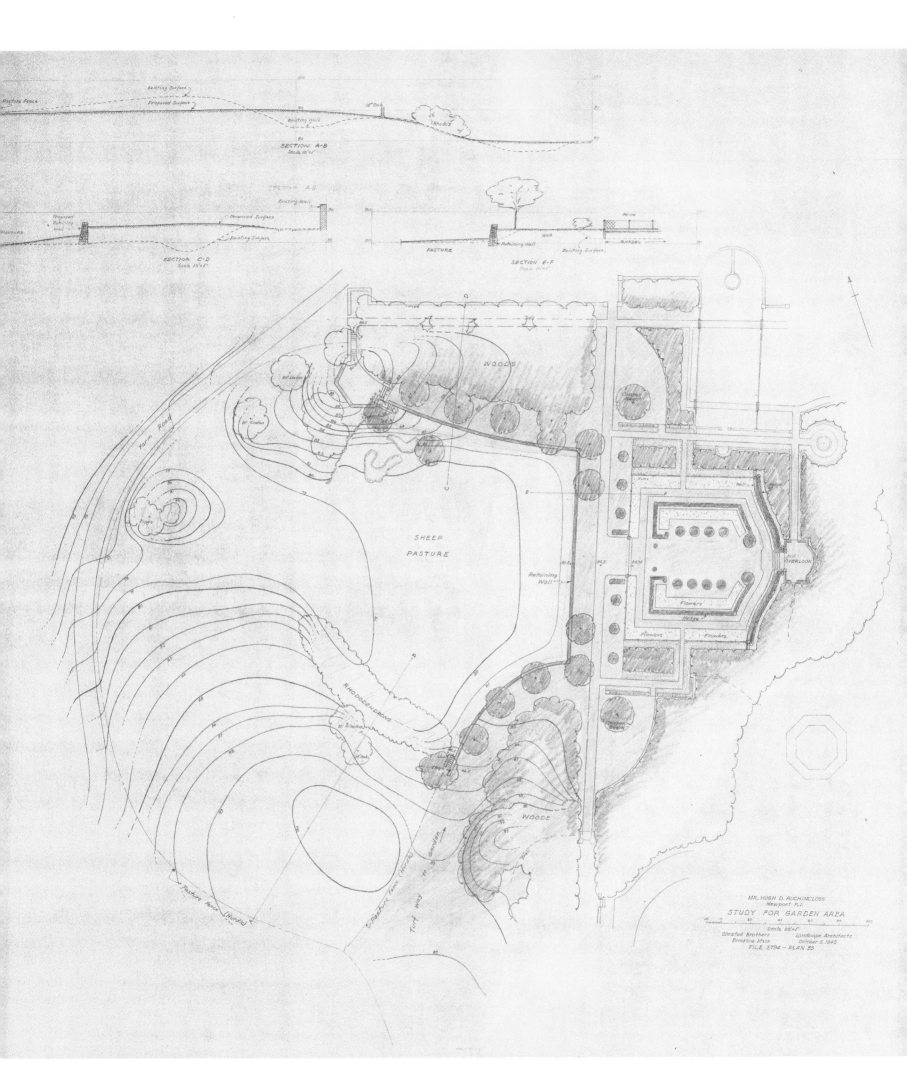

SECTION A-B
Scale 15"=1'

SECTION C-D
Scale 15"=1'

SECTION E-F
Scale 15"=1'

WOODS

SHEEP
PASTURE

Farm Road

RHODODENDRONS

WOODS

Retaining
Wall

Flowers

Flowers   Flowers

Hedge

OVERLOOK

Pasture Fence (Hurdle)

Feature Fence (Hurdle)

Tuft way

MR. HUGH D. AUCHINCLOSS
Newport R.I.
STUDY FOR GARDEN AREA
Scale 20'=1'
Olmsted Brothers   Landscape Architects
Brookline Mass   October 5, 1945
FILE 3794 – PLAN 33

Fig. 201 (above)
Robert Yarnall Richie,
Bonniecrest, 1932–34,
photograph
Robert Yarnall Richie
Photograph Collection,
Negative Series 0091, DeGolyer
Library, Southern Methodist
University

Fig. 202 (opposite)
Olmsted Brothers, *Outline Map
of Newport*, 1913
United States Department of
the Interior, National Park
Service, Frederick Law Olmsted
National Historic Site

to install a sunken garden (ca. 1955) adjacent to the house. Brilliant red geraniums and electric yellow chrysanthemums set in stone borders served as a frame for roses in a traditional plan, in keeping with the main house, yet with a modernist approach in the use of simple bands of flowers in solid, bold colors.[159]

The Olmsted Brothers' use of evergreens at Hammersmith Farm to provide privacy and protection from high winds was also evident in the landscape they created for Mr. and Mrs. Stuart Duncan at Bonniecrest (1914), a Jacobean-style house designed by John Russell Pope. Set atop the rocky outcroppings at the very edge of Newport harbor, the house serenely commands its site due to the architect's mastery of proportion and scale in the terraces that anchor the building, and the rich plantings selected by the Olmsteds effortlessly integrate structure and topography (Fig. 201). Thirteen varieties of juniper and seven varieties of cypress, including hinoki, boulevard, and gold threadleaf, were selected for the grounds, which contained a total of 140 cultivars of trees and shrubs.[160] The rich composition of these plantings blended with the weathered half-timbering and aged brick of the house and brought the soft natural colors and mellowed architectural textures into harmony.

With over thirty Newport projects to their credit, the Olmsted brothers, and their father, Olmsted Sr., made a major impact on the landscape of Newport through their planning of large-scale estates and intimate gardens, and their siting of houses on complex topographies from stony precipice to ocean-side meadow. Other designers, such as Eugene Baumann, Ernest Bowditch, Rose Standish Nichols, Samuel Parsons Jr., and Jacques Gréber, along with the scores of unnamed and unknown gardeners, created a collection of landscapes ranging from the picturesque to the classical, causing Lucius Davis to comment that the city appeared to be "a park of which these private estates constitute distinct features."[161] Newport's private and privileged Gilded Age gardens, however, did not comprise the sole work of these designers; many of them were also involved in creating public versions of Eden in the form of parks, tree-lined boulevards, and suburban subdivisions. The Olmsted Brothers undertook just such a project for the Newport Improvement Association in 1913, addressing a series of urban issues encompassing the challenges of traffic congestion, the preservation of scenic vistas, the management and propagation of the urban forest composed of street trees, and the need for public access to natural resources via parks and beaches. Frederick Law Olmsted Jr. began his report for the Improvement Association with compelling language:

There is much that is sordid, shabby and ugly in Newport; there is much that seems vulgarly ostentatious, there is also a great deal that is charming . . . when I go over the whole ground, deliberately, critically, impartially, I am surprised and pleased to find in how large measure

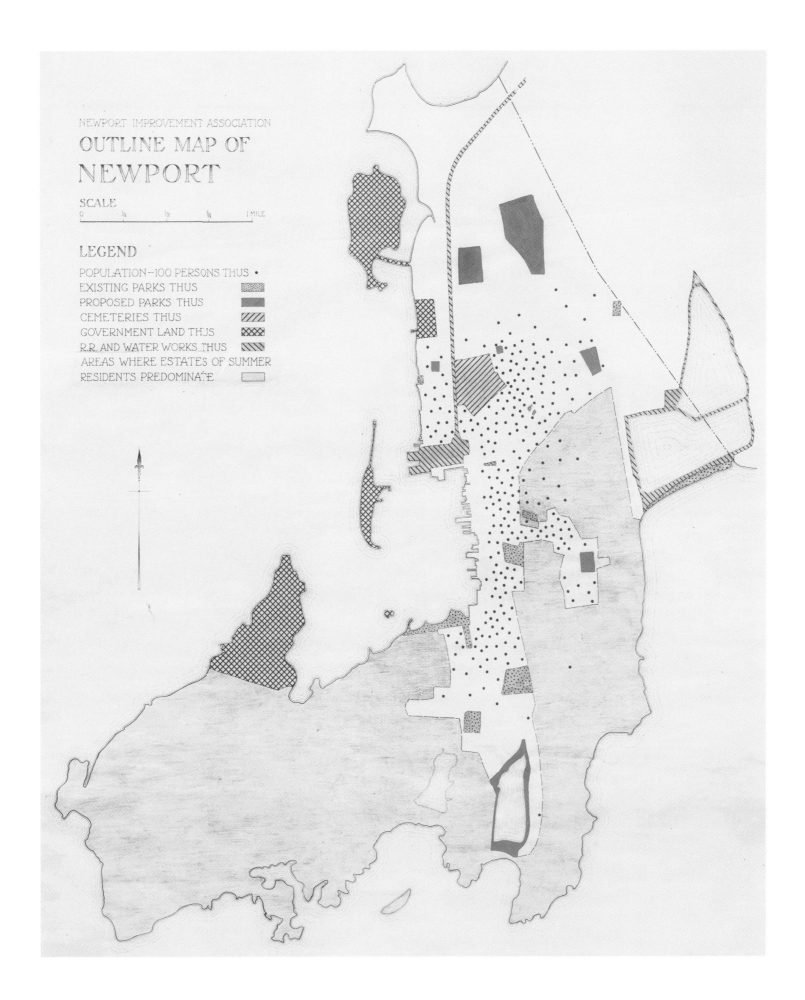

NEWPORT IMPROVEMENT ASSOCIATION

OUTLINE MAP OF
NEWPORT

SCALE

0   ¼   ½   ¾   1 MILE

LEGEND

POPULATION—100 PERSONS THUS   •
EXISTING PARKS THUS
PROPOSED PARKS THUS
CEMETERIES THUS
GOVERNMENT LAND THUS
R.R. AND WATER WORKS THUS
AREAS WHERE ESTATES OF SUMMER
RESIDENTS PREDOMINATE

Newport retains the picturesque charm which, with its climate and harbor, won for it that distinction as an agreeable place.[162]

The report assessed the character of the streetscapes of the city, the role of the urban forest in defining the quality of specific districts, and access to open space. The Olmsteds were extraordinary designers of private estates, public parks, and tree-lined parkways, and their study of Newport drew upon decades of the firm's experience in their own numerous projects and upon the principles established by their father, Frederick Law Olmsted Sr., in Central Park, New York; Prospect Park, Brooklyn; and the integrated park and road system in Boston known as the "Emerald Necklace."[163] They looked at Newport as an entire living organism and, while pragmatic in terms of proposals for traffic congestion, they considered aesthetics in their recommendations for street widenings and in emphasizing the significance of preserving nature and scenery in a city. It was not only the spectacular views of cliffs and ocean that they extolled but the intimacy of the small street, as Frederick Law Olmsted Jr. wrote:

It is this scenery which most continuously and immediately affects the lives of the residents and most strongly impresses the visitor . . . I venture to believe that it was the inherent human

By E.C.W.   June 14, 1913   1824-129

HALIDAN AVENUE.

By E.C.W.   June 14, 1913   1824-130

ON MILL STREET NEAR SPRING LOOKING NORTHWEST.

By E.C.W.   June 14, 1913   1824-131

POND AVENUE.

By E.C.W.   June 14, 1913   1824-132

POND AVENUE.

By E.C.W.   June 14, 1913   1824-133

POND AVENUE.

Fig. 205
E. C. W., Shepard Avenue, 1913,
photograph
United States Department of
the Interior, National Park
Service, Frederick Law Olmsted
National Historic Site

*quality of the old town of Newport itself, and the charming
and picturesque expression which this quality had wrought for
itself through the centuries in the form of streets and houses and
gardens, and of the trees which embowered them all—that it
was this kind of scenery far more than the larger scenery of the
shore and the hills. . . . which led people to seek Newport as a
place of residence.*[164]

The Olmsteds' photographic portfolio recorded ancient trees
on streets and in side yards, and views from one side garden to the
next, illustrating how these modest spaces contributed to the urban
forest, providing shade in a densely built district (Figs. 202–8). This
was the gentle scale they viewed as essential to a nurturing cityscape
and humane urban planning. The maps and photographs compiled
by the Olmsteds form a significant repository of images of the
historic tree canopy, providing a rare connection to the past. By the
early 1900s, Newport's first generation of urban trees had reached
their peak growth. In 1913, the Olmsted Brothers were essentially
documenting the mature nineteenth-century landscape of the city
at a critical point when several generations of trees were nearing the
end of their lifespan. Defining the character of distinct districts, in
terms of the scale of their buildings, thoroughfares, and greenery,
guided Frederick Law Olmsted Jr.'s objectives in preserving and
enhancing neighborhoods by systematic tree planting. He found
many areas with a "lamentable absence of the trees" and proposed
a city-wide solution: "If the Improvement Association were to offer
the necessary trees and vines, together with skilled advice and assistance in setting them out,
there can be no question that enough of the residents, along the streets that are now bare, would
avail themselves."[165]

Olmsted's plans, which were democratic in word and spirit, outlined the needs of every
part of the city, with the main objective of ensuring that Newport capitalized on all of its assets,
both natural and constructed, and that the greatest number of people benefited from urban
improvements. In his assessment of parks, Olmsted observed, "it appears that Newport already
has a reasonably satisfactory area and distribution of parks in the central and southern sections,
but it is almost totally lacking in parkland north of Washington Square."[166] Drawn to the bucolic
quality of Miantonomi Hill, Olmsted advocated for this setting to become a public park for the
northern end of Newport. The photographs taken of the area are not merely documentary, they
are romantic and softly lit; one image depicts a lone figure embedded in nature (Fig. 209), which
inspired a proposal.

Fig. 206 (above)
E. C. W., Clark Street
near Mary Street, 1913,
photograph
United States Department
of the Interior, National
Park Service, Frederick Law
Olmsted National Historic
Site

Fig. 207 (left)
Pelham Street, 1913,
photograph
United States Department
of the Interior, National
Park Service, Frederick Law
Olmsted National Historic
Site

overleaf:

Fig. 208 (left)
E. C. W., Side gardens, 1913,
photograph
United States Department
of the Interior, National
Park Service, Frederick Law
Olmsted National Historic
Site

Fig. 209 (right)
H. D. Perkins, Miantonomi
Hill, 1913, photograph
United States Department
of the Interior, National
Park Service, Frederick Law
Olmsted National Historic
Site

By E.C.W.   June 14, 1913   1824-118

SIDE YARD ON PROSPECT HILL STREET.

By E.C.W.   June 14, 1913   1824-119

SIDE YARD ON PROSPECT HILL STREET.

By E.C.W.   June 14, 1913   1824-120

SIDE YARD PROSPECT HILL STREET

By E.C.W.   June 14, 1913   1824-121

SIDE YARD PROSPECT HILL STREET.

By E.C.W.   June 14, 1913   1824-122

SIDE YARD PROSPECT HILL STREET.

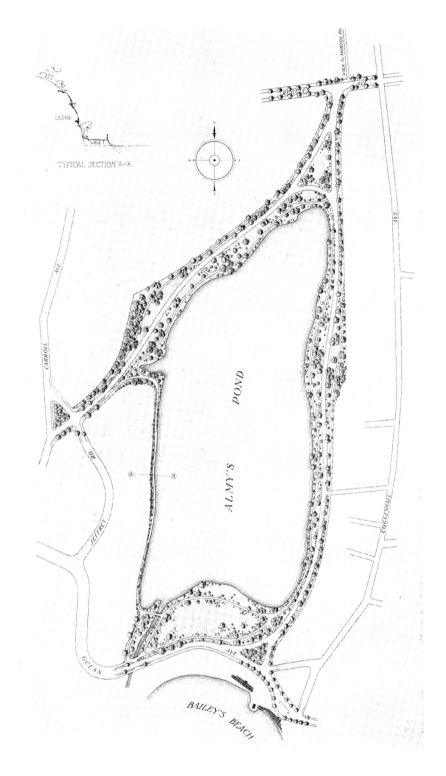

Fig. 210
Olmsted Brothers, Proposal for Almy's Pond, 1913
United States Department of the Interior, National Park Service, Frederick Law Olmsted National Historic Site

It is a beautiful wooded hill easily accessed from every part of the city, affording woodland and meadow scenery. . . . Furthermore, on this hilltop was once a fort which lends added interest and value . . . For it may be accepted as a good general park policy to preserve as far as possible for the use and enjoyment of the people such landscape features as are of unusual geological and historical interest.[167]

The Olmsted Brothers made recommendations for other parks in Newport, such as a plan for winding, tree-lined paths around the wetlands of Almy's Pond on the southern coast (Fig. 210). They envisioned a tree-lined boulevard in their scheme for widening Bath Road and a revised planting plan for Easton's Beach at its terminus in an effort to create a unified traffic plan with public access to open spaces (Fig. 211). Not all of their proposals were immediately acted upon, but their philosophy of preserving historic character, conserving natural resources, creating humane green spaces on residential streets, widening and greening main traffic arteries, and coherently developing public parks influenced future developments in Newport. Miantonomi Memorial Park was created in 1923 with a stone tower by McKim, Mead and White as a focal point. Bath Road was widened in the 1920s and again in the 1940s, receiving its double rows of trees and the new name of Memorial Boulevard in honor of the men and women who served in World War II (Fig. 212). Born of a commitment to picturesque scenery on the part of Andrew Jackson Downing, their father, Frederick Law Olmsted Sr., and their own interests in nature and its benefits in the human environment, the Olmsted Brothers set Newport on a course for the remainder of the twentieth and twenty-first centuries and beyond, focusing attention on the need to create a harmony between the natural and the constructed in the urban environment. The Olmsteds' work encapsulates the many sides of the Gilded Age. On Newport's estates, they crafted private versions of Eden within public view, either seen tantalizingly from the street or published by a curious press. In public, on Newport's streets, they managed the urban tree canopy and preserved scenery as an Eden for all.

Fig. 211 (above)
Olmsted Brothers, Bath
Road widening, 1913
United States Department
of the Interior, National
Park Service, Frederick
Law Olmsted National
Historic Site

Fig. 212 (left)
Auguste Miller, Plan for
Bath Road World War II
memorial and tree
planting, 1945
United States Department
of the Interior, National
Park Service, Frederick
Law Olmsted National
Historic Site

CASE STUDY

BLOOMING BEAUTY
Floral Culture and Fashion during the Gilded Age

Rebecca Kelly

Fashion Historian

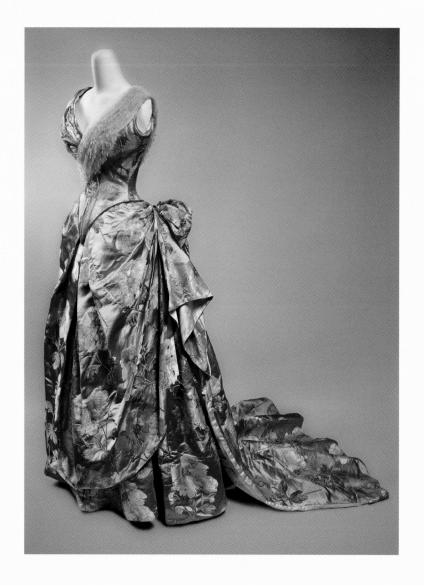

She had her own little triumph of an evening for everybody asked who that beautiful girl was and more than one gallant of the old Newport families felt himself adorned and distinguished to walk with her on his arm . . . We now have the image of Mary as she stood in her little hat and wreath of rose-buds, her fluttering ribbons and rich brocade, as it were a picture framed in the doorway with her back to the illuminated garden.

—Harriet Beecher Stowe, *The Minister's Wooing*, 1859

Wearing, carrying, and exchanging flowers are age-old customs. Some of the earliest fashion impulses in humans were certainly satisfied by using elements of nature, such as flowers, as adornments. When evaluating the long and connected histories of horticulture and fashion, the Victorian and Gilded Ages stand out for their extravagance and creativity (Fig. 213). Newport's cottages were decorated inside and out with flowers; their residents likewise were not to be forgotten in the realm of floral décor. Seaside summer living encouraged relaxed resort fashions, and this peak season for flowers ensured their role in the social whirl's sartorial splendor. The desire for corsages, boutonnières, nosegays, wreaths, crowns, and garlands added to the endless summer tasks for estate gardeners and florists. The expense of hot house blooms may have relegated them to a rare luxury in winter, but spring and summer months brought a profusion of floral wonders within the easy grasp of many.

Wearing blooms for their aesthetic or scented pleasure is expected, yet another compelling use of flowers during the Gilded Age was communication. Scholars of floriography, the language of flowers, speculate that the connotations of some flowers stretch far back to antiquity. Ancient meanings endured in religious ceremonies, medicinal practices, and folk traditions. The language of flowers known today was codified in the early nineteenth century. Several French publications were the first to assign specific meanings to an exhaustive list of blooms, from anemones to zinnias and everything in between. English-language manuals were quick to follow.

Corsages, Posies, Wreaths, and Dress Trimmings

Small bouquets, called nosegays, posies, or tussie mussies, became missives. Groupings intentionally compounded flowers' individual meanings. It is amusing to speculate about the veiled or bold messages communicated through the seemingly innocent and ephemeral blossoms of a Newport summer.

In an 1880 portrait painted by Raimundo de Madrazo y Garreta, Alice Gwynne Vanderbilt wears a corsage of red and pink roses tucked into the bodice of her gown (Fig. 214). Pink roses suggest grace and beauty, while cherry-red roses indicated merriment, and sweetness of character derived from good works. This portrait hangs today at Mrs. Vanderbilt's summer house, The Breakers, and gives visitors a sense of her style and character.

Today, carrying flowers or wearing a corsage is reserved for an occasion. In Newport's gilded past, flowers were an integrated part of everyday dress and living (Fig. 215). Nosegays were gifted among friends, given as favors at balls, and sent to debutantes by prospective suitors. Imagine a heart aflutter to receive a bouquet of roses combined with additional elements to solidify a message of love and romance. However, a posy with French marigolds or lavender may have been a warning, indicating feelings of distrust, envy, or jealousy.

Posies, like so many aspects of Gilded Age life, were intended to be conspicuous. Queen Victoria is said to have popularized fine silver and bejeweled holders for small bouquets. Some holders doubled as stands to display flowers in reception rooms. Holders and pins allowed young women to wear and carry flowers more easily. The popular press contributed to the growing interest in flower meanings as ladies' magazines discussed and illustrated floral etiquette.

Fig. 213 (opposite)
House of Worth, Evening gown of apricot satin brocade with yellow and gold-tone peony pattern, worn by Ella Rives King of Kingscote, Newport, ca. 1890, photograph
The Preservation Society of Newport County

Fig. 214 (below)
Raimundo de Madrazo y Garreta, Mrs. Cornelius Vanderbilt, oil on canvas, 1880
The Preservation Society of Newport County

Fig. 215
Gustave Janet, Toilette de course, Fashion Plate 85 from *La Mode Artistique*, ca. 1876, lithograph
The University of Rhode Island, Historic Textile and Costume Collection, 2001.09.01 (II)

Fancy Dress and Flowers

In addition to everyday dress, floral themes for balls, and particularly those in fancy-dress, were very popular (Fig. 216). Fancy-dress balls required all invitees to come in elaborate costumes. These occasions generated specific excitement; etiquette books abounded to assist in an inspired costume choice. Occasionally, a fancy-dress ball may have had an explicit theme, but guests were free to choose more often than not. Hence, Henry VIII, Hamlet, Marie Antoinette, a personification of summer, a lady gardener, and a pair of Spanish dancers perhaps all whirled on the same dance floor.

The manual *Fancy Dresses Described* by Ardern Holt was published in numerous editions during the Gilded Age and proposed costume ideas ranging from history and literature to

La Mode Artistique

par Gustave Janet.

TOILETTE DE BAL

Fig. 216
Gustave Janet, Toilette de bal,
Fashion Plate 53 from *La Mode
Artistique*, ca. 1876, lithograph
The University of Rhode Island,
Historic Textile and Costume
Collection, 2001.09.01 (y)
Flowers were often used in hair
ornaments and dress garlands
as well as hand-carried tussie
mussies at balls.

mythology and folk dress. The sixth edition, published in 1896, described more than 1,200 costumes. Taking on a flower's guise was recommended as an easy and charming costume. Illustrations instruct specifically on becoming "a rose garden" or a "bunch of sweetpeas" (Fig. 217). The fashion press indicates Newport residents followed Holt's prescriptions closely. Newspaper and other accounts well document costume balls where ladies appeared as roses and gardenias. At one such party, hosted by Mrs. Hermann Oelrichs of Newport and New York, featured in *Vogue*, Miss Elsie De Wolfe, famed actress and interior designer, was dressed "in a French costume of light blue taffeta trimmed with garlands of flowers. A wreath of roses in her powdered hair . . . and Mrs. Edward Thomas, as a gardenia, wore a white gown trimmed lavishly with natural gardenias."[1]

Fig. 20.—LADY GARDENER.

Fig. 40.—SUMMER.

Fig. 34.—ROSE GARDEN.

Fig. 42.—BUNCH OF SWEET PEAS.

Fig. 217
Miss Lillian Young, a
Lady Gardener, Summer,
a Rose Garden, and a
Bunch of Sweet peas,
from Ardern Holt, *Fancy
Dresses Described* (1896),
lithographs
Private Collection

Boutonnières

Gentlemen were in no way excluded from wearing floral fancies. The nineteenth century brought a radical shift in men's fashions. Once hallmarks of stylish men, floral-patterned silk coats and profusions of lace trimmings were relocated to women's wardrobes. A plain yet well-tailored cloth frock coat was the new signifier of a well-dressed man. The lapels of these coats were a blank canvas ready and awaiting decoration. The abundance of summer flowers in Newport perhaps tempted many to pluck a blossom and thread it through a buttonhole to enliven bland fashions with a bit of ephemeral gaiety.

Flowers worn on a jacket lapel are often called *boutonnières*, or simply buttonholes. Men's fashion historian Nick Foulkes writes that, "towards the end of the nineteenth century, the boutonnière was widely accepted as the mark of a man who was careful in his dress. A man would select a fresh boutonnière in much the same way he would wear a freshly laundered shirt or a pair of polished shoes."[2]

One Newport resident, Alfred Gwynne Vanderbilt, was known to consistently wear a boutonnière (Fig. 218). *Vogue* magazine reported on the dashing sportsman and his participation in a coaching club event:

Fig. 218
Tennis at Newport—Alfred Vanderbilt at the wheel of his machine, 1913, photograph
Library of Congress

> *The drive was made from New York to Newport, and Sunday was to be passed at the Vanderbilt farm, which is some miles from Newport itself. The stages were comparatively easy, and the first night's stop was made in New London. . . . Mr. Vanderbilt and his guard had boutonnières of carnations in the Vanderbilt colors. . . . the weather was excellent, good time was made, and the trip was generally most enjoyable.*[3]

Numerous portraits document Vanderbilt's propensity for the boutonnière. He was in good company, as many images have captured Newport's fashionable gentlemen wearing flowers on their lapels while enjoying an afternoon of driving or watching tennis.

Famed French essayist and arbiter of style Barbey d'Aurevilly, who proclaimed himself "Knight of the order of springtime," declared, "I sacrifice a rose each evening to my buttonhole"[4] It seems that the Newport set was eager to establish their own order, one that honored the summertime, showcasing the horticultural bounty of the city by the sea in endlessly clever ways.

Notes

1 "Society in Fancy Dress," *Vogue*, February 1, 1911, 18.

2 Umberto Angeloni, ed., *The Boutonniere: Style in One's Lapel* (New York: Universe Publishing, 2000), 28.

3 "As Seen by Him," *Vogue*, October 30, 1909, 704.

4 J. Barbey d'Aurevilly, *Deuxième Memorandum (1838) et quelque pages de 1864* (Paris: Ancienne Library Tresse & Stock, 1906), 91, author's translation.

The Working Landscape
GARDENERS AND GREENHOUSES

All the gardeners were gentlemen. They all dressed up. One tried to out-dress the other. And it was something else. And they were all friendly.

—John Burrows, interview, 2000

Gardeners, nursery owners, and florists flourished in Victorian and Gilded Age Newport. They were part of an emerging industry and an evolving creative community, an interconnected society based on the practice of horticulture as a business, a science, and an art. As the farms and meadowlands of the colonial landscape became the summer estates, urban gardens, and public parks of the nineteenth and early twentieth centuries, gardeners and suppliers of plant materials were in constant demand. Whether the supervisor of a formal French parterre at a private palace on the cliffs or a nursery owner planting trees on a narrow street in the heart of the city, all who participated in these projects were part of a burgeoning American interest in gardening. Their story is one of labor, invention, adaptation, and collegiality.

Taste and technology were interdependent forces affecting the work of Newport gardeners and those in related horticultural professions. Industrial advancements in the construction of greenhouses (generally referred to at the time as glass houses), and the use of Wardian cases for transporting plants, allowed for the propagation of imported flowers, trees, and shrubs from across the globe (Figs. 219 and 220). Taste was driven by technological advancement. With an abundance of cultivars at their disposal, the landscape gardeners of mid-nineteenth century Newport carpeted flower beds with the brilliant colors of begonias, chrysanthemums, and geraniums and filled conservatories with exotics such as ferns, palms, and orchids. By the 1880s, a new aesthetic arose along with the profession of landscape architecture, which focused more on design than on specific flowers and shrubs. The Victorian taste for color was to be tempered: plants were to be more subtle, the landscape more natural. In this period, the gardener was often not as involved in the initial planning phase; rather, they worked with the new breed of professional, the landscape architect, assisting with installation and nurturing the plan to maturity. Frederick Law Olmsted wrote to Mariana Griswold Van Rensselaer to share his concern that once he left a project others might add trivial plantings and destroy his entire

Fig. 219
Greenhouse, Belair, ca. 1870, photograph
Newport Historical Society, P8959

Fig. 220
Robert Yarnall Richie, Three grand estates
and their greenhouses, cutting and
vegetable gardens, ca. 1935, photograph
Robert Yarnall Richie Photograph
Collection, Negative Series: 0606,
DeGolyer Library, Southern Methodist
University
Great Victorian and Gilded Age
estates required extensive gardens
for flowers and vegetables, and large
greenhouses and palm houses to aid in
the propagation of imported and exotic
species, all a major presence in the
Newport landscape. Seen here are the
main house of Wakehurst (center) and
its cutting and vegetable gardens (lower
left); Ochre Court (upper left) and its
cutting and vegetable gardens, and three
greenhouses (lower right); and Vinland
(top/center) and its hennery/gardener's
house, and cutting and vegetable gardens
(below the main house of Ochre Court).

scheme.[168] While property owners and landscape designers were prime decision makers, head gardeners were also forces to be reckoned with. Harold Hill Blossom of the Olmsted Brothers firm reported Mrs. John Nicholas Brown's need for a new head gardener at Harbour Court: "she does not want a man who would take the whole scheme of direction out of her hands entirely."[169] In practice, Newport landscapes were the product of the overall plan of the landscape architect, the taste of the owners, the horticultural skills of gardeners, and the specimens provided by nurseries—a combination of artful visions and everyday maintenance.

Nurseries and Florists

The rare trees and brilliantly hued flowers that adorned the genteel villas of the mid-1800s were provided by a growing list of nurseries. Many summer residents retained their own estate gardeners and built magnificent greenhouses and palm houses, such as those at Belair, By-the-Sea, and Elm Court (Figs. 221–25), but this expensive proposition did not suit all cottage owners. The nursery industry, which fostered and promoted in great measure the use of diverse plants, both native and imported, had grown exponentially during the period 1850 to 1880, and Newport reflected this trend. In 1858, there were four listed florists and nurseries in the city; in 1880, the directory listed seventeen florists, four landscape gardeners, and one firm self-described as "practical gardeners."[170]

Fig. 221
Greenhouse and garden, Elm Court, ca. 1905, photograph Courtesy of Rodney Merrill

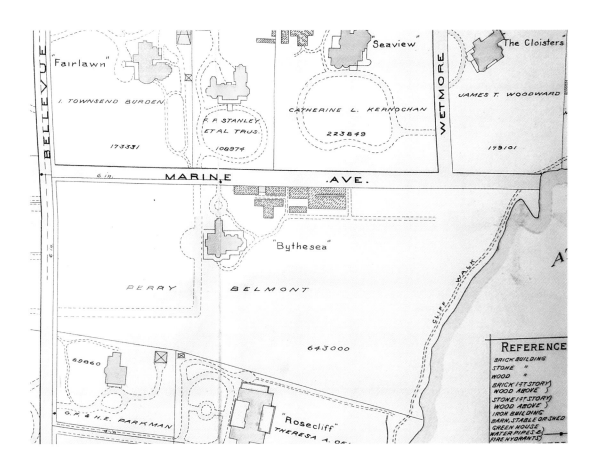

Fig. 222 (left)
Belmont greenhouses, in yellow
with black lines (detail), from
L. J. Richards and Co., *Atlas of
the City of Newport* (1907)
Newport Historical Society
Photograph courtesy of
the Preservation Society of
Newport County

Fig. 223 (below)
Greenhouse and bowling alley,
Belair, ca. 1880, photograph
Newport Historical Society,
P8948

Fig. 224 (right)
Greenhouses and lily pond,
Fairholme, ca. 1900,
photograph
Newport Historical Society,
P5734

Fig. 225 (below)
Gardens, Goat Island,
ca. 1890, photograph
Newport Historical Society,
P9573

Fig. 226
Galvin Nurseries, ca. 1855,
photograph
Newport Historical Society,
2010.2

Thomas Galvin established his firm in the 1850s, growing to eight greenhouses by 1867, when his advertisements featured "A Fine Collection of New and Rare Plants, Trees and Shrubs" (Fig. 226).[171] Competition thrived in Newport with the continued construction of summer cottages following the Civil War. In 1892, J. Hodgson appears in the *Newport Directory* as somewhat of an interloper on the Newport scene, self-described as "The Fifth Avenue Floral Establishment . . . with nursery greenhouses and Branch Store on the corner of Bellevue and LeRoy Avenues, Newport."[172] Hodgson's floral displays took the city by storm, being featured at the most opulent balls of the period, notably at The Elms.[173] He also maintained a shop on Bellevue Avenue in the midst of the summer colony to serve as a destination for his fashionable clientele (Figs. 227 and 228).

By 1901, Thomas Galvin and Sons, not to be left behind by the glamour of Hodgson's, advertised themselves as "Landscape Gardeners and Florists," offering "to citizens of Newport, a large variety of Forest Trees and Shrubs, Choice Flowers and Hot House fruits. Having had an experience of many years in their profession, they feel confident to satisfy all who may favor them in orders. Particular attention paid to laying out gardens, etc."[174] Their account books list deliveries for trees, shrubs, plants, and flowers. They also note laurel trees, palms, rubber plants, ferns, and hydrangeas in large tubs rented out for the summer season, and fees for annual

Fig. 227 (above)
Hodgson's Botanical Garden,
Bellevue Avenue, ca. 1900,
illustration
Newport Historical Society,
91.34

Fig. 228 (right)
Flower shop at Hodgson's
Botanical Garden, Bellevue
Avenue, ca. 1900, photograph
Newport Historical Society,
2015.002

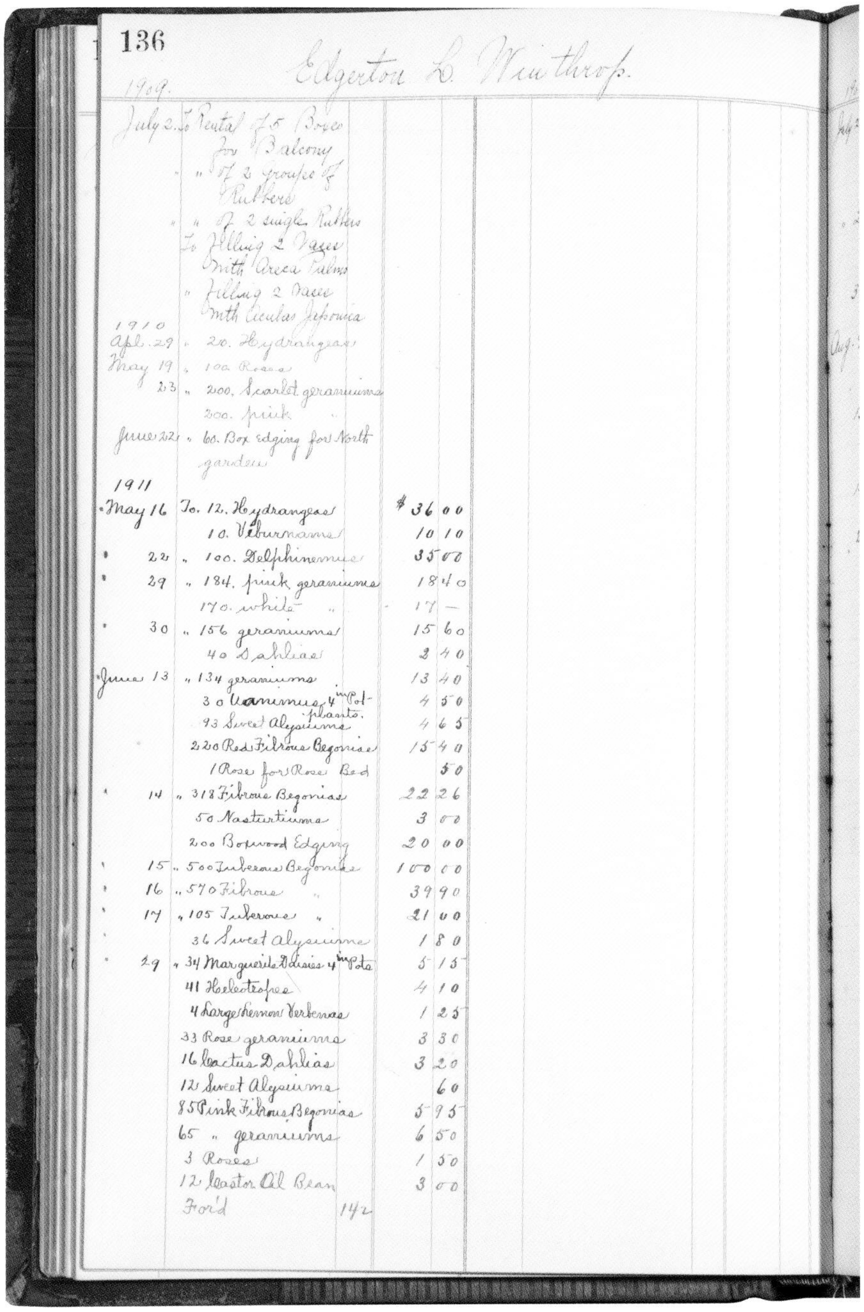

Fig. 229
Plant lists, Galvin Nurseries
Ledger, 1909–16
Redwood Library and
Athenaeum

installations of red and pink geraniums, begonias, and dahlias. For example, between 1911 and 1914, they supplied to Egerton Winthrop's Bellevue Avenue cottage a selection of potted palms, hydrangeas in tubs, hanging baskets of fuchsia, scarlet and pink geraniums, delphiniums, dahlias, red begonias, heliotropes, roses, lemon verbena, viburnum, sweet alyssum, and boxwood edging (Fig. 229).[175] Winthrop was a connoisseur of art and friend to Edith Wharton, who lived nearby at Land's End. His discerning judgement of color and scale in his gardens certainly was shared with Wharton in their discussion of art and design. Similar horticultural specimens, particularly hanging baskets of flowers, were delivered by Galvin's to Mrs. William Watts Sherman, who did not maintain greenhouses on her property.[176] Bright red and pink bedding flowers, brilliant blue hydrangeas, and green ferns and palms appeared to anchor every house. Such were the

Fig. 230
Lawn roller, Newport Casino,
ca. 1900, photograph
Newport Historical Society,
P8018

essential tones and textures of Newport's Gilded Age gardens, as recorded by one of the city's most successful nurseries. So great was demand to maintain the grounds of summer houses and supply plants for grand parties that new businesses entered the scene (Fig. 230). The firm of T. J. Brown, established in 1901, is a study in the evolution of the horticultural profession in Newport as gardeners and estate owners navigated the social and economic changes of the first half of the twentieth century.[177] The firm began with basic hauling of coal ash and the delivery of manure to what appeared to be the entire list of the Social Register (Fig. 231). According to the firm's day books, between April and June they were fully scheduled for deliveries of manure, loam, seed, and potting soil as gardeners prepared lawns and propagated flowers during the spring.[178] Throughout the summer, they hauled ash and supplied gardeners with occasional day labor when required. By the 1920s, T. J. Brown expanded into wholescale garden plantings and maintenance as many estates reduced their labor forces. The firm supplied roses and dahlias for the gardens of Dr. Alexander Hamilton Rice at Miramar (Fig. 232) and worked for decades with Mrs. Harold Brown, her estate gardeners, and the Olmsted Brothers on the installation of and subsequent additions to her gardens.[179]

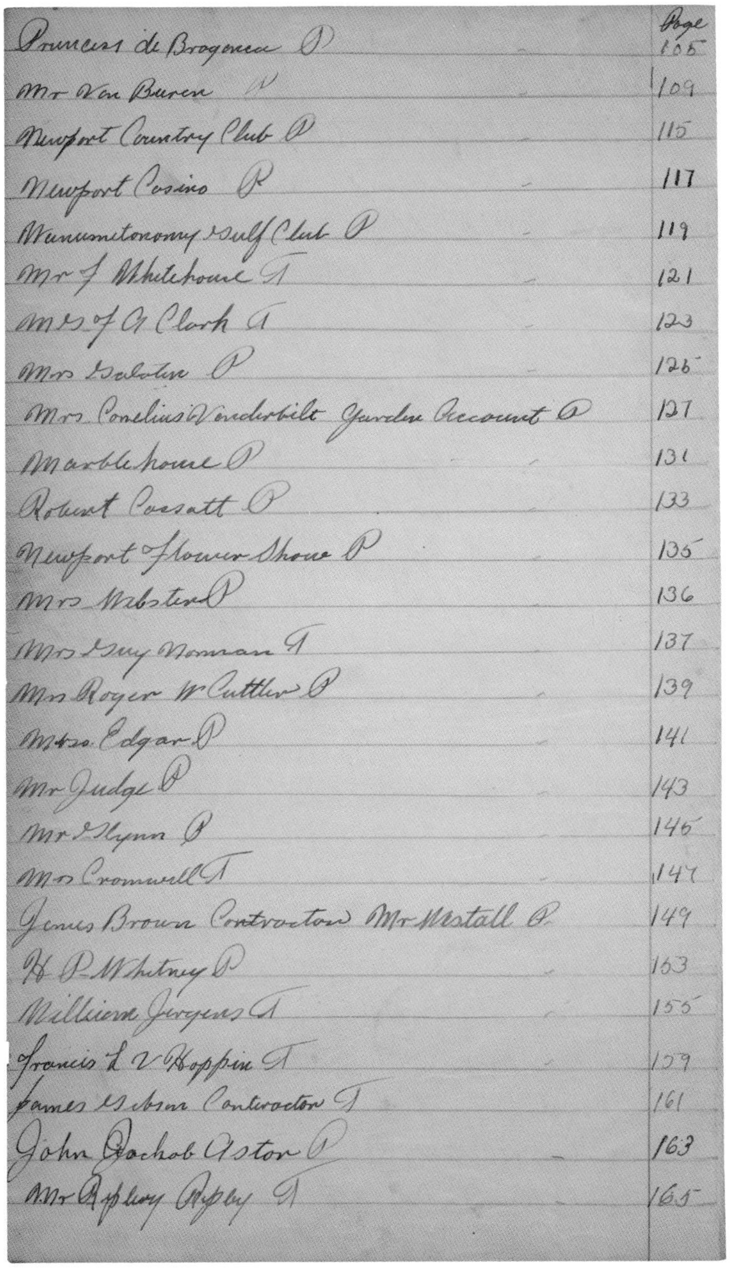

	Page
Princess de Brogonza P	105
Mr Van Buren P	109
Newport Country Club P	115
Newport Casino P	117
Wanumetonomy Golf Club P	119
Mr J Whitehouse T	121
Mrs J A Clark T	123
Mrs Galatin P	125
Mrs Conelius Vanderbilt Garden Account P	127
Marble house P	131
Robert Cassatt P	133
Newport Flower Show P	135
Mrs Webster P	136
Mrs Guy Norman T	137
Mrs Roger W Cutler P	139
Miss Edgar P	141
Mr Judge P	143
Mr Glynn P	145
Mrs Cromwell T	147
James Brown Contractor Mr Mestall P	149
H P Whitney P	153
William Jurgens T	155
Francis L V Hoppin T	159
James Gibson Contractor T	161
John Jacob Astor P	163
Mr Ripley Ripley T	165

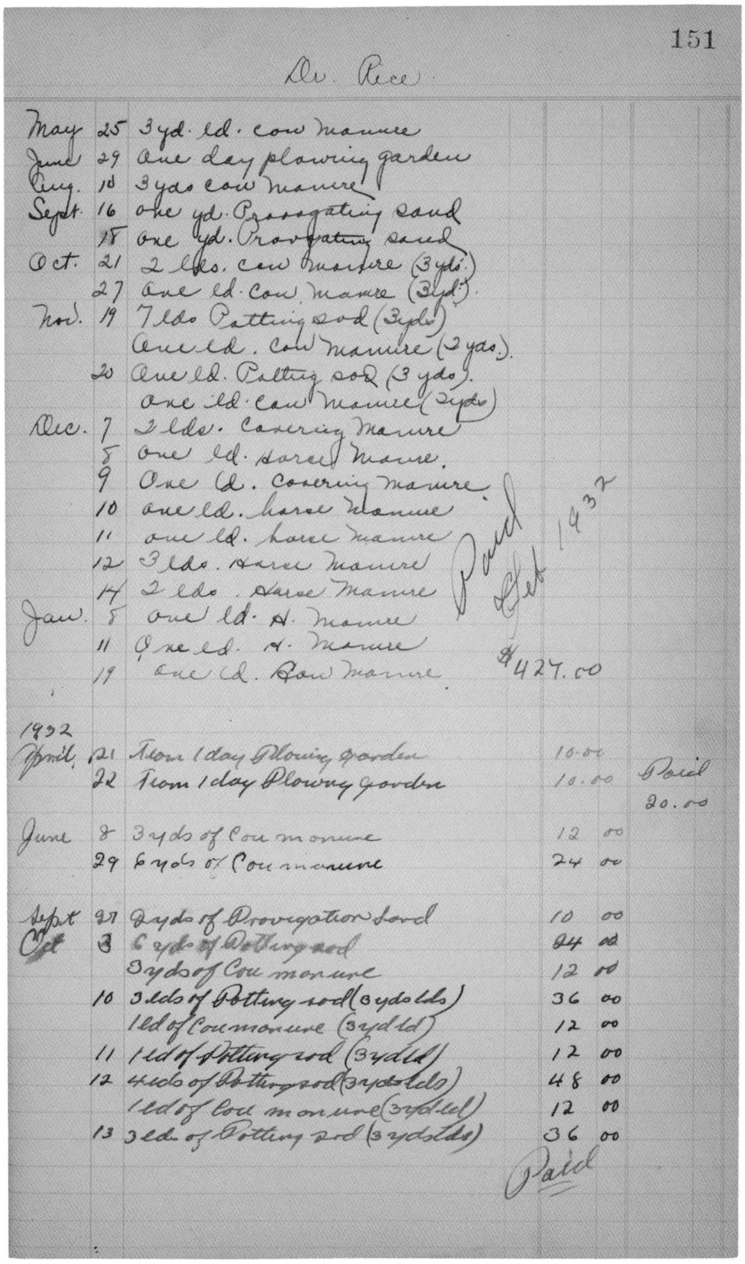

151

Dr. Rice

May	25	3 yd. ld. cow manure		
June	29	One day plowing garden		
Aug.	10	3 yds cow manure		
Sept.	16	one yd. Propagating sand		
	18	one yd. Propagating sand		
Oct.	21	2 lds. cow manure (3 yds)		
	27	One ld. cow manure (3 yd)		
Nov.	19	7 lds Potting sod (3 yds)		
		One ld. cow manure (2 yds)		
	20	One ld. Potting sod (3 yds)		
		one ld. cow manure (3 yds)		
Dec.	7	2 lds. Covering manure		
	8	One ld. horse manure		
	9	One ld. Covering manure		
	10	one ld. horse manure		
	11	one ld. horse manure		
	12	3 lds. horse manure		
	14	2 lds. horse manure		
Jan.	8	one ld. H. manure		
	11	One ld. H. manure		
	19	one ld. cow manure	$427.00	Paid Feb 1932
1932				
April	21	Team 1 day Plowing garden	10.00	
	22	Team 1 day Plowing garden	10.00	Paid 20.00
June	8	3 yds of Cow manure	12 00	
	29	6 yds of Cow manure	24 00	
Sept	27	2 yds of Propagation sand	10 00	
Oct	3	~~6 yds of Potting sod~~	~~24 00~~	
		3 yds of Cow manure	12 00	
	10	3 lds of Potting sod (3 yds lds)	36 00	
		1 ld of Cow manure (3 yd ld)	12 00	
	11	1 ld of Potting sod (3 yd ld)	12 00	
	12	4 lds of Potting sod (3 yds lds)	48 00	
		1 ld of Cow manure (3 yd ld)	12 00	
	13	3 ld of Potting sod (3 yds lds)	36 00	
			Paid	

Estate Gardeners

Newport's estates were overseen by head gardeners, who functioned as the superintendents for buildings and grounds and lived year round in the city. They employed from five to fifteen assistants and were charged with maintaining lawns, growing flowers for the house and gardens, and, if the grounds were designed by a landscape gardener or architect, remaining faithful to the general plan of the site as its trees and shrubs matured (Fig. 233). The head gardener had to adapt and master the growing of grass, plants, and trees in varying topographies and microclimates, whether atop a rocky summit, nestled in a cove exposed to the sea, or in a protected valley. In a resort devoted to pleasure, a place to see and be seen, where visual presentation of house and gardens was paramount, the gardener served as the key creator and caretaker. Each season, the press took note of preparations for another social whirl and its demands for polished perfection.

Fig. 231 (above left)
T. J. Brown client list,
T. J. Brown Day Book, 1927
Courtesy of T. J. Brown

Fig. 232 (above right)
Plant list for Dr. Rice at
Miramar, T. J. Brown Day Book,
1927
Courtesy of T. J. Brown

Her new robe of vivid green, artfully brocaded with flowers of every hue, is without a speck or crease to mar its aristocratic elegance. . . . Every villa has been furbished until it looks as though just erected. . . . The grass is everywhere a precisely shaven lawn, and the roads and pathways seem too nice to step upon. The grand old trees and spreading bushes, clustering in such profusion in every lot, are clad in a luxuriance of foliage that suggests a hothouse training. The apparently studied picturesqueness of the cliffs also gives a notion of the landscape gardener's skills, and the bordering sea has a fresh and limpid appearance, as though it too had passed through the hands of the renovator.[180]

The Newport head gardener did not exist in isolation. In the period between the Civil War and World War II, over five hundred gardeners were at work in the city at any given time.[181] They formed a close-knit community, both collegial and competitive in a resort built for show. Richard Gardner, Robert Burrows, and John "Jack" Yule are three individuals representing the breadth, talent, and specializations required in the ever-changing role of estate gardener for over a century, from the 1880s to the 1980s.

Fig. 233 (opposite)
Frances Benjamin Johnston,
Gardener, Beacon Hill, 1917,
photograph
Library of Congress

Fig. 234
Richard Gardner, ca. 1890,
photograph
Newport Historical Society,
P575

Richard Gardner: Gardener Extraordinaire and Leader in the Field

Richard Gardner played a central role among Newport's gardeners, guiding the training of many apprentices who went on to flourish in the field and fostering the art and craft of his profession as a founder of the Newport Horticultural Society (Fig. 234). He served as head gardener at The Breakers from 1882 until 1895, witnessing a period of active redesign of the estate. Pierre Lorillard hired Gardner, who continued in the service of Cornelius Vanderbilt when he purchased the property in 1885. Mr. Vanderbilt ordered greenhouses from Lord and Burnham of New York, purveyors of the most state-of-the art structures of the era, with Gardner coordinating the installation with the landscape designer Ernest Bowditch.[182] Gardner directed the daily maintenance of the grounds according to the plans developed by Bowditch and propagated flowers in the

Fig. 235
Fairlawn staff, ca. 1890,
photograph
Courtesy of Harry Eudenbach
John T. Allan, head gardener, is
on the far left.

greenhouses for the elaborate beds lining the serpentine path and dotting the lawns. In 1895, he left The Breakers to work for Newport Nurseries, specializing in roses. He continued to be a major presence in Newport garden circles. A postscript to Gardner's tenure at The Breakers is the story of his staff members, all of whom worked within the system he established for the estate, each head gardener serving as an assistant before their promotion, learning about the methods for cutting and rolling lawns, edging paths, and propagating flowers and plants. His apprentices also achieved positions as head gardeners at other Newport estates.[183] John T. Allan began as an assistant gardener under Gardner, who also hired Alexander MacLellan to work at the greenhouses in 1883 after a seed store sent his resume to The Breakers (Fig. 235).[184] Often, employment was found through seed stores and traveling plant salesman, who learned of available positions. After one year of apprenticeship with Gardner, MacLellan took over as head gardener at Stoneacre, the new house being built for John W. Ellis one block away, working to implement the new landscape design by Frederick Law Olmsted.[185] The apprentice system formed the essential mode of training for a new gardener. These positions included oversight not only of the grounds but of the entire property. Gardeners were called upon to have technical and managerial skills in addition to their horticultural talents. One gardener recalled, "You couldn't apply for one of those chief gardener's jobs if you didn't have twenty-five years experience . . . a head gardener had a white shirt with gold cuff links and he carried a cane."[186]

Robert Laurie, previously a planting foreman under Ernest Bowditch, became head gardener at The Breakers upon Gardner's departure.[187] Laurie then worked with Ernest and James Bowditch on the redesign of the grounds to accommodate the building of a new house by architect Richard Morris Hunt from 1893 to 1895. He maintained the parterres according to Bowditch's plan: alyssum, ageratum, and Tom Thumb edged in Irish ivy on the southwest parterre, with trumpet vine and clematis on the adjoining pergola; wichuriana roses on the northwest parterre. Laurie was also tasked with yet more greenhouse installations when the old structures were moved to Coggeshall Avenue. These projects, due to their grand scale and the fame of the Vanderbilt name, were subjects of national interest, as reported in the *New York Times*.

> *Cornelius Vanderbilt's new greenhouses are attracting great attention from cottages and professional florists. The houses . . . are stocked with rare specimens, and among the many beautiful greenhouses connected with Newport's magnificent summer residences, easily take the lead . . . there is a potting house . . . There are also six houses of equal size, including a Palm House stocked with a great variety of rare exotics. In one of the houses there is what is known as the Australian glory pea, a curious flower, which is very rare in this country . . . in another part of the house is an abundance of begonias. Another house is filled with Gloxinias . . . while another house in its entirety is given up to the cultivation of maiden-hair fern, of which Mrs. Vanderbilt is very fond. Another house is filled with fuchsias . . . later on, when the Vanderbilts return to New York, a large boxful will be cut each morning and sent to them to decorate their Fifth Avenue residence.[188]*

Frederick Carter assumed the head gardener role on Laurie's retirement and remained until 1931. He was succeeded by his assistant, William "Billy" Murphy, who oversaw the grounds and greenhouses for fifty-one years, until 1982, in that period serving under Mrs. Vanderbilt, her daughter Countess László Széchenyi, and the Preservation Society of Newport County, which acquired the estate in 1976.[189] Although ownership changed and the task of head gardener was filled by successive generations, a historical continuity remained due to the apprenticeship system. John "Echo" Burrows succeeded Billy Murphy as head gardener for the Preservation Society in 1982 and trained the next generation. Thus, the greenhouses of The Breakers, lauded in the *New York Times* at their opening, remain among the oldest structures of their type still in continuous operation in Newport.

Robert Burrows: The Life of an Estate

Mrs. Harold Brown's continual improvements to her Bellevue Avenue estate provided an endless round of chores for her head gardener, who was in charge of lawn care, greenhouse management, and the flower and vegetable gardens, as well as working with landscape architects and the purveyors of horticultural specimens. The grounds were showcases for changing floral displays, while the greenhouses became a veritable beehive of activity, with flowers and vegetables

Fig. 236
Robert Burrows (left), John
"Echo" Burrows (center), and
an unidentified guest (right),
ca. 1935, photograph
Courtesy of Jane Burrows

delivered daily to the main house. With two flower gardens, a woodland, a bowling green, and a collection of specimen trees, the estate required a multifaceted superintendent, a role filled by Robert Burrows, born in Scotland and trained at Kew Gardens in London.[190] "He had a little potting shed, and a little greenhouse," recounted Burrows's son, John "Echo" Burrows (Fig. 236). "And all the gardeners used to meet there, and they had a good relationship, all of them. They started work at 7am. The head gardener for Mrs. Brown had 4 or 5 helpers."[191]

The care and attention Mrs. Brown lavished on the grounds is apparent in the Bartlett Tree Survey conducted in 1939 in response to damage done by the 1938 hurricane. The estate trees suffered little impact from the storm due to their protected location away from the ocean, but Mrs. Brown ordered the survey for the general health of the site. Mr. Burrows specialized in the care of trees, so he worked closely with Bartlett on the survey. The estate had fine examples of weeping beech planted by the Olmsted Brothers, who were engaged often by Mrs. Brown to return to the estate to amend the gardens. Burrows worked with the Olmsteds and also ordered supplies from the Newport landscape firm of T. J. Brown. Not only did the grounds have to be presented perfectly, but so did the head gardener himself, in a gray suit, tie, and straw hat. "They never wore work clothes," recalled Echo Burrows. "There was a guy who was a bulb man from England. He used to sell bulbs to all these gardeners. And he also, as a side line, sold material for suits. And they had a friend that was a tailor, so he used to make the suits for him. Oh, they were all dressed up guys."[192]

Robert Burrows possessed great ability, but he also owed a great deal to coincidence, specifically because of his name. Mrs. Brown generally hired staff only with last names beginning with the letter B, aligning with her own name, according to Echo Burrows: "Brothrow was the chauffeur; Bailey was the butler. Babbidge was the personal maid . . . Burns was the house man."[193] The life of a Newport estate, and that of its head gardener, as exemplified by Robert Burrows, was based on methodical maintenance and an artful eye, and was subject to the preferences of the estate owner. Mrs. Brown's landscape was a product of high-minded aesthetic theories and horticultural practices, but these august forces were also tempered by individual predilections, the unpredictable daily changes of weather, and the temperamental conditions of soil, drainage, and pests. Head gardeners needed to be many things to many people and work with the overriding power of nature. In doing so, they crafted and maintained their own versions of Eden within the confines of their respective estates.

John "Jack" Yule: Generations of Gardeners

Expertise in horticulture distinguished six generations of Scottish gardeners in the Yule family. John "Jack" Yule's grandfather worked at St. Andrew's Golf Links in Scotland and came to the United States to work as head groundskeeper at the Newport Country Club.[194] His son,

Alexander, became head gardener for Mr. and Mrs. J. Edgar Monroe at Rosecliff in 1947. Raised in a world of gardeners, his son, John "Jack" Yule, began as an assistant gardener at the Cushing estate, The Ledges, where he spent eighteen years before moving on in 1974 to become head gardener for Mr. and Mrs. Russell B. Aitken at Champ Soleil. Jack Yule became an expert at cultivating roses, becoming president of the Rose Society and a fellow of the Royal Horticultural Society (Fig. 237). Among his favorite specimens were Chicago, Chicago Peace, and varieties in ivory, pale yellow, and pink, the hues that predominated in the estate's rose garden and throughout the house.[195] He also developed Annie Laurie and Irene, hybrids in honor of the ladies who made Champ Soleil their home.[196] Beyond the garden walls, he also served as a popular host for a radio program, "The Potting Shed" for WADK Newport, demonstrating how the estate gardener in the late twentieth century could expand his influence even further than his forebears.

Fig. 237
John "Jack" Yule, ca. 1980, photograph
Courtesy of Tommy Downes

A Community of Gardeners: The Newport Horticultural Society

In 1890, Richard Gardner founded the Newport Horticultural Society with his two former assistants, John T. Allan and Alexander MacLellan, and the florist Arend Brandt.[197] The organization quickly became the official gathering point of the city's gardeners, florists, and nursery owners (Fig. 238) and sponsored annual flower shows at the Newport Casino, featuring categories for the display of single specimens, such as roses, sweet peas, dahlias, gladioli, and hot-house fruits (Fig. 239). Estate owners gained in prestige along with their prize-winning head gardeners, and, in 1911, they founded the Newport Garden Club to promote horticultural expertise. Now Newport had organizations for its gardeners and its patrons of gardening, who engaged in both lively collegiality and competition. The gardeners, Echo Burrows recalled, "were always, you, know, one was trying to outdo the other a lot of times. . . . And I can remember hollering at each other, 'mine are better than yours!' . . . There was a lot of camaraderie."[198] At the 1912 show, Robert Livingston Beekman of Land's End won for a specimen palm by his gardener John B. Urquhart; first prize for an arrangement of outdoor roses went to Robert Goelet and his gardener Cole Robertson, with second prize to August Belmont and his gardener John Forbes.[199] William Gray, head gardener for Mr. and Mrs. William B. Leeds of Rough Point, reigned as a major champion. He won several awards at Newport Horticultural Society Flower Shows, exhibited sweet peas at the annual gathering of the American Sweet Pea Society in New York at the Museum of Natural History, won prizes from the New York Horticultural Society, and received *Garden Magazine*'s Achievement Award.[200] In 1914, the grounds of Chateau-sur-Mer played host to the Newport Horticultural Society's Flower Show. Much like the trees collected from across the globe by estate owners, the theme of the flower show was "gardens of the world," with exhibits of Dutch, French, and Italian gardens (Fig. 240).

Lay Out for 2nd Open Air Flower Show
Newport Garden Ass'n & Horticultural Society
in
Grounds of Hon. G.P. Wetmore, Bellevue Avenue, Newport, R.I.
June 24-25-26th 1914

H.W. Hankewl, invt: et del. Newport R.I. La 1914.

Fig. 238
(opposite, top)
Newport
Horticultural
Society, 1932,
photograph
Courtesy of T. J.
Brown

Fig. 239
(opposite, bottom)
Newport Flower
Show, Newport
Casino, 1927,
photograph
Newport Historical
Society, P9517

Fig. 240 (right)
Plan for the
Newport Flower
Show, Chateau-sur-
Mer, 1914
The Preservation
Society of Newport
County

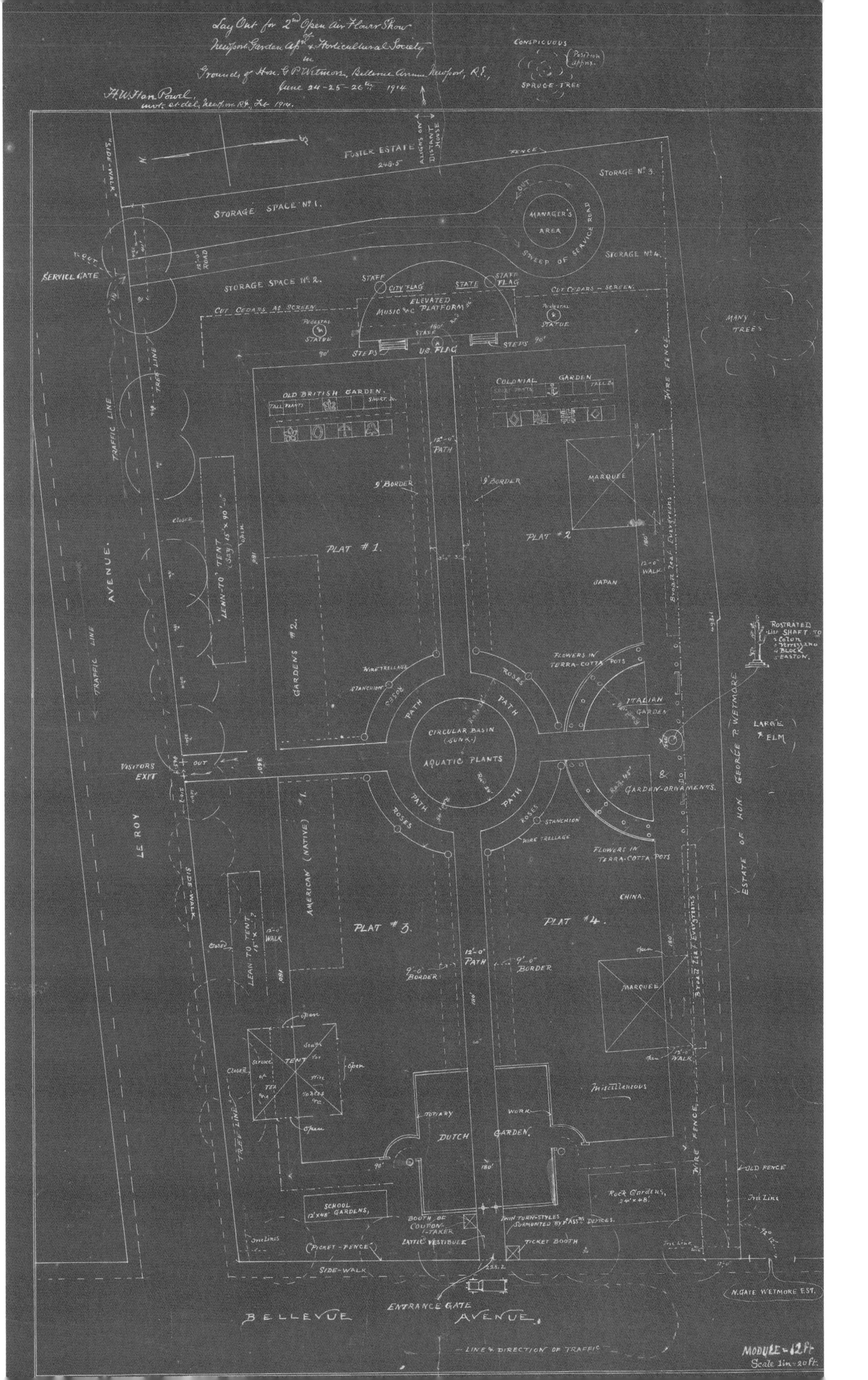

Fig. 241 (opposite, top)
Harold Hill Blossom, Vegetable
garden, Beacon Hill, 1915,
photograph
United States Department of
the Interior, National Park
Service, Frederick Law Olmsted
National Historic Site

Fig. 242 (opposite, bottom)
Frances Benjamin Johnston.
Mowing the lawn in the Blue
Garden, Beacon Hill, 1917,
photograph
Library of Congress

Fig. 243 (left)
Frances Benjamin Johnston,
Gardener, Beacon Hill, 1917,
photograph
Library of Congress

Increasing awareness of the significance of Newport's designed landscapes and horticultural practices, featured in the annual Flower Show, prompted the Newport Garden Club to commission photographs of the city's gardens in the 1920s. Edward Van Altena took glass lantern slides of estate gardens, which were then hand colored.[201] Mr. and Mrs. Arthur Curtiss James followed suit, commissioning the pioneering photographer Frances Benjamin Johnston to document their Beacon Hill gardens and the daily tasks of their estate gardeners (Figs. 241–43). While in Newport, Johnston, who worked in partnership with Mattie Edwards

Hewitt, also photographed The Elms and The Breakers (Fig. 244). She rose to fame with her position as White House photographer for several presidents, including Theodore Roosevelt,

and became noted for her images of society figures, her curated exhibition of photographs by women artists at the Universal Exposition in Paris in 1900, and her images of diverse scenes from tattooed sailors to female mill workers.[202] In the 1930s, Johnston was awarded a Carnegie Corporation grant to photograph the rural architecture of the American South, reflecting her interest in vernacular buildings and their landscape settings. These photographers created an invaluable record of Newport at the height of its horticultural opulence. In color and composition, they preserved the work of generations of estate gardeners, nursery owners, and florists who were the laborers in Newport's Eden (Figs. 245–47).

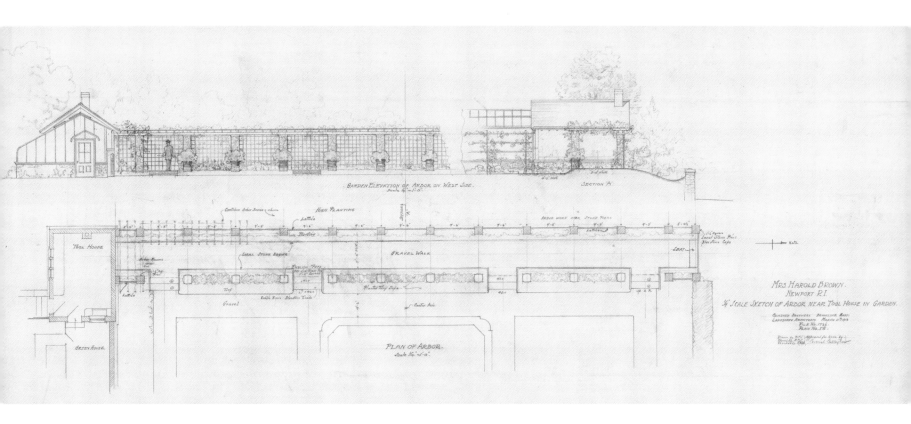

Fig. 244 (opposite, top)
Frances Benjamin Johnston, View towards one of the main gates, The Elms, ca. 1920, photograph
Library of Congress
Architect Horace Trumbauer sunk the service drive below the grade of the lawn to prevent the working aspects of the house from having a visual impact on the grounds.

Fig. 245 (opposite, bottom)
Michael Pignatelli, Superintendent of The Elms, ca. 1950, photograph
Gift of Gloria Pignatelli, The Preservation Society of Newport County

Fig. 246 (above)
Olmsted Brothers, *Sketch of Arbor near Tool Shed in Garden*, Harold Brown Estate, 1913
United States Department of the Interior, National Park Service, Frederick Law Olmsted National Historic Site

Fig. 247 (right)
Olmsted Brothers, *Arrangement of Trained Fruit Trees on Vegetable Garden Wall*, Chateau-sur-Mer, 1916
United States Department of the Interior, National Park Service, Frederick Law Olmsted National Historic Site

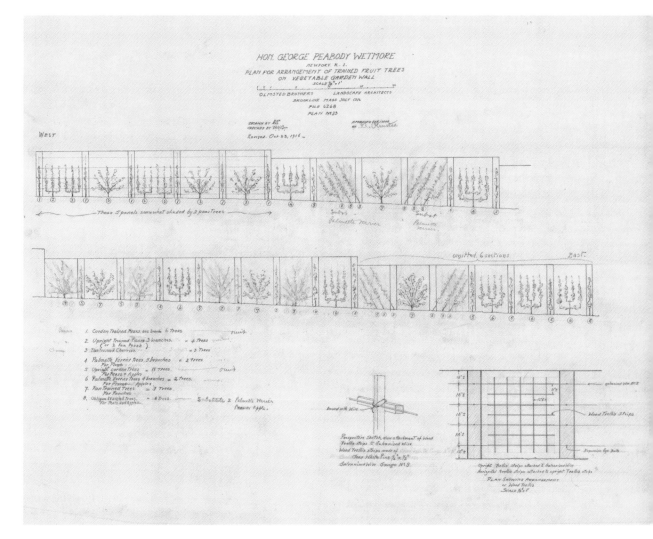

The Age of the New
MODERNISM IN THE LANDSCAPE

The town was Newport, Rhode Island, U.S.A., Earth, Solar System, Milky Way . . . the walls were those of the
Roomford estate . . . well-endowed as Mrs. Roomford was, she still did troubling things . . . like having the gates
of the estate bricked up, like letting the famous formal gardens turn into New England jungle.
—Kurt Vonnegut Jr., *The Sirens of Titan*, 1959

Modernity in its triumphant period during the mid-twentieth century appeared to pass by Newport, a time capsule cloaked in its own historical dress. The rich architectural heritage and scenic beauty remained, but was there a place for the new? Anything is possible. Kurt Vonnegut set the beginning of his 1959 futuristic novel *The Sirens of Titan* in Newport, where the character of Malachi Constant, the richest man in the world, arrives to meet Mr. Roomford.

> *The Roomford mansion was marble, an extended reproduction of the banqueting hall of*
> *Whitehall Palace in London. . . . It was surely one of the greatest essays on density since*
> *the Great Pyramid of Khufu. In a way it was a better essay on permanence than the Great*
> *Pyramid, since the Great Pyramid tapered to nothingness as it approached heaven. Nothing*
> *about the Roomford mansion diminished as it approached heaven.*[203]

The mansion is a symbol of humankind's hubris and the starting point for a complex science fiction story that offers both comedy and drama, as well as a Martian invasion. Before achieving his dream to go into space, however, Constant encounters the Roomford garden, itself a metaphor for history and decay.

> *Rising on both sides of the path was the green jungle the gardens had become . . . Standing*
> *now in the topmost, in the smallest of the baroque fountain's bowls, standing with his feet in*
> *the ruins of birds' nests, Malachi Constant looked out over the estate, and over a large part*
> *of Newport and Narragansett Bay. He held up his watch to sunlight, letting it drink in the*
> *wherewithal that was to solar watches what money was to Earth men.*[204]

Garden, Warren residence, ca. 1950, from Peter Shepheard, *Modern Gardens* (1953), photograph

Vonnegut's fiction captured much of the reality, and the popular perception, of Newport in the late twentieth century. Two world wars, an economic depression, and changing social and cultural norms had left the city a decaying relic of the past. The colonial center of town showed signs of commercial decline, with areas of blight. Many Victorian and Gilded Age houses and gardens, no long viewed as sustainable, were reduced in scale or overgrown, and some had been entirely abandoned. From the 1940s through the 1970s, The Reefs on Brenton Point, Beacon Hill on the heights high above Ocean Avenue, and Chetwode on Bellevue Avenue eventually stood as burned-out ruins in derelict landscapes.

History may have weighed heavily on Newport, but modernity did make its presence felt in the form of an extraordinary garden created for an individual apparently at ease with past, present, and future. In 1949, Katherine Urquhart Warren commissioned the English landscape architect Christopher Tunnard to design a garden for her Federal-era house in the heart of town overlooking Touro Park and the Stone Tower. As a patron of art, a board member of the Museum of Modern Art, and a founder and president of the Preservation Society of Newport County, Katherine Warren collected and commissioned the new and dedicated herself to saving the old. Her garden, a modern landscape with references to the past set against a historic house, reflected both interests.

Christopher Tunnard was an ideal choice to envision and craft the Warren garden since it required the union of art and nature, two topics that were his specialty. His book *Gardens in the Modern Landscape* (1938), which influenced generations of designers, articulated his interest in English and Japanese gardens as art forms and the importance of integrating art in the garden— the foundation of the Warren garden plan.[205] Tunnard believed gardens could be both functional and meditative, serving the body and the soul. In his study for the Sculpture Garden at the Museum of Modern Art in 1939, he focused on works of art set within a composition of clipped trees and plants near the building, and greenery with more naturalistic forms at a distance, encouraging viewers to sit, talk, relax, and ponder together or alone.[206] In the Warren garden plan, Tunnard worked with an intimate space of sixty-five feet by forty-two feet. Jean Arp's bronze sculpture *Chimerical Font* (1947) was a focal point, set in a pool in the corner of the composition (Figs. 248 and 249). Two fountains edged in clipped boxwood, yew, and ivy form one side of the scheme. Pleached lime trees and arborvitae served as tall backdrops against the white-painted cement block wall. This combination of water, greenery, and stone derives from classical landscapes, while the shrubs, precisely clipped in the shape of question marks and semicolons, conjure the mood of Surrealism, their sinuous contours aligning with the Abstract Expressionism of the Arp sculpture. Past and future become one in this small space, serene in its historic references, while embracing the modern. The garden is a master work, a testament to Tunnard's commitment to the integration of architecture, art, and landscape, which inspired his work and writing.

As a counterpoint to the avant-garde forms embedded in the soil of the Warren garden, Champ Soleil (1927), an eighteenth-century-French-inspired house on Bellevue Avenue, presents a landscape with traditional classical features by Umberto Innocenti and Richard Webel.[207] The Tuscan-born Innocenti, expert in plant selection, worked with intuition honed by practical experience in all things growing. Webel, Harvard educated, winner of the Rome Prize affording three years at the American Academy in Rome, brought classical precision to the planning process. Established in 1931, their firm prospered and they became prominent estate designers on Long Island and beyond. The grounds of Champ Soleil, created around 1945, are an essay in subtlety. Low grass terraces serve as a transition from house to lawn, which features flowering trees, such as dogwood, azalea, and rhododendron, and rose gardens.

> *It is work founded not on a desire for formal invention or new design languages, but on the diligent habits of tried and perfected ways. The firm sought value not from novelty but from predictability and permanence.*[208]

This green space is classicism chastened and simplified for the mid-century modern era. It bears none of the grandiose scale and elements of its nearby Gilded Age estates. While modernism did prevail in the mid-twentieth century, a strong classical tradition still made itself felt in the landscape design of some practitioners. Tunnard himself, though a champion of the new, advocated for the integration of architecture and its natural setting that is inherent in the classical tradition:

> *Today, modern architecture may fairly be said to have won its first battles all over the world, but in very few of them has it had any assistance from landscape architecture. Even now, one sees many great modern buildings whose setting is an incongruous medley of dwarf walls, crazy paving, and all the tricks of the Edwardian landscape gardener . . . This is more unfortunate because modern architecture needs the landscape architect. One of the best qualities of the modern movement is its increasing awareness of the connection between the space within buildings and the space around them, and of the interdependence of building and site.*[209]

What is old is new again. Tunnard's words evoke the architectural and landscape traditions of centuries recast in the mold of modernism. As he evolved as a designer, he became interested not only in individual buildings and gardens but in the combination of the two in urban planning. In 1960, as part of the firm of Tunnard and Harris, he produced a report on Newport for the Preservation Society of Newport County.[210] Either of her own accord or influenced by Tunnard, Katherine Warren expressed the Preservation Society's interest in a plan for Newport's landscape as well its architecture, a visionary idea at a time when saving the built environment of the city was an overwhelming need.[211] Tunnard insisted that the appreciation of scenery was vital:

Fig. 248
Garden, Warren residence, ca. 1950, from Peter Shepheard,
Modern Gardens (1953), photograph

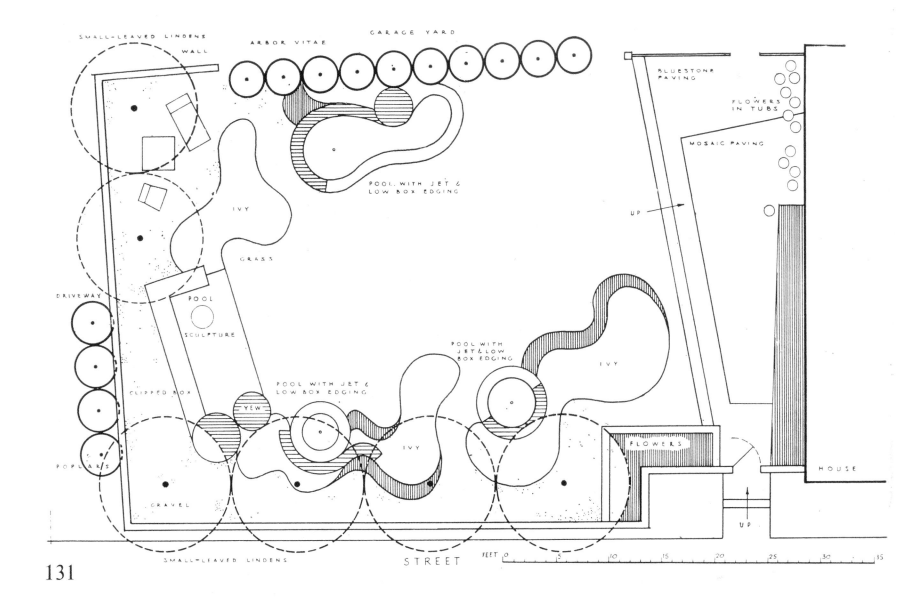

SMALL-LEAVED LINDENS
ARBOR VITAE
GARAGE YARD
WALL
BLUESTONE PAVING
FLOWERS IN TUBS
MOSAIC PAVING
POOL WITH JET & LOW BOX EDGING
IVY
UP
GRASS
IVY
DRIVEWAY
POOL
SCULPTURE
POOL WITH JET & LOW BOX EDGING
POOL WITH JET & LOW BOX EDGING
CLIPPED BOX
YEW
IVY
FLOWERS
POPLARS
HOUSE
GRAVEL
UP
SMALL-LEAVED LINDENS
STREET
FEET 0   5   10   15   20   25   30   35

131

Our surroundings are being destroyed and we are losing all the qualities of what used to be called "scenery." . . . When a landscape is considered to be "scenic," its esthetic qualities are somehow better served. Only when a proper appreciation of scenery returns can destruction be halted and the esthetic content restored to our cities and countryside, to what we build and what we plan.[212]

Fig. 249
Plan for the garden, Warren residence, ca. 1950, from Peter Shepheard, *Modern Gardens* (1953)

Of Tunnard's many proposals, his scheme for a park in downtown Newport, in front of Trinity Church (1726), featuring open green space with an underground parking garage, illustrates his interest in landscapes of meditation and functionality. Tunnard's park was eventually realized not by him but by the Newport Restoration Foundation, which created Queen Anne Square in the early 1970s. In 2013, it became the subject of landscape art as the site

"To Trinity. After church, Loulie and I read up in studio and later took a lovely walk & got wildflowers. Talked in evening." Anna F. Hunter's Diary, 1891

of Maya Lin's *The Meeting Room* installation (Figs. 250 and 251), comprising three foundations referencing colonial-era structures with text from historic documents carved into the thresholds of each.[213] The issues raised by Tunnard and Harris relating to the creation and maintenance of parks and green spaces such as Queen Anne Square, public access to nature, and traffic congestion were the same as those first addressed by Frederick Law Olmsted Jr. in his 1913 improvement plan, and they are still relevant today.

Tunnard and Warren's shared interest in modern art and landscape could be considered a single instance in mid-twentieth-century Newport, the dream of lone visionary figures. To a great extent this was true, except for a remarkable event in 1974 called *Monumenta*, an exhibition of large-scale modernist sculpture set against Newport's landscape. In a city noted for its historical layers, for the generations of artists and writers who were inspired by its landscape, the introduction of abstract works of art created an interface between old and new. The exhibition's director, Sam Hunter, specifically aimed to use Newport's built and natural setting as a backdrop:

> Monumenta *dramatizes the interaction of past and present in a dialogue of sculpture and natural or architectural site. Today's authentic sculptural expression can be expected*

to illuminate and echo the architectural ambitions of a bygone age . . . The exhibition was conceived with two primary objectives in mind, to match sculpture and site, and to provide a balanced reading of large-scale sculpture today in a variety of mediums.[214]

Among the artists and works featured in the exhibition were Willem de Kooning's *Clamdigger* (1972), Barbara Hepworth's *River Form* (1965), Henry Moore's *Two Piece Reclining Figure No. 9* (1967), Louise Nevelson's *Night Tree* (1971), Claes Oldenburg's *Geometric Mouse, Scale X* (1971), and Alexander Calder's *Lightening* (1970).[215] Works were exhibited across the city, on the grounds of historic estates such as Chateau-sur-Mer (1852), where Richard Fleischner created *Sod Maze*, an abstract composition of earth mounds laid in a circular pattern 125 feet in diameter. The soft green turf undulated across the ground, interacting with the massive rusticated granite façade of the towering Victorian house and the soft texture of the surrounding beeches and Turkish oaks. In the Ocean Drive district, Anne Healy displayed *Hot Lips*, nylon fabric and stainless steel wire formed into lips suspended over a cove with the soaring roofs and chimneys of the French-style château Seafair (1937) rising on the hill behind. The juxtaposition of the old and the new, the natural and the artful, made for a striking and, often times, challenging presentation.

Fig. 251
Alexander Nesbitt, *The Meeting Room* by Maya Lin, Queen Anne Square, 2016, photograph

Newport is quite properly celebrated for its scenic beauty and for its unique ensemble of architectural monuments, the numerous colonial houses and great mansions which dot the landscape and provide visible testimony to a rich and enduring cultural heritage. . . . Thus, the bald confrontation between this noble repository of formal New England culture and fifty uncompromising, large-scale sculptures, stamped with the look of the industrial age, might be expected to generate certain environmental tensions.[216]

Fig. 252
William Trost Richards, *Cove* (detail), 1875, oil on canvas
Private Collection

This tension came to the fore in a specific way in Christo's installation *Ocean Front Project for Covering the Cove at King's Beach, Newport, August, 1974*, which consisted of 150,000 square feet of white polypropylene fabric floating on King's Beach, illuminating the half-moon contour of the rocky shoreline. As waves came and went, the rhythms of the ocean filled the fabric, floating one moment then clinging to the rocks the next.

> *The contradictory notion of the "temporary monument" is a crucial aspect of Christo's entire esthetic. The term was first applied by Christo himself . . . The covered King's Beach cove had a mystery and romantic sweep, evoking paintings such as* Die Gescheiterte Hoffnung *[The Sea of Ice] and* Monch am Meer *[Monk by the Sea] by Caspar David Friedrich. . . . The Newport project was also intimately related to the landscape in that the natural forms were accentuated by the fabric—in a sense made more visible, rather than altered or disguised.*[217]

Ocean Front Project was "the controlled transformation of a vast expanse of marine nature into pure visual poetry and enthralling theater."[218] This use of the rocks and ocean for artful objectives was part of a historical trajectory. Harriet Beecher Stowe's heroine, Mary, in *The Minister's Wooing* (1859), came to contemplate her future on this same rocky shoreline, sensing the power of the ocean and her place in the universe. William Trost Richards depicted the rock formations of this area in his 1874 watercolor *Cove* (Fig. 252). A century later, Christo, with *Ocean Front Project*, yet again reinterpreted this setting, land and sea acting as a canvas for forms and materials that evoked the sublime rhythms of nature, as Richards and Stowe had done before him. Gianfranco Gorgoni, an Italian photographer renowned for documenting the major land art of mid- to late twentieth-century masters of modernism, came to Newport to record the process of creation and final iteration of *Ocean Front Project* (Fig. 253). The entire installation process from beginning to end was captured in black and white images: the monumental effort of aligning the fabric with the waves; the finished product responding to the movement of water, clinging to the solidity of rocks. Gorgoni's work is based on one artist experiencing the art of another, itself a form of art. His photographs record the fleeting nature of *Ocean Front Project*. The installation was dismantled, but the images live on.

The art historian Sally Yard interviewed Christo and his partner Jeanne-Claude about the ephemeral nature of their work:

> Sally Yard: "I suspect you wouldn't want your large pieces to last, even if they could."
> Christo: "No. They could not really, in any case."
> Jean-Claude: "It depends on which piece."
> Christo: "It is very difficult to determine. I cannot think of one piece that could be called permanent."[219]

Fig. 253
Gianfranco Gorgoni,
Ocean Front Project
by Christo and Jeanne-
Claude, King's Beach,
1974, photograph
Estate of Gianfranco
Gorgoni

Fig. 254
Alexander Nesbitt, *Sod Maze*
by Richard Fleischner, Chateau-
sur-Mer, 1974, photograph

Monumenta left viewers to find their own meaning as abstract large-scale sculptures brought attention to natural settings but did not provide any overt interpretations or direct messages. Sam Hunter wrote, "Christo's ocean front cove, covered by 14,000 square yards of polypropylene fabric, and Fleischner's sod maze, 125 feet in diameter (Fig. 254), are meant to be experienced as landscape rather than optically isolated art objects. The mind-boggling grandiosity which these two projects only begin to hint at contains elements of irony as well as high seriousness."[220] Irony was to be found in the confrontation of the art and its setting, seriousness in the message of looking at art and the world in different ways. Was it entirely novel, however? The abstract art may have been new, but the land and the sea and the artist's interaction with them were not.

Culture continually made its mark on Newport's landscape as each generation viewed it through the lens of its own aesthetic values. Styles change; creativity appears to be eternal. Christo's installation was, like nature itself, ephemeral. Earth is timeless, and art is timely; each enriches the other. Certain periods, such as the Victorian and Gilded Ages, have left more impressions on Newport's landscape than others (Figs. 255 and 256). Modernity had only a few moments, but they were powerful and provided lessons for the future about how the landscape can continue to inspire and engage.

Fig. 255 (left)
Tree canopy of Stone Villa (left)
overhanging Bellevue Avenue,
ca. 1900, photograph
Library of Congress

Fig. 256 (below)
Removal of a tree from the
shopping center parking lot,
once part of the grounds
of Stone Villa, ca. 1960,
photograph
Newport Historical Society, P88

Living Legends
THE HISTORIC TREES OF NEWPORT

To gaze again at the glorious trees of Newport—lofty, sheltering, and varied. The climate, but not the soil of Eastern Rhode Island, was favorable to the growth of large and exotic trees. It was explained that a whole generation of learned scientists had derived pleasure from planting foreign trees on this Aquidneck Island.
—Thornton Wilder, *Theophilus North*, 1973

The trees of Newport stand as sentinels, bearing silent witness to the past and the present, and serving as a living form of hope for the future. They are the product of interest in global exploration, collecting, and propagation. The southern portion of Aquidneck Island, which makes up the land mass of Newport, was essentially deforested by the time of European settlement in the seventeenth century. Thus, the story of Newport's trees is one of importation and experimentation with new non-native specimens.

During the colonial period, fruit trees were prized for both their utility and their beauty, the centerpieces of boxwood-framed garden beds. Streets were rarely lined with trees. European cities offered few prototypes of urban green spaces. The classical approach to city planning, emphasizing a grid of streets and squares, did not encourage greenery, which was relegated to private gardens; parks evolved out of private royal gardens made public over time and at the discretion of monarchs.[221] Thus, the builders of colonial Newport did not necessarily bring with them a well-established practice of urban tree planting. Houses directly abutted the streets, leaving little space for planting, though there was an early trend to name streets after trees. The 1680 plan for Philadelphia and the 1725 map of the Point in Newport are examples this.[222] Chestnut, Walnut, Elm, and Poplar Streets on the Point, however, never had trees to live up to their names. There were some exceptions in other American cities: in 1723, English elms were set along Tremont street in Boston, forming a grand promenade known as the "great mall."[223] By the end of the eighteenth century, the fashion for English picturesque landscape design took hold in the United States and cities began to be populated by trees. The American elm appeared on urban streets and, in the country, in front of houses, usually set symmetrically at either side of a main door. Physically hardy with a columnar structure and broad leaf canopy ideally suited for a streetscape, the elm became the signature tree of numerous New England towns and cities—such as Portsmouth, New Hampshire; Cambridge and Concord, Massachusetts; and

Roselle McConnell, Turkish oak and weeping beech, Chateau-sur-Mer, 2020, photograph

Fig. 257
E. C. W., Washington Street,
1913, photograph
United States Department of
the Interior, National Park
Service, Frederick Law Olmsted
National Historic Site

Portland, Maine—and spread consistently westward.[224] The practical merits of the tree were extolled: "an avenue of elms is never somber, however cool and shadowy it may be. It does not shut out the light and air, but merely tempers them."[225] Newport followed this fashion for elms, and the tree appeared in gardens and along streets, as documented in nineteenth-century photographs (Fig. 257).

The emphasis on trees as primary elements, in a landscape burgeoned in the United States during the course of the nineteenth century, inspired by the English writer John Claudius Loudon and the American Andrew Jackson Downing. On the subject of the elm tree, Downing declared that for beauty, grace, and grandeur it had no equal in New England, and encouraged his readers to serve as "apostles of taste" in the appropriate use of these and other specimens.[226]

Fig. 258
Childe Hassam, *Duke Street*,
1901, pen and ink and crayon
on light blue paper
Carnegie Museum of Art,
Pittsburgh, Andrew Carnegie
Fund, 07.14.19

Their luxuriant leafy arms, swaying and waving to and fro, will make more convincing gestures than any member of congress or stump speaker, and if there is any love of nature dormant in the dusty hearts of the villagers, we prophecy that in a very short time there will be such a general yearning after green trees, that the whole place will become a bower of freshness and verdure.[227]

On their spiritually uplifting qualities, he proclaimed, "It is quite extraordinary . . . what sermons they will preach."[228] Virtue, self-improvement, reform, and reinvigoration were sacred to Downing, a man on a mission who had witnessed the remarkable expansion of tree varieties on offer during the first half of the nineteenth century as steam power allowed for the quicker

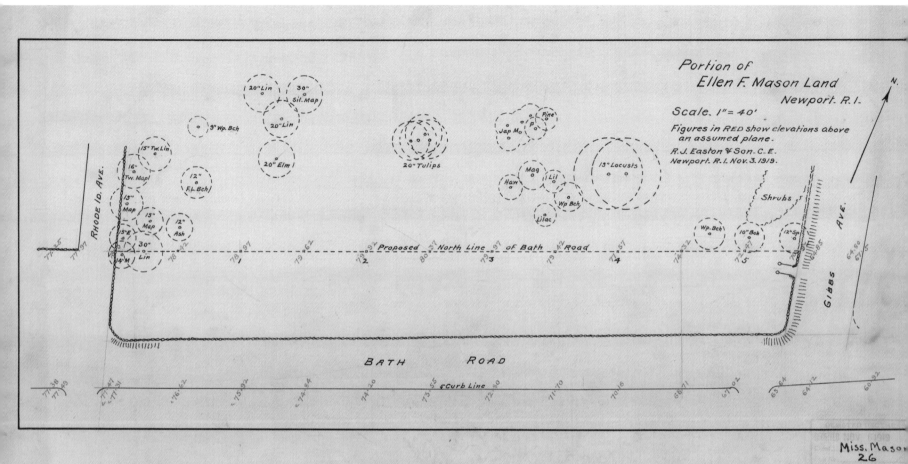

Fig. 259
Olmsted Brothers, *Portion of Ellen F. Mason Land*, plan for tree planting, Miss Ellen Mason Estate, ca. 1920
United States Department of the Interior, National Park Service, Frederick Law Olmsted National Historic Site
This plan illustrates the attention to detail paid to a variety of trees forming the main features of the landscape, including each tree marked (some in abbreviated form), such as ash, linden, weeping and Fernleaf beech, elm, Japanese maple, locust, and hawthorn.

importation by rail and ship of many types of new specimens. With the rural cemetery movement of the 1830s, the formation of tree societies in the 1840s, and the ensuing development of public parks in the 1860s, trees became a focal point of landscape settings, allowed to grow to their full expanse and appreciated as objects of cultural significance.

Newport's public streets, parks, and private gardens displayed an expanding variety of trees by the 1870s (Fig. 258). The once open, windswept meadowlands of the city were planted with imported specimens, aided by the increasing number of nurseries in Newport and the connections many residents had with the newly established Arnold Arboretum in Boston. George Champlin Mason duly noted this increasing prominence of trees in the city (Figs. 259 and 260).

Standing out in strong relief, we see the ash and the lime, the broad-leafed magnolia, and serrated foliage of the deciduous cypress, the variegated horse-chestnut, and the strong-leafed oak. These, with the tulip-tree, the Norway and sugar maples, and the well-known varieties of evergreens, make a charming background for the rarer specimens more prominently placed on the open lawn, the weeping ash, the Salisburia, the purple beech, the cut-leafed birch, and other well-known trees of rare beauty, so grouped as to produce an infinite variety of hues and shades of green.[229]

Fig. 260
Linden gate, Henry Marquand
Estate, ca. 1880, photograph
Library of Congress
Young oak trees (right) and
potted palms (left) stand on the
lawn of a house designed by
Richard Morris Hunt for Henry
Marquand.

Mason singled out the Italianate villa (1845) of Edward Leroy King, which had been featured in Andrew Jackson Downing's *The Architecture of Country Houses* (1852), for its fine specimens: "down long vistas the dark leaves of the purple beech mingle with those of the maple and oak; and the linden and chestnut, the cypress and holly, all find ample space to grow and expand on the broad acres set apart for their culture."[230] The acquisition and arrangement of trees on the grounds of Newport's estates became an exercise in discerning taste and horticultural expertise, and the subject of critiques. Enter Mariana Griswold Van Rensselaer, who in her book *Art Out of Doors* (1893), included the purple beech on her list of "eccentric and therefore dangerous trees."[231] She believed the overuse of such showy specimens compromised the subtle art of designing a landscape the way an artist would plan a painting, with foliage rather than paint providing color, light, and form.

Fig. 261 (right)
Tree moving, ca. 1905,
photograph
Courtesy of T. J. Brown
John "The Tree Mover" Martin,
in a long coat (right), directs
the planting.

Fig. 262 (below)
Roselle McConnell, Weeping
beech, Chateau-sur-Mer, 2020,
photograph

Fig. 263 (opposite)
Robert Yarnall Richie, Grafton
W. Minot's Oakwood estate
and Mrs. James B. Haggin's
Villa Rosa estate, 1932–34,
photograph
Robert Yarnall Richie
Photograph Collection,
Negative Series: 0612, DeGolyer
Library, Southern Methodist
University
Oakwood (bottom) was
celebrated for its rare trees.
Villa Rosa (center left) was
demolished in the early 1960s.

In order to achieve the appearance of a landscape of ancient trees, specimens of great maturity were planted and moved, calling upon the legendary figure of John "The Tree Mover" Martin, born in Newport in 1874 and moving monumental trees by the late 1890s (Fig. 261).[232] Catherine Lorillard Wolfe placed a fernleaf beech at the foot of the front door of her cliffside

estate, Vinland (1884), and Senator George Peabody Wetmore requested evergreens from the Olmsted Brothers in 1915 when they designed the main entrance to Chateau-sur-Mer.[233] The result was a fine weeping hemlock that is a living legend today.

Throughout Newport, in parks, in private estates, and on city streets, tree cultivation continued until, by the 1930s, Newport hosted a mature urban forest (Fig. 262). The renowned photographer Robert Yarnall Richie, whose work featured in *Life*, *National Geographic*, *Time*, and *Scientific American*, made the treescapes and houses of Newport his subject in a series of aerial photographs taken between 1932 and 1934. Documenting the nineteenth- and

twentieth-century tree plantings of the city's estates, Richie's images would prove to be an invaluable record after storms took their toll on the landscape (Figs. 263–70). The hurricane of 1938 occurred when the majority of the tree canopy was seventy-five years old. One of the most powerful storms on record to hit the area, this was followed by others in 1954 and thereafter. The south coast and the estates along the east-facing cliffs of Newport suffered losses, but the city, remarkably, retains the majority of its historic treescape. Thriving regardless of time and the tumults of weather, the trees of Newport deserve the worthy moniker of "Living Legends."

Fig. 264 (right)
Robert Yarnall Richie, Frederick
Prince's Marble House estate, 1932–34,
photograph
Robert Yarnall Richie Photograph
Collection, Negative Series: 0589,
DeGolyer Library, Southern Methodist
University
The serpentine borders of trees,
depicted here in their mature form, is a
picturesque manner of landscape design
fusing with the classically inspired
entrance drive and terrace of Marble
House.

Fig. 265 (below)
Robert Yarnall Richie, Vincent Astor's
Beechwood estate, 1932–34, photograph
Robert Yarnall Richie Photograph
Collection, Negative Series: 0587,
DeGolyer Library, Southern Methodist
University

Fig. 266 (left)
Robert Yarnall Richie, Hermann Oelrich Jr.'s Rosecliff estate, 1932–34, photograph
Robert Yarnall Richie Photograph Collection, Negative Series: 0603, DeGolyer Library, Southern Methodist University
Richie's photographs are valuable documents of Newport's mature treescapes prior to the Hurricane of 1938.

Fig. 267 (below)
Robert Yarnall Richie, Mrs. Elsie Hutton's Shamrock Cliff estate, 1932–34, photograph
Robert Yarnall Richie Photograph Collection, Negative Series: 0589, DeGolyer Library, Southern Methodist University

Fig. 268 (above)
Robert Yarnall Richie, Mrs. Walter B. James's Rockhurst estate,
1932–34, photograph
Robert Yarnall Richie Photograph Collection, Negative Series:
0646 RI, DeGolyer Library, Southern Methodist University
Rockhurst was demolished in the mid-twentieth century.

Fig. 269 (opposite, top)
Robert Yarnall Richie, Mrs. E. G. Slater's Hopedene estate, 1932–34,
photograph
Robert Yarnall Richie Photograph Collection, Negative Series:
0638 RI, DeGolyer Library, Southern Methodist University
The tree-lined drive and formal flower garden at Hopedene were
designed by Beatrix Farrand, noted landscape designer and the only
woman among the original founders of the American Society of
Landscape Architects. Her aunt, Edith Wharton, introduced her to
Newport circles. Farrand is credited with two other Newport designs:
the formal garden at Wakehurst and the gardens at the Alfred Coats
House.

Fig. 270 (below)
Robert Yarnall Richie, Mrs.
Lewis Cass Ledyard's Sunset
Ridge estate (left) and Lewis C.
Ledyard Jr.'s Broadlawns estate,
1932–34, photograph
Robert Yarnall Richie
Photograph Collection,
Negative Series: 0638 RI,
DeGolyer Library, Southern
Methodist University
Broadlawns (right) is a
significant landscape, the site
of the revived "Point of Trees,"
a grove of elms that historically
served as a navigation
landmark once visible to sailors
from the sea.

CASE STUDY

THE SENTINELS OF EDEN
An Arborist's View of Newport and its Trees

Chris Fletcher

Arborist

Newport has a quality that appears innately predestinate. Many visiting the city for the first time sense, consciously or not, the mysteries of its past within the leafy canopy and primordial character of its urban forest (Fig. 271). Initially, we may not know exactly what speaks to us. This book explores the premise that Newport is an American Eden, an idea projected onto the land by European settlers. I myself knew that I had discovered a fabled site when I started work as an arborist in Newport, becoming a wanderer within the New World garden. I saw artistic forms, light, color, and texture in landscapes maintained by fellow arborists, horticulturists, gardeners, and lovers of all growing things.

In the late 1980s, a group of Newport citizens committed themselves to celebrating, preserving, and propagating Newport's legacy of trees. Their view of the city as an arboretum is heir to the ideas of the Scottish botanist and landscape designer John Claudius Loudon and his concept of the arboretum, which he defined as a collection of trees selected for their scientific study and arranged with a view to their special beauty. In the late eighteenth and nineteenth centuries, the fashion for collecting trees from around the world and arranging them according to family, genus, and species emerged in the United States. The first shipments of Asian plant material arrived in Boston and Long Island, acquired by Dr. George Rogers Hall of Bristol, Rhode Island, in 1861. Among the first species to be planted in Newport were magnolia, sawara cypress, umbrella pine, and Japanese zelkova.

Of the many species cultivated, the European beech can justly be called Newport's signature tree. One in particular is exceptional. At Chepstow, a fernleaf beech rises from an artificial mound, causing the roots to cascade visibly over the edges (Figs. 272 and 273). Its trunk soars to a height of approximately eighty feet with limbs that sweep back down to the ground as they spread to a comparable width, while others rise like a candelabra. Offspring sprout from branches that have touched the ground, protecting their elders from the scalding sun. As groups walk underneath the canopy of this tree, each person tends to look around in amazement. The coolness of the shade is striking. People often notice the carvings on the trunk and limbs—vandalism, in fact. Beech trees have often been used for the inscription of names and dates throughout the ages.

"Millions of years ago, the northern European continent was connected to North America," I tell people, recounting how this tree was first planted as an ornament on an estate and now reigns as a museum relic. "When the plates separated, Europe was left with a forest of many types of beech—green European, weeping, copper, and fernleaf—while North America had only one variety. The legacy of tree collecting in places like Newport reintroduced these beeches to the New World."

People enter Newport's Eden as they walk beneath its tree canopies. There are many living sentinels within this green enclave: the Japanese sophora, Sargent's weeping hemlock, and the Turkish oaks at Chateau-sur-Mer; the London plane trees at Braga Park; the Japanese katsura and the hornbeam at Merrillton—I've seen its skirt in its prime, whispering in the winds, so I know the stories it could tell; the three zelkova trees at the National Museum of American Illustration; and the melancholy English yew at Rough Point spreading its lonely arms across the wintery windswept landscape of a storm-tossed coastline. Loudon would have marveled at the variety of trees in Newport, which now embraces the botanical science and benefits from the aesthetics of an arboretum (Figs. 274–85).

Fig. 271
Roselle McConnell,
Fernleaf beech (*Fagus sylvatica* 'Asplenifolia'),
Redwood Library and
Athenaeum, 2020,
photograph

273

Fig. 272
Roselle McConnell, Fernleaf beech (*Fagus sylvatica* 'Asplenifolia')
(detail of canopy), Chepstow, 2020, photograph

Fig. 273
Roselle McConnell, Fernleaf beech (*Fagus sylvatica* 'Asplenifolia'),
Chepstow, 2020, photograph

Fig. 274 (left)
Roselle McConnell, Turkish oak (*Quercus cerris*), Rough Point, 2020, photograph
The Turkish oak was imported in small numbers to the western hemisphere from Southeastern Europe and Asia in the nineteenth century. Its low spreading limbs and wide trunk distinguish it from other oak species.

Fig. 275 (opposite, top)
Roselle McConnell, Sargent's weeping hemlock (*Tsuga canadensis* 'Pendula'), Chateau-sur-Mer, 2020, photograph
This tree has matured to its maximum breadth and scale. Its dark dense canopy protects the trunk from heat and other environmental stresses. Hemlock is a species native to the Northeast. This weeping form is not found in the natural environment but has been bred by generations of horticulturists.

Fig. 276 (opposite, bottom)
Roselle McConnell, Japanese pagoda tree, also referred to as a scholar tree (*Styphnolobium japonicum*), Chateau-sur-Mer, 2020, photograph
The Japanese pagoda tree is noted for its weeping pendular form.

Fig. 277 (above)
Roselle McConnell, European hornbeam (*Carpinus betulus*), Merrillton, 2020, photograph
Similar to beeches, hornbeams have a mature profile of multiple branches reaching to the ground. They are also used as clipped hedges.

Fig. 278 (left)
Roselle McConnell, Katsura (*Cercidiphyllum japonicum*), Merrillton, 2020, photograph
The katsura, native to Japan, is an example of the collecting spirit of the nineteenth century, in which trees and plants from across the globe were of interest to gardeners and homeowners.

Fig. 279 (opposite, top)
Roselle McConnell, Gingko (*Gingko biloba*), Beaulieu, 2020, photograph
Gingko biloba is considered a living fossil, unchanged for millions of years, and cultivated in China for at least two thousand years. It is not specifically a hardwood, a pine, or a fern, but is considered to be within all three classifications. The tree is defined by evenly stratified limbs and finely textured leaves.

Fig. 280 (opposite, bottom)
Roselle McConnell, Plane trees (*Platanus × acerifolia*), Braga Park, 2020, photograph
The London plane tree is especially adapted to urban environments. These majestic specimens are from the 1870s.

Fig. 281 (above)
Roselle McConnell, Blue Atlas cedar
(*Cedrus atlantica*), The Breakers,
2020, photograph
"This beautiful conifer deserves
more recognition than it seems
to get at present. Some erroneous
ideas as to his hardihood, I believe,
are partly responsible for its not
being used in ornamental planting
more than it is. It has stood 14
degrees below zero here in Rhode
Island, which would lead one to
assume it may be classed as a fairly
hardy tree . . . yet, in the Spring, it
broke out in its natural steel blue as
beautiful as ever." Frederic Carter,
head gardener of The Breakers,
writing in "Practical Horticultural
Notes," *Journal of the International
Garden Club* 3 no. 1 (March 1919).

Fig. 282 (opposite, bottom left)
Roselle McConnell, Blue Atlas
cedar (*Cedrus atlantica*)
(detail), The Breakers, 2020,
photograph

Fig. 283 (opposite, bottom right)
Nick Garcia-Belong, Mongolian
oak (*Quercus mongolica*), 2020,
photograph
Private collection
Native to Siberia, Mongolia,
and Japan, this rare tree is an
example of the fascination for
Asian specimens in the late
nineteenth century.

Fig. 284 (left)
Roselle McConnell, Japanese
Zelkovas (*Zelkova serrata*),
Stoneacre, 2020, photograph

Fig. 285 (below)
E. C. W., Horse-chestnut
(*Aesculus hippocastanum*),
Touro Street, 1913, photograph
Frederick Law Olmsted National
Historic Site

Eden Preserved and Propagated

We have glanced at Newport as it was a hundred years ago, as it was fifty years ago, and as it is today. What will be its appearance fifty years hence?
—George Champlin Mason, *Newport and Its Cottages*, 1875

What remains of the past, what exists in the present, and what is hoped for in the future are the driving forces behind the mission to preserve and propagate Newport's urban forest, its designed landscapes, and its natural scenery (Fig. 286). The Newport Tree Conservancy, founded in 1987, is dedicated to these issues and has created a community-wide arboretum with the support of the city, organizations, and residents. With over thirty accredited sites, Newport has more arboreta than any city in the world and is designated by ArbNet as a Level II arboretum. Among the treasures in these arboreta are mature specimens, such as the Squarrosa falsecypress at Weetamoe, one of the tallest Turkish oaks in New England at Oakwood, a silver linden at Miramar, and a century-old Kwanzan cherry tree at The Whim.

The accomplishments in preserving the city's historic trees are impressive but there is still much to be done. The Heritage Tree Program, the Newport Herbarium, The Newport Project with Roger's High School, the Tree Planting Program, and the accreditation program for private properties are key initiatives that address past, present, and future.

The Heritage Tree Program ensures the integrity of historic landscapes by propagating genetic lines unique to the historically significant, aging trees in Newport. The relationship between Newport's buildings, streets, gardens, and parks and their plantings is an essential feature of the city. As institutions and individuals invest in restoring historic buildings, the landscapes that surround them must also be preserved and sustained. Horticulture can be a powerful tool to maintain the legacy of natural assets. By perpetuating the DNA of a tree that has stood through significant memory, not only is the lineage of the specimen preserved but the authenticity of its setting is also maintained (Figs. 287 and 288). In efforts to preserve trees for the future, the Heritage Tree Program supports various propagation techniques to reproduce new trees in order to maintain their legacy. One of these techniques is grafting, whereby a piece

Roselle McConnell, Ginkgo, 2019, photograph

Fig. 286 (above)
Rhode Island Avenue, 1914, photograph. United States Department of the Interior, National Park Service, Frederick Law Olmsted National Historic Site

Fig. 287 (below left)
Roselle McConnell, Blue Atlas cedar (foreground) and weeping beech (background) (detail), 2019, photograph

Fig. 288 (below right)
Roselle McConnell, Fernleaf beech (detail), 2019, photograph

Fig. 289 (left)
Students and Newport Tree Conservancy staff before the fernleaf beech at Redwood Library, the subject of their tree propagation project, 2018, photograph
The Newport Tree Conservancy

Fig. 290 (below)
Kristyn Woodland (left) and Jose Cortes (right) with the tree propagated from the fernleaf beech in front of Redwood Library and Athenaeum, 2019, photograph
The Newport Tree Conservancy

of twig section, known as a scion, of the heritage tree is joined to a seedling host plant, referred to as a rootstock. Once the graft heals, the clonal scion takes over as the new tree. This results in a specimen that is genetically identical to the historic parent tree (Figs. 289 and 290).

The Newport Herbarium is an archival project conducted with Salve Regina University and Roger Williams High School, resulting in a library of botanical information in the form of pressed, dried, and annotated plant specimens. This is a critical resource for biodiversity, ecological, and evolutionary research studies. Newport's students, volunteers, and residents participate in the collecting and labeling process. The result is a work of utility, as a reference source for those interested in the city's horticultural history, a font of beauty, and an inspiring collection of extraordinary natural specimens that have been cultivated in Newport.

Utility and beauty are at the core of Newport's horticultural and landscape history, from the pragmatic layouts of orchards of the colonial era that provided food for the table to the romantic sentiments behind the tree collections in Victorian landscapes, and the desire for historical fantasy that inspired the opulent high-style gardens of the Gilded Age. The practical benefits of a healthy urban forest and thriving ecosystem and the personally elevating qualities of being in natural surroundings are a continuation of the age-old values of utility and beauty.

Conclusion

THE LEGACY AND FUTURE OF EDEN

Today, Newport bears the marks of those who shaped it in both words and deeds. It is not a landscape of the wild, it is a landscape of culture, embodying the beliefs, hopes, desires, and pleasures of generations. The natural and the human-made co-exist and intertwine. Turn the pages of an eighteenth-century horticulture book and witness the classical inspiration for geometric remnants of the garden at Malbone. Walk under a beech planted by the romantics of the Victorian age, as a breeze catches the branches and makes them gently sway, and be enveloped in its green bower as people have been for over a century, or sit among the clipped lindens of an allée ornamented with marble busts of the four seasons in a system of classical lines beloved of the Beaux Arts designers of the Gilded Age. All of these places and experiences exist in Newport and are the sum total of centuries of human endeavor manifested on the land. Each path, each tree, each flower signifies a cultural moment, however grand or modest, a representation of what an individual or an entire age valued in its relationship to nature. The designers, gardeners, arborists, artists, patrons, and critics who created, praised, condemned, preserved, and propagated the features of Newport's landscapes were all cultural arbiters. They each imposed their visions on the place. Their legacy is present in gardens and natural sites, and preserved in books, photographs, paintings, and all of the creative productions of the human hand and mind. But what of the future? In 1875, George Champlin Mason stated,

> The natural features of the region will remain unchanged; the same rocks will frown upon the sea; the same purple haze rest at eventide upon the land-locked harbor; the same veil of ocean-mist temper the brightness of the noontide sun, and tide rise and fall on the sandy beach with the same rhythmical flow; the storm thunder with the same loud turbulence; but, meanwhile, what changes will the hand of man have wrought?[234]

Frances Benjamin Johnston,
Sculpture of Venus, The Elms,
ca. 1920, photograph
Library of Congress

(above)
E. C. W., Newport side yard,
1913, photograph
United States Department of
the Interior, National Park
Service, Frederick Law Olmsted
National Historic Site

(right)
E. C. W., Dearborn Street, 1913,
photograph
United States Department of
the Interior, National Park
Service, Frederick Law Olmsted
National Historic Site

One cannot predict the future of Newport's landscape, since nature is in continual flux. So too is the image of Eden. Each generation has interpreted this idea and ideal on its own terms. What remains in Newport are the layers of that interpretation across the land, a record, however fleeting, of humankind's relationship with the earth. These may serve as a memory of the past, a model for the present, and an inspiration for the future.

Masque of the Blue Garden, Beacon Hill, 1913, photograph Redwood Library and Athenaeum

NOTES

1 The vision of North America as a new Eden evolved from a wilderness to be cultivated, as it was seen by early European settlers in the seventeenth century, to untamed nature to be worshipped, in the late eighteenth and nineteenth centuries. Roderick Nash, *Wilderness and the American Mind* (New Haven, CT: Yale University Press, 1967); Keith Thomas, *Man and the Natural World* (New York: Pantheon, 1983); Perry Miller, *Errand into the Wilderness* (New York: Harper and Row, 1964); Henry Nash Smith, *Virgin Land* (Cambridge, MA: Harvard University Press, 1950); C. Vann Woodward, "The Fall of the American Adam," *New Republic* (December 2, 1981), 13.

2 Robert Pogue Harrison, *Gardens: An Essay on the Human Condition* (Chicago and London: University of Chicago Press, 2008), x.

3 Jedidiah Morse, *The American Geography; or A View of the Present Situation of the United States* (Elizabeth Town, NJ: Printed by Shepard Kullock for the author, 1789), 202.

4 *Secretary of the Interior's Standards for the Treatment of Historic Properties with Guidelines for the Treatment of Cultural Landscapes.* National Park Service, U.S. Department of the Interior, 1996. https://www.nps.gov/tps/standards/four-treatments/landscape-guidelines/index.htm.
The National Park Service identifies four categories of cultural landscapes: historic designed landscapes, historic vernacular landscapes, historic sites, and ethnographic landscapes.

5 J. M. Omernick, "Ecoregions of Rhode Island," U.S. Geological Survey (2009), 2–4, https://bplant.org/region/1383. The Environmental Protection Agency (EPA) collaborated with the Massachusetts Department of Environmental Protection (MA DEP) to draft an ecoregion classification for Massachusetts, Rhode Island, and Connecticut. The EPA designates Rhode Island as part of the Northeastern Coastal Zone and Atlantic Coastal Pine Barrens Level III Ecoregions; only Block Island is in the latter, with the rest of the state in the former. Rhode Island is within three Level IV draft ecoregions—the Southern New England Coastal Plains and Hills (western two-thirds of the state), the Narragansett/Bristol Lowland (eastern third of the state), and Cape Cod/Long Island Ecoregion (Block Island).

6 Jim Turenne, *Soils of Eastern Rhode Island* (Warwick, RI: Natural Resources Conservation Service, US Department of Agriculture, 2016).

7 Turenne, *Soils of Eastern Rhode Island*.

8 Thomas Wentworth Higginson, *Oldport Days* (Boston, MA: James R. Osgood and Company, 1873), 241–42.

9 Mariana Griswold Van Rensselaer, "Newport I," *Garden and Forest* 1 (November 28, 1888).

10 S. B. Sutton, ed., *Civilizing American Cities, Writings on City Landscapes* (New York: Da Capo Press, 1997), 270. Olmsted is expressing his views on landscape in a letter to the Rev. S. H. Willey from Olmsted, Vaux and Co., June 29, 1866.

11 Lucius D. Davis, "Ornamental Shrubs," in *Gardens and Gardening* (New York: G. P. Putnam's Sons, 1899), 95–98.

12 Peter Shepheard, *Modern Gardens* (London: Architectural Press, 1953), 80.

13 Lawrence C. Wroth, *The Voyages of Giovanni da Verrazzano, 1524–1528* (New Haven, CT: Yale University Press, 1970), 133–34.

14 Wroth, *Voyages of Giovanni da Verrazzano*, 134.

15 Records of the Island of Rhode Island and Providence Plantations in New England, 1638–1644, accession number C#00206, Rhode Island State Archives, Providence.

16 Newport Town Meeting Records, 1679–1776, book 2007, p. 27, Newport Historical Society, Newport, RI. Peter Easton and John Clarke's executors laid out the burying ground in 1681.

17 Nicholas Easton, Last Will and Testament, 1674, vault A, box 82, folder 6, Newport Historical Society, Newport, RI. William Brenton in *A History of Brenton's Neck*, by Elizabeth C. Brenton (Newport, RI: Printed by John P. Sanborn, 1877). Benjamin Church, Deeds, Land Evidence Records, City Hall, Newport, RI.

18 Brenton, *A History of Brenton's Neck*, 7.

19 "An Agreement of Several of the Free Inhabitants of Rhode Island, etc. Concerning the Purchasing of a Certain Island Called Qunonaqutt," March 10, 1657, MS. A2006.461.001, Jamestown Historical Society, Jamestown, RI. In 1657, group of 101 men became "Proprietors," forming a company that sought to acquire land to satisfy their common need for grazing land for their livestock and purchasing "Quononaqutt" Island from Chief Cashasaquont of the Narragansett Indian tribe. The largest Proprietor shares, one-twentieth, went to William Coddington and Benedict Arnold of Newport.

20 Census of Newport, Rhode Island, 1774, Rhode Island Historical Society, Providence, RI.

21 Akeia A. F. Benard, "The Free African American Cultural Landscape of Newport, 1774–1826" (PhD thesis, University of Connecticut, 2008), 180–287. The list of enslaved African Americans in Newport households is based on the 1774 Census of Newport (Rhode Island Historical Society).

22 Caesar Lyndon Accounts and Diaries, MS. 9004, Rhode Island Manuscripts; Accounts Marriages, and Letters, Newport 1761–1770, Rhode Island Historical Society, Providence.

23 Benard, "The Free African American Cultural Landscape of Newport, 1774–1826," 205.

24 Benard, 163.

25 W. P. Cutler and J. P. Cutler, *Life, Journals and Correspondence of Reverend Manasseh Cutler, L.L.D.* (Cincinnati, 1888), 68–69, in *The Architectural Heritage of Newport, Rhode Island, 1640–1915*, by Antoinette Downing and Vincent J. Scully Jr., 2nd ed. (New York: Clarkson Potter), 43.

26 Richard Bradley, *A Survey of the Ancient Husbandry and Gardening* (London: Benjamin Motte, 1725).

27 Batty Langley, *Pomona, or the Fruit-Garden Illustrated* (London: G. Strahan, R. Gosling, W. Mears, F. Clay, D. Browne, B. Motte, and L. Gilliver, J. Stagg, J. Osborne, and C. Davis, 1729).

28 Philip Miller, *The Gardeners Kalendar* (London: John Rivington, 1743). Philip Miller, *The Gardeners Dictionary*, 2 vols. (London: Philip Miller, 1743).

29 "Solomon Drowne's Journal," *Newport Historical Magazine* 1, no. 2 (October 1880): 67–68.

30 Downing and Scully, *The Architectural Heritage of Newport*, 38.

31 Joseph Jacob Probate Inventory, October 3, 1781, NP 1:37, Newport Probate Records, City Hall, Newport, RI.

32 Downing and Scully, *The Architectural Heritage of Newport*, 40.

33 "Rhode Island in 1750," *Rhode Island Historical Society Collections* 13, no. 2 (April 1920): 61. Downing and Scully, *The Architectural Heritage of Newport*, 41.

34 *Deed of Liberty Tree and of the Land Upon Which It Stands*, April 14, 1766, object number FIC.2016.073.001, Newport Historical Society, Newport, RI. The title page of the deed states that it was drawn by Henry Marchant, esquire, and copied by William Ellery.

35 "History Bytes: Newport's Liberty Tree," March 18, 2016, Newport Historical Society, https://newporthistory.org/history-bytes-newports-liberty-tree/.

36 Edward F. Andrews, "Creature of Mimic and Imitation: The Liberty Tree, Black Elections, and the Politicization of African Ceremonial Space in Revolutionary Newport, Rhode Island," *Radical History Review* 99 (Fall 2007): 26. John R. Tschirch, *Newport: The Artful City* (London: D. Giles Limited, 2020), 111.

37 God's Little Acre: America's Colonial African American Cemetery, accessed February 19, 2021, http://www.colonialcemetery.com/.

38 "Naming Traditions," God's Little Acre: America's Colonial African American Cemetery, accessed February 19, 2021, http://www.colonialcemetery.com/names/.

39 Downing and Scully, *The Architectural Heritage of Newport*, 41.

40 Edward C. Carter II, ed., *The Virginia Journals of Benjamin Henry Latrobe, 1795–1798* (New Haven, CT: Yale University Press, 1977), 1:165.

41 Theresa O'Malley, "Landscape Gardening in the Early National Period," in *Views and Visions, American Landscape before 1830*, by Edward J. Nygren and Bruce Robertson, exh. cat. (Washington, DC: Corcoran Gallery of Art, 1986), 145.

42 Thomas L. Campanella, *The Republic of Shade, New England and the American Elm* (New Haven and London: Yale University Press, 2003), 30.

43 George Champlin Mason, *Newport and Its Cottages* (Boston: James R. Osgood and Co., 1875), 40.

44 The real estate holdings and subdivisions of developers and major land owners are documented in G. M. Hopkins, *City Atlas of Newport, Rhode Island* (Philadelphia, 1876, 1883); and L. J. Richards and Co., *Atlas of the City of Newport* (Springfield, MA, 1893, 1907).

45 Mason, *Newport and Its Cottages*, 29.

46 Norman T. Newton, *Design on the Land* (Cambridge, MA: Harvard University Press, 1971), 211–15.

47 Newton, *Design on the Land*, 216–17.

48 Nygren and Robertson, *Views and Visions*, 56–58.

49 Andrew Jackson Downing, *A Treatise on the Theory and Practice of Landscape Gardening, Adapted to North America; With a View to the Improvement of Country Residences*, 2nd ed. (New York: Wiley; London: Putnam, 1844), 21.

50 Downing, *A Treatise on the Theory and Practice of Landscape Gardening*, 10.

51 Jacob Weidenmann, *Beautifying Country Homes* (New York: Orange, Judd and Co., 1870), plate XIII.

52 Newton, *Design on the Land*, 308.

53 Weidenmann, *Beautifying Country Homes*, plate XIII.

54 William Alex and George B. Tatum, *Calvert Vaux, Architect and Planner* (New York: Ink, Inc., 1994), 63, 114.

55 Calvert Vaux, *Villas and Cottages* (New York: Harper and Brothers, 1872), 67. "Life at Newport," *New York Times*, September 3, 1860.

56 Weidenmann, *Beautifying Country Homes*, plate XV.

57 Downing, *A Treatise on the Theory and Practice of Landscape Gardening*, 89.

58 Downing, 107.

59 Vaux, *Villas and Cottages*, 329.

60 Vaux, 328.

61 Walter Barrett, *The Old Merchants of New York City* (New York: Carleton, 1872), 299.

62 Letter from Robert Christie to George Peabody Wetmore, May 3, 1897, Box 5, MS. 798, George Peabody Wetmore Papers, Rhode Island Historical Society, Providence.

63 Census of Newport, Rhode Island, 1865, U.S. Bureau of Census Records, Rhode Island Historical Society, Providence.

64 *Newport Daily News*, May 18, 1891.

65 *Newport Daily News*, May 18, 1891.

66 F. Paul L. Veeder II, "The Outbuildings and Grounds of Chateau-sur-Mer," *Journal of the Society of Architectural Historians* 29, no. 4 (1970): 316.

67 Harold Hill Blossom, Report on visit to Chateau-sur-Mer, September 18, 1915, Olmsted job number 06268, Olmsted Archives, National Park Service, Frederick Law Olmsted National Historic Site, Brookline, MA.

68 John Cairns biography, in *The Wetmore Family and their Domestics at Chateau sur Mer*, by Holly Collins (Newport, RI: Preservation Society of Newport County, 2000).

69 Lucinda Brockway, *RI Designed Landscapes, 1830–1950* (unpublished research report), 32.

70 Downing, *A Treatise on the Theory and Practice of Landscape Gardening*, 12.

71 Mason, *Newport and Its Cottages*, 51.

72 Katherine Duffy, "From Virtuous Visions to Rubbish and Rats: A Natural History Society in Gilded Age Newport," *Newport History: Journal of the Newport Historical Society* 85, no. 273 (Newport: Newport Historical Society, 2016), 29.

73 Virginia Galvin Covell, "A Critical Examination of the Town and Country Club of Newport, Rhode Island," (master's thesis, University of Rhode Island, 1964), 3.

74 Duffy, "From Virtuous Visions to Rubbish and Rats," 28.

75 "The Newport Natural History Society," *Newport Daily News*, July 13, 1883.

76 *Proceedings of the Newport Natural History Society, 1884–1885* (Newport, RI: Davis and Pitman, 1885), 37–46.

77 Duffy, "From Virtuous Visions to Rubbish and Rats," 32.

78 J. H. Browne, "The Queen of Aquidneck," *Harper's New Monthly Magazine* 1 (August 1874).

79 Henry James, "The Sense of Newport," *Harper's Monthly Magazine* 23, no. 675 (August 1906): 345.

80 Harriett Beecher Stowe, *The Minister's Wooing* (New York: Derby and Jackson, 1859), 507.

81 Stowe, *The Minister's Wooing*, 67–68.

82 Stowe, 272.

83 Stowe, 132.

84 Stowe, 19–20.

85 Stowe, 67.

86 Mason, *Newport and Its Cottages*, 89.

87 Mason, 376.

88 George Champlin Mason, untitled editorial, *Newport Mercury*, October 17, 1857, 2. Mason advocated for a road on the south coast of Newport in the early 1850s, beginning a decades-long campaign to achieve this dream. See George Champlin Mason, untitled editorial, *Newport Mercury*, July 26, 1851, 4.

89 S. L. Minot, *Map of Ocean Avenue*, September 9, 1863, book 35, p. 313, Land Evidence Records, City Hall, Newport, RI.

90 Frederick Law Olmsted, Letter to the Board of Commissioners of the Central Park, January 22, 1861. Also quoted in Frederick Law Olmsted, Jr. and Theodora Kimball, eds. *Frederick Law Olmsted: Landscape Architect, Vol. I* (New York: G. P. Putnam's Sons, 1922), 310.

91 Frederick Law Olmsted and John Charles Olmsted, "Plan for Subdivision of Properties in Newport RI Belonging to Mrs. Edward King, J.H. Glover, Esq., The Hon. C.S. Bradley, G. Gordon King," 1885, Plat Book 1, pp. 30–31, Land Evidence Records, City Hall, Newport, RI. C. S. Bradley, G. G. King, and John H. Glover, Olmsted job number 0681, National Park Service, Frederick Law Olmsted National Historic Site, Brookline, MA. The King-Glover-Bradley plat followed a number of predecessors in planned

picturesque communities, including Glendale in Cincinnati, Ohio (1851); Llewellyn Park (1852) and Short Hills (1874) in New Jersey; and Lake Forest in Illinois (1856).

92 Mariana Griswold Van Rensselaer, "Newport II," *Garden and Forest* 1 (December 5, 1888), 483.

93 Olmsted job numbers are as follows: Theodore M. Davis, 0684; William Dorsheimer, 1073; J. R. Busk, 1299, National Park Service, Frederick Law Olmsted National Historic Site, Brookline, MA. The job files include drawings and photographs.

94 Charles A. Birnbaum and Robin Karson, *Pioneers of American Landscape Design* (New York: McGraw-Hill, 2000), 287–89.

95 Olmsted and Olmsted, "Plan for Subdivision of Properties," 30–31.

96 Walter Howe, *The Garden* (New York: Knickerbocker Press; London: G. P. Putnam's Sons, 1890).

97 John R. Howe, "Historical Summary," in *The Flora of Berry Hill*, by Bruce Howe (Newport, RI: Bruce Howe, 1992), 4. Birnbaum and Karson, *Pioneers of American Landscape Design*, 287. The other major landscaped component of the Ocean Drive district is the Newport Country Club. In 1894, Scottish-born William F. Davis (1863–1902) came as the golf professional to Newport Country Club, where he built a nine-hole members' course and a six-hole beginners' course; see Geoffrey S. Cornish and Ronald E. Whitten, *The Architects of Golf: A Survey of Golf Course Design from Its Beginnings to the Present, with an Encyclopedic Listing of Golf Architects and Their Courses* (New York: HarperCollins, 1993), 238. Albert Warren Tillinghast (1874–1942), one of the most-successful early twentieth-century design-build golf architects, remodeled Davis's original nine and added the second nine to bring the course to its current eighteen-hole configuration.

98 Howe, "Historical Summary," 5.

99 Howe, "Historical Summary," 2–7; Bruce Howe, "The Flora of Berry Hill," in *The Flora of Berry Hill*, 49–63.

100 "Blending an Estate with the Landscape," *Country Life* 44 (August 1923). Wyndham and Roslyn were designed by architect William Ralph Emerson, according to the *Newport Mercury*, June 28, 1890.

101 Ernest Bowditch, "The Year 1881 at the Office," *Office-Work Personalities II*, no. 6. Bowditch Family Papers, Philips Library, Peabody Essex Museum, Salem, MA.

102 Ernest Bowditch, *Office Work-Personalities II*, no. 5, Bowditch Family Papers, Peabody Essex Museum, Salem, MA.

103 George William Sheldon, *Artistic Country Seats* (New York: D. Appleton and Company, 1887), 143–46.

104 Frederick Law Olmsted, letter to Elizabeth Baldwin Whitney, December 16, 1890, in *Civilizing American Cities: Writings on City Landscapes*, ed. S. B. Sutton (New York: Da Capo Press, 1997), 13.

105 Mariana Griswold Van Rensselaer, "Newport I," *Garden and Forest* 1 (November 28, 1888), 470–71.

106 Van Rensselaer, "Newport I," 470–71.

107 Frederick Law Olmsted, letter to Mariana Griswold Van Rensselaer, May 17, 1887, Olmsted Associates Records. Manuscript Division, Library of Congress, Washington, DC ; Mariana Griswold Van Rensselaer, "Landscape Gardening VII," *Garden and Forest* 1 (April 11, 1888), 75; Van Rensselaer, "Newport II," 483.

108 Judith K. Major, *Mariana Griswold Van Rensselaer: A Landscape Critic in the Gilded Age* (Charlottesville and London: University of Virginia Press, 2013), 51.

109 Mariana Griswold Van Rensselaer, "The Artistic Aspect of Trees IV," *Garden and Forest* 1 (October 3, 1888), 524–55.

110 Major, *Mariana Griswold Van Rensselaer*, 81.

111 Frederick Law Olmsted, letter to Mariana Griswold Van Rensselaer, June 29, 1888, Olmsted Associates Records, Manuscript Division, Library of Congress, Washington, DC.

112 Van Rensselaer, "Newport II," 482–83.

113 A. H. Olmsted, Wildacre, Newport, RI, Olmsted job numbers 2221 and 2261, National Park Service, Frederick Law Olmsted National Historic Site, Brookline, MA.

114 John Russell Pope, letter to Olmsted Brothers, August 21, 1931; see also letters to Olmsted Brothers, October 1, 1931, and October 30, 1931, Olmsted Associates Records, Manuscript Division, Library of Congress, Washington, DC.

115 Easton's Beach, Olmsted job number 1211, National Park Service, Frederick Law Olmsted National Historic Site, Brookline, MA; Newport Land Trust, Newport, RI, Olmsted job number 1070, National Park Service, Frederick Law Olmsted National Historic Site, Brookline, MA.

116 Ogden Goelet, Olmsted job number 1203, National Park Service, Frederick Law Olmsted National Historic Site, Brookline, MA.

117 Keith Morgan, Introduction, in *Charles Eliot, Landscape Architect* (Amherst: University of Massachusetts Press, 1999), xxxv.

118 Ignasi de Sola Morales, "The Beaux Arts Garden," in *The Architecture of Western Gardens*, ed. Monique Mosser and George Teyssot (Cambridge: MIT Press, 1991), 399.

119 James H. Bowditch, letter to Cornelius Vanderbilt, January 23, 1896, The Preservation Society of Newport County Archives, Newport, RI.

120 Ernest Bowditch, "First Office," *Office Work-Personalities II*, no. 3, Bowditch Family Papers, Phillips Library, Peabody Essex Museum, Salem, MA.

121 Richard Morris Hunt, *Drawing of the Southwest Façade of The Breakers*, April 20, 1893, no. 791801.48, American Architectural Foundation, Washington, DC. A pergola is drawn in pencil above the semicircular projection in the center of the façade.

122 Lucius Davis, *Gardens and Gardening* 1, no. 7 (1896): 111.

123 Barr Ferree, *American Estates and Gardens* (New York: Munn and Company, 1904), 65–66.

124 Pierre de Nolhac, *Versailles and the Trianons* (New York: Dodd, Mead and Company, 1906), 147.

125 Edith Wharton, *Italian Villas and Their Gardens* (New York: Century Company, 1904), 12.

126 Wharton, *Italian Villas and Their Gardens*, 12.

127 Louis Auchincloss, *Profile of a Gilded Age* (New York: Charles Scribner's Sons, 1988), 53.

128 Edith Wharton, *A Backward Glance* (New York: Curtis Publishing Company, 1933), 103.

129 Paul Bourget, *Outre Mer Impressions of America* (New York: Charles Scribner's Sons, 1896), 50.

130 Mark Twain, "What Paul Bourget Thinks of Us," *North American Review* 160, no. 458 (January 1895): 50–52.

131 Edwin J. Emerson, "Newport in the Lead," *Automobile Magazine* 1 (October 1899): 10.

132 "Magnificent Newport," *Munsey's Magazine*, 1900.

133 *Newport Journal and Weekly News*, August 23, 1907.

134 Ogden Codman Jr., garden plans for Martha Codman, 1908–10: garden plan (AR022.001.005.001.003.039), plot plan for trees (AR022.001.005.001.003.041), plot plan including garden (AR022.001.005.001.003.040), Ogden Codman Jr. architectural collection, Historic New England, Boston.

135 Isabelle Gournay, "Revisiting Jacques Gréber's *L'Architecture aux Etats-Unis*: From City Beautiful to Cite-Jardin," *Urban History Review* 29, no. 2 (March 2001): 6–19.

136 Jacques Gréber, *L'Architecture aux Etats-Unis* (Paris: Payot et Cie, 1920), 65–67.

137 James T. Maher, *The Twilight of Splendor: Chronicles of the Age of Splendor* (Boston: Little, Brown and Co., 1975), 65. For Gréber's work in Canada, see David Gordon, "Jacques Gréber, Urbaniste et Architecte," *Urban History Review* 29, no. 2 (March 2001): 3–5.

138 James, "The Sense of Newport," 354.

139 "Masque of the Blue Garden," *Newport Daily News*, August 16, 1913.

140 Pierre-Andre Lablaude, *The Gardens of Versailles* (London: Zwemmer, 1995), 28.

141 Arleyn A. Levee, *The Blue Garden, Recapturing an Iconic Newport Landscape* (Newport, RI: Blue Garden and the Redwood Library and Athenaeum, 2016), 13. *The Masque of the Blue Garden Scrapbook*, a compilation of photographs, thankyou notes, and newspaper clippings celebrating the event at the Blue Garden, Beacon Hill House, Newport, RI, August 15, 1913, Gift of Hayward F. Manice, Redwood Library and Athenaeum, Newport, RI.

142 Arthur Curtiss James, Olmsted job number 03558, National Park Service, Frederick Law Olmsted National Historic Site, Brookline, MA.

143 W. F. Anderson, "Farm Buildings of Arthur Curtiss James, Esq., Newport, RI, Grosvenor Atterbury and Stowe Phelps, Associate Architects," *Architectural Forum* 34 (February 1921), 55–58. John Taylor Boyd Jr., "Picturesque Farm, Architecture on Newport Estate: Surprise Valley Farm, Estate of Arthur Curtiss James," *Arts & Decoration* 30 (March 1929): 60–61, 100, 125. "Surprise Valley Farm," *Country Life* 45 (April 1924): 50–53. "Farm Group, Estate of Mr. Arthur James, Newport, RI.," *Architect* (March 9, 1928), 713–15.

144 Levee, *The Blue Garden*, 99.

145 Lida Rose McCabe, "Surprise Valley Farm," *Country Life* 45 (April 1924): 50–53.

146 Judith Tankard, "Rose Standish Nichols, A Proper Bostonian," *Arnoldia* 59, no. 4 (1999): 26–27.

147 Tankard, "Rose Standish Nichols," 28. Ellen Mason, Olmsted job number 00257, National Park Service, Frederick Law Olmsted National Historic Site, Brookline, MA.

148 Major, *Mariana Griswold Van Rensselaer*, 15.

149 *Garden and Forest* 6 (August 2, 1893), 322.

150 Charles Adams Platt, *Italian Gardens* (New York: Harper and Brothers, 1894), 15–16.

151 Wharton, *Italian Villas and Their Gardens*, 17.

152 Harold Brown, Olmsted job number 1726, National Park Service, Frederick Law Olmsted National Historic Site, Brookline, MA.

153 Mrs. Harold Brown, letter to Olmsted Brothers, November 10, 1912, Olmsted job number 1726, Olmsted Associates Records, Manuscript Division, Library of Congress, Washington, DC.

154 John Nicholas Brown, Olmsted job number 1220, National Park Service, Frederick Law Olmsted National Historic Site, Brookline, MA.

155 Harold Hill Blossom, report on meeting with Mr. and Mrs. Hugh D. Auchincloss, May 26, 1910, Olmsted job number 3794, Olmsted Associates Records, Manuscript Division, Library of Congress, Washington, DC.

156 Blossom, report on meeting with Mr. and Mrs. Hugh D. Auchincloss, May 26, 1910.

157 Blossom.

158 Hugh D. Auchincloss Jr., letter to Olmsted Brothers, April 10, 1945. The drawings for the Hammersmith Farm Project are in Olmsted job number 3794, Olmsted Associates Records, Manuscript Division, Library of Congress, Washington, DC.

159 Clare Lise Kelly, *Montgomery Modern* (Riverdale, MD: Maryland-National Capital Park and Planning Commission, 2015), 194. Boris Timchenko designed the landscapes of the Watergate Complex (1964) and was chief architect of the National Capital Flower Show and Garden Show. He also served on the First Lady's Committee for a More Beautiful National Capital during the Johnson administration.

160 Stuart Duncan, Olmsted job number 5432, National Park Service, Frederick Law Olmsted National Historic Site, Brookline, MA.

161 Davis, *Gardens and Gardening*, 111.

162 Frederick Law Olmsted Jr., *Proposed Improvements for Newport, Rhode Island* (Cambridge, MA: University Press, 1913), 1.

163 Birnbaum and Karson, *Pioneers of American Landscape Design*, 272.

164 Olmsted, *Proposed Improvements for Newport*, 5.

165 Olmsted, 12.

166 Olmsted, 12.

167 Olmsted, 26.

168 Major, *Mariana Griswold Van Rensselaer*, 83.

169 Harold Hill Blossom, report on Mrs. John Nicholas Brown's request for a gardener for her Newport estate, Harbour Court, August 25, 1914, Olmsted job number 6268, Olmsted Associates Records, Manuscript Division, Library of Congress, Washington, DC.

170 *Boyd's Newport City Directory* (Newport, RI: William H. Boyd, 1858). *Newport Directory* (Newport, RI: J. A. and R. A. Reid, 1880).

171 *Boyd's Newport City Directory*; Galvin and Geraghty, advertisement, in *Newport Directory* (1867).

172 *Newport Directory* (1892), 411.

173 *Newport Journal and Weekly News*, August 23, 1907.

174 *Newport Directory* (1901).

175 Galvin Nurseries Ledger, 1909–1916, Redwood Library and Athenaeum, Newport, RI.

176 Galvin Nurseries Ledger.

177 T. J. Brown, interview (interviewer unknown), February 2021, Newport Tree Conservancy, Newport, RI.

178 T. J. Brown Day Books, 1905–1945, Private Collection of T. J. Brown, Newport, RI.

179 T. J. Brown Day Books.

180 "Newport Cottages Ready," *New York Times*, June 16, 1879.

181 Harry Eudenbach. *The Estate Gardeners of Newport, A Horticultural Legacy* (Newport, RI: Harry J. Eudenbach, 2010).

182 Ernest W. Bowditch, letter to Lord and Burnham Co., October 8, 1886, The Preservation Society of Newport County Archives, Newport, RI. Richard Gardner, letter to Lord's Horticultural Manufacturing Co., February 6, 1887, The Preservation Society of Newport County Archives, Newport, RI.

183 Eudenbach, *The Estate Gardeners of Newport*, 39.

184 Eudenbach, 44–45.

185 John W. Ellis, Olmsted job number 1015, National Park Service, Frederick Law Olmsted National Historic Site, Brookline, MA.

186 Lisa Hammel, "A Vanishing Breed: The Head Gardeners of Newport," *New York Times*, September 3, 1967.

187 "Local Briefs," *Newport Daily News*, September 17, 1895.

188 "The Vanderbilt Greenhouses," *New York Times*, November 8, 1896.

189 Eudenbach, *The Estate Gardeners of Newport*, 120.

190 John Burrows, interview (interviewer unknown), Harold Brown Villa, August 8, 2000, The Preservation Society of Newport County Archives, Newport, RI.

191 Burrows, interview.

192 Burrows, interview.

193 Burrows, interview.

194 *Newport Journal and Weekly News*, April 12, 1902.

195 Jack Yule, interview by Thomas Downes, February 7, 2021, Newport Tree Conservancy, Newport, RI.

196 Irene Roosevelt Aitken, interview by John Tschirch, February 10, 2021, Newport Tree Conservancy, Newport, RI.

197 Newport Horticultural Society Records, Redwood Library and Athenaeum, Newport, RI.

198 Burrows, interview.

199 *Newport Journal and Weekly News*, June 12, 1912.

200 *Newport Journal and Weekly News*, July 13, 1914.

201 Terry Borton, "Outstanding Colorists of American Magic Lantern Slides," *Magic Lantern Gazette, A Journal of Research* 26, no. 1 (Spring 2014): 7–8.

202 Bettina Berch, *The Woman Behind the Lens: The Life and Work of Frances Benjamin Johnston, 1864–1952* (Charlottesville and London: University of Virginia Press, 2003), 35.

203 Kurt Vonnegut Jr., *The Sirens of Titan* (New York: Delacore, 1959), 11.

204 Vonnegut, *The Sirens of Titan*, 1.

205 Christopher Tunnard, *Gardens in the Modern Landscape* (London: Architectural Press, 1938). Marc Treib, *Thinking a Modern Landscape Architecture, West and East* (Novato, California: ORO Editions, 2020), 102–3. Birnbaum and Karson, *Pioneers of American Landscape Design*, 396–97.

206 Treib, *Thinking a Modern Landscape Architecture*, 108.

207 Irene Roosevelt Aitken, interview (interviewer unknown), Champ Soleil, Newport, February 10, 2021, Newport Tree Conservancy, Newport, RI.

208 Gary Hilderbrand, *Making a Landscape of Continuity: The Practice of Innocenti and Webel* (Cambridge, MA: Harvard University Graduate School of Design, 1997).

209 Shepheard, *Modern Gardens*, 16. Tunnard worked with Henry Hope Reed on *American Skyline: The Growth and Form of Our Cities and Towns* (New York: New American Library, 1955).

210 Tunnard and Harris, *A Preservation Planning Report on Newport, RI*, prepared for the Preservation Society of Newport County, January 1960, The Preservation Society of Newport County Archives, Newport, RI.

211 Mrs. George Henry Warren and Harold Talbot, interview (interviewer unknown), July 16, 1970, The Preservation Society of Newport County Archives, Newport, RI.

212 Christopher Tunnard, *A World with a View: An Inquiry into the Nature of Scenic Values* (New Haven, CT: Yale University Press, 1978), 3. See also Treib, *Thinking a Modern Landscape Architecture*, 117.

213 The Queen Anne Square Maintenance Trust, an offshoot of the Newport Restoration Foundation, commissioned the new park installation by Maya Lin in collaboration with landscape designer Edwina van Gal and stone carver and calligrapher Nick Benson. See Maya Lin, Edwina von Gal, and Nicholas Benson, "Artists' Statement," *The Meeting Room: An Installation by Maya Lin*, 2013, https://queenannesquare.com/about/.

214 Sam Hunter, ed., *Monumenta: A Biennial Exhibition of Outdoor Sculpture, Newport, Rhode Island, August 17 through October 13, 1974* (Newport: Monumenta Newport, Inc., 1974), 5.

215 The *Monumenta* catalogue has a complete list of the artists included in the exhibition. See Hunter, *Monumenta*, 94–96.

216 Hunter, 5.

217 Sally Yard, *Christo Oceanfront* (Princeton, NJ: Art Museum, Princeton University, 1975), 19.

218 Hunter, *Monumenta*, 11.

219 Yard, *Christo Oceanfront*, 29.

220 Hunter, *Monumenta*, 8.

221 Campanella, *The Republic of Shade*, 108. Christopher Tunnard, *The City of Man* (New York: Charles Scribner's Sons, 1970), 240–43.

222 Samuel Easton, plan of Easton's Point, 1725, Newport Historical Society, Newport, RI.

223 Campanella, *The Republic of Shade*, 103. Nathaniel B. Shurtleff, *A Topographical and Historical Description of Boston* (Boston: Noyes, Holmes and Co., 1872), 326.

224 Campanella, *The Republic of Shade*, 99.

225 "An Avenue of Elms," *Garden and Forest* 6 (April 19, 1893): 172.

226 Downing quoted in Campanella, *The Republic of Shade*, 91.

227 Andrew Jackson Downing, "Trees in Towns and Villages," *Horticulturist* 1 (March 1847): 394, quoted in Campanella, *The Republic of Shade*, 91.

228 Andrew Jackson Downing, "On the Improvement of Country Villages," *Horticulturist* 3 (June 1849): 546, quoted in Campanella, *The Republic of Shade*, 91.

229 Mason, *Newport and Its Cottages*, 40.

230 Mason, 22.

231 Mrs. Schuyler Van Rensselaer, *Art Out of Doors: Hints on Good Taste in Gardening* (New York: Charles Scribner's Sons, 1893), 282. Major, *Mariana Griswold Van Rensselaer*, 51.

232 Eudenbach, *The Estate Gardeners of Newport*, 150.

233 Harold Hill Blossom, report on meeting with Senator George Peabody Wetmore, September 18, 1915, Olmsted job number 6268, Olmsted Associates Records, Manuscript Division, Library of Congress.

234 Mason, *Newport and Its Cottages*, 367.

BIBLIOGRAPHY

Aitken, Irene Roosevelt. Interview by John Tschirch, Champ Soleil, Newport, February 10, 2021. Newport Tree Conservancy, Newport, RI.

Alex, William, and George B. Tatum. *Calvert Vaux, Architect and Planner.* New York: Ink, Inc., 1994.

"An Agreement of Several of the Free Inhabitants of Rhode Island, etc. Concerning the Purchasing of a Certain Island Called Quononaqutt [Conanicut]. March 10, 1657. MS. A2006.461.001. Jamestown Historical Society, Jamestown, RI.

"An Avenue of Elms." *Garden and Forest* 6 (April 19, 1893). https://www.biodiversitylibrary.org/item/107147#page/190.

"An Interesting Problem." *American Gardening* 18, no. 116 (March 1897).

Anderson, W. F. "Farm Buildings of Arthur Curtiss James, Esq., Newport, RI, Grosvenor Atterbury and Stowe Phillips, Associate Architects." *Architectural Forum* 34 (February 1921).

Andrews, Edward. "Creature of Mimic and Imitation: The Liberty Tree, Black Elections and the Politicization of African Ceremonial Space in Revolutionary Newport, Rhode Island." *Radical History Review* 99 (Fall 2007).

Angeloni, Umberto, ed. *The Boutonniere: Style in One's Lapel.* New York: Universe Publishing, 2000.

"As Seen by Him." *Vogue,* October 30, 1909.

Auchincloss, Hugh D., Jr. Letter from Hugh D. Auchincloss Jr. to the Olmsted Brothers, April 10, 1945. Olmsted job number 03794. Olmsted Associates Records. Manuscript Division, Library of Congress.

Auchincloss, Louis. *Profile of a Gilded Age.* New York: Charles Scribner's Sons, 1988.

Bailey, Joseph I., and Alfred Smith. Deed: Joseph I. Bailey and Alfred Smith, Grantors, to William A. Sweet. Grantee, September 7, 1852. Book 30, pp. 59–60. Land Evidence Records. City Hall, Newport, RI.

Bailey, L. H. *Cyclopedia of American Horticulture.* New York: Macmillan Company, 1900.

Barbey d'Aurevilly, Jules Amédée. *Deuxième Memorandum (1838) et quelque pages de 1864.* Paris: Ancienne Library Tresse & Stock, 1906. https://gallica.bnf.fr/ark:/12148/bpt6k9754144n.

Barrett, Walter. *The Old Merchants of New York City.* New York: Carleton, 1872.

Bartlett, John R. *Census of the State of Rhode Island, 1774.* Providence, RI: Knowles, Anthony and Co., State Printers, 1858.

Bayles, Richard M., ed. *History of Newport County.* New York: L. E. Preston, 1888.

Benard, Akeia A. F. "The Free African American Cultural Landscape of Newport, 1774–1826." PhD thesis, University of Connecticut, 2008.

Berch, Bettina. *The Woman Behind the Lens: The Life and Work of Frances Benjamin Johnston, 1864–1952.* Charlottesville and London: University of Virginia Press, 2000.

Blaskowitz, Charles. *A Topographical Chart of the Bay of Narraganset in the Province of New England.* July 22, 1777. Engraved and printed by Wm. Faden.

"Blending an Estate with the Landscape." *Country Life* 44 (August 1923).

Blossom, Harold Hill. Drawings for Hammersmith Farm Project, undated. Olmsted job number 03794. National Park Service, Frederick Law Olmsted National Historic Site, Brookline, MA.

Blossom, Harold Hill. Report on meeting with Mr. and Mrs. Hugh D. Auchincloss, May 26, 1910. Olmsted job number 03794. Olmsted Associates Records. Manuscript Division, Library of Congress.

Blossom, Harold Hill. Report on meeting with Senator George Peabody Wetmore, September 18, 1915. Olmsted job number 06268. Olmsted Associates Records. Manuscript Division, Library of Congress.

Blossom, Harold Hill. Report on Mrs. John Nicholas Brown's request for a gardener for her Newport estate, Harbour Court, August 25, 1914. Olmsted job number 01220. Olmsted Associates Records. Manuscript Division, Library of Congress.

Blossom, Harold Hill. Report on visit to Chateau-sur-Mer, September 18, 1915. Olmsted job number 06268. National Park Service, Frederick Law Olmsted National Historic Site, Brookline, MA.

Birnbaum, Charles A., and Robin Karson. *Pioneers of American Landscape Design.* New York: McGraw-Hill, 2000.

Borton, Terry. "Outstanding Colorists of American Magic Lantern Slides." *Magic Lantern Gazette, A Journal of Research* 26, no. 1 (Spring 2014).

Bourget, Paul. *Outre Mer Impressions of America.* New York: Charles Scribner's Sons, 1896.

Bowditch, Ernest. "First Office." *Office-Work Personalities II*, no. 3. Bowditch Family Papers, 1881–1918. Phillips Library, Peabody Essex Museum, Salem, MA.

Bowditch, Ernest. *Office-Work-Personalities II*, no. 5. Bowditch Family Papers, 1881–1918. Phillips Library, Peabody Essex Museum, Salem, MA.

Bowditch, Ernest. "The Year 1881 at the Office." *Office Work Personalities II*, no. 6. Bowditch Family Papers, 1881–1918. Phillips Library, Peabody Essex Museum, Salem, MA.

Bowditch, James. Letter from James H. Bowditch to Cornelius Vanderbilt, January 23, 1896. The Preservation Society of Newport County Archives, Newport, RI.

Bowditch, Ernest. Letter from Ernest W. Bowditch to Lord and Burnham Co., October 8, 1886. The Preservation Society of Newport County Archives, Newport, RI.

Boyd, John Taylor, Jr. "Picturesque Farm Architecture on Newport Estate: Surprise Valley Farm, Estate of Arthur Curtiss James." *Arts and Decoration* 30 (March 1929).

Boyd's Newport City Directory. Compiled by William H. Boyd. Newport, RI: William H. Boyd, 1856–58.

Boyd's Newport City Directory. Compiled by Andrew Boyd. Newport, RI: A. J. Boyd, 1863, 1867, 1869–70, 1871–72, 1878–79.

Bradley, C. S., King, G. G., and Glover, John H. Olmsted job number 00681. National Park Service, Frederick Law Olmsted National Historic Site, Brookline, MA.

Bradley, Richard. *A Survey of the Ancient Husbandry and Gardening.* London: Benjamin Motte, 1725.

Brenton, Elizabeth C. *A History of Brenton's Neck.* Newport, RI: Printed by John P. Sanborn, 1877.

Broadlawns, Cultural Landscapes Report, prepared by Place Studios, LLC. December 20, 2018.

Brockway, Lucinda A. "The Historic Designed Landscapes of Newport County." *Newport History* 64, no. 219 (1991). https://digitalcommons.salve.edu/newporthistory/vol64/iss219/2.

Brown, Harold. Olmsted job number 3794. National Park Service, Frederick Law Olmsted National Historic Site, Brookline, MA.

Brown, Harold, Mrs. Letter from Mrs. Harold Brown to Captain Cotton, September 18, 1912. Olmsted job number 1726. Olmsted Associates Records. Manuscript Division, Library of Congress.

Brown, Harold, Mrs. Letter from Mrs. Harold Brown to Olmsted Brothers, January 12, 1912; letter from Mrs. Harold Brown to Captain Cotton, October 19, 1912. Olmsted job number 1726. Olmsted Associates Records. Manuscript Division, Library of Congress.

Brown, John Nicholas. Olmsted job number 1220. National Park Service, Frederick Law Olmsted National Historic Site, Brookline, MA.

Browne, J. H. "The Queen of Aquidneck." *Harper's New Monthly Magazine* 1 (August 1874).

Burrows, John. Interview (interviewer unknown), Harold Brown Villa, Newport, August 8, 2000. The Preservation Society of Newport County Archives, Newport, RI.

Busk, J. R. Olmsted job number 1299. National Park Service, Frederick Law Olmsted National Historic Site, Brookline, MA.

Campanella, Thomas L. *The Republic of Shade: New England and the American Elm.* New Haven and London: Yale University Press, 2003.

Carter, Edward C., II, ed. *The Virginia Journals of Benjamin Henry Latrobe, 1795–1798.* Vol. 1. New Haven: Yale University Press, 1977.

Carter, Frederic. "Practical Horticultural Notes." *Journal of the International Garden Club* 3, no. 1 (March 1919).

Census of Newport, Rhode Island, 1774. Rhode Island Historical Society, Providence, RI.

Census of Newport, Rhode Island, 1865. U.S. Bureau of Census Records. Rhode Island Historical Society, Providence, RI.

Champlin, Richard. "Newport Estates and Their Flora." *Journal of Newport History* 53, part 2, no. 178 (Spring 1980).

Christie, Robert. Letter from Robert Christie to George Peabody Wetmore, May 3, 1897. Box 5, MS. 798. George Peabody Wetmore Papers. Rhode Island Historical Society, Providence, RI.

Codman, Ogden, Jr. Garden plan, 1/8 inch scale, residence of Martha Codman, Bellevue Ave. and Berkeley, "Berkeley Villa," Newport, RI, 1908–10. Reference code AR022.001.005.001.003.039. Ogden Codman, Jr. architectural collection. Historic New England, Boston. https://www.historicnewengland.org/explore/collections-access/gusn/268519/.

Codman, Ogden, Jr. Plot plan including garden, 1/8 inch scale, residence of Martha Codman, Bellevue Ave. and Berkeley, "Berkeley Villa," Newport, RI, 1908–10. Reference code AR022.001.005.001.003.040. Ogden Codman, Jr. architectural collection. Historic New England, Boston. https://www.historicnewengland.org/explore/collections-access/gusn/268520/.

Codman, Ogden, Jr. Plot plan (trees): J. P. Cotton to Ogden Codman, 1 inch to 16 feet scale, residence of Martha Codman, Bellevue Ave. and Berkeley, "Berkeley Villa," Newport, RI, 1908. Reference code

AR022.001.005.001.003.041. Ogden Codman, Jr. architectural collection. Historic New England, Boston. https://www.historicnewengland.org/explore/collections-access/gusn/268521/.

Collins, Holly. *The Wetmore Family and Their Domestics at Chateau sur Mer.* Newport, RI: Preservation Society of Newport County, 2000.

Cornish, Geoffrey, and Ronald E. Whitten. *The Architects of Golf: A Survey of Golf Course Design from Its Beginnings to the Present, with an Encyclopedic Listing of Golf Architects and Their Courses.* New York: HarperCollins, 1993.

Covell, Virginia. "Town and Country Club." Typed thesis, 1964. Newport Historical Society, Vol. 2086.

Cutler, W. P., and J. P. Cutler. *Life, Journals and Correspondence of Reverend Manasseh Cutler, L.L.D.* Cincinnati, 1888, 68–69. In *The Architectural Heritage of Newport, Rhode Island, 1640–1915.* By Antoinette Downing and Vincent J. Scully Jr. 2nd ed. New York: Clarkson Potter, 1967.

Davis, L. D. "The Gardens of Newport—1." *American Garden: An Illustrated Journal of Horticulture* 12, no. 6 (June 1891).

Davis, Lucius. *Gardens and Gardening* 1, no. 7 (1896).

Davis, Lucius D. "Ornamental Shrubs." In *Gardens and Gardening.* New York: G. P. Putnam's Sons, 1899.

Davis, Theodore M. Olmsted job number 0684. National Park Service, Frederick Law Olmsted National Historic Site, Brookline, MA.

Deed of Liberty Tree and the Land Upon Which It Stands, April 14, 1766. Object number FIC.2016.073.001. Newport Historical Society, Newport, RI. https://collections.newporthistory.org/Detail/objects/13962.

de Nolhac, Pierre. *Versailles and the Trianons.* New York: Dodd, Mead and Company, 1906.

de Sola Morales, Ignasi. "The Beaux Arts Garden." In *The Architecture of Western Gardens.* Edited by Monique Mosser and George Teyssot. Cambridge: MIT Press, 1991.

Desmarais, Jane. *Monsters Underglass: A Culture History of Hothouse Flowers.* London: Reaktion Books, 2018.

Downing, Andrew Jackson. "Domestic Notices: The Mildest Climate in the United States." *Horticulturist* 6, no. 12 (December 1851).

Downing, Andrew Jackson. "On the Improvement of Country Villages." *Horticulturist* 3 (June 1849).

Downing, Andrew Jackson. *A Treatise on the Theory and Practice of Landscape Gardening, Adapted to North America; With a View to the Improvement of Country Residences.* 2nd ed. New York: Wiley; London: Putnam, 1844.

Downing, Andrew Jackson. "Trees in Towns and Villages." *Horticulturist* 1 (March 1847).

Dorsheimer, William. Olmsted job number 1073. National Park Service, Olmsted National Historic Site, Brookline, MA.

Duffy, Katherine. "From Virtuous Visions to Rubbish and Rats: A Natural History Society in Gilded Age Newport." *Newport History: Journal of the Newport Historical Society* 85, no. 273 (2016). https://digitalcommons.salve.edu/newporthistory/vol85/iss273/4/.

Duncan, Stuart. Olmsted job number 5432. National Park Service, Frederick Law Olmsted National Historic Site, Brookline, MA.

Easton, Nicholas. Last Will and Testament, 1674. Vault A, box 82, folder 6. Newport Historical Society, Newport, RI.

Easton, Samuel. Plan of Easton's Point, 1725. Newport Historical Society, Newport, RI.

Easton's Beach. Olmsted job number 01211. Landscape design and road improvements. National Park Service, Frederick Law Olmsted National Historic Site, Brookline, MA.

Elliott, Maud Howe. *This Was My Newport.* 1944; reprint, Salem, NH: Ayer Company, 1990.

Ellis, John W. Olmsted job number 01015. National Park Service, Frederick Law Olmsted National Historic Site, Brookline, MA.

Emerson, Edwin J. "Newport in the Lead." *Automobile Magazine* 1 (October 1899).

Eudenbach, Harry. *The Estate Gardeners of Newport, A Horticultural Legacy.* Newport, RI: Harry J. Eudenbach, 2010.

"Farm Group, Estate of Mr. Arthur James, Newport, RI." *Architect* (New York), March 9, 1928.

Ferree, Barr. *American Estates and Gardens.* New York: Munn and Company, 1904.

Frank, John L. H. "The American Beauty." *Gardener's Monthly and Horticulturist* 29, no. 344 (August 1887).

Galvin Nurseries Ledger, 1909–1916. Redwood Library and Athenaeum, Newport, RI.

Garden and Forest 6 (August 2, 1893), 322.

Gardner, Richard. Letter from Richard Gardner to Lord's Horticultural Manufacturing Co., February 6, 1887. The Preservation Society of Newport County Archives, Newport, RI.

Gibbs, Wolcott. "Wanted—A Hand-book of Horticulture." *Garden and Forest* 1 (April 4, 1888). https://www.biodiversitylibrary.org/item/107709#page/81.

God's Little Acre: America's Colonial African American Cemetery. Accessed February 19, 2021. http://www.colonialcemetery.com.

Goelet, Ogden. Olmsted job number 01203. National Park Service, Frederick Law Olmsted National Historic Site, Brookline, MA.

Gordon, David. "Jacques Gréber, Urbaniste et Architecte," *Urban History Review* 29, no. 2 (March 2001).

Gournay, Isabelle. "Revisiting Jacques Gréber's L'Architecture aux Etats-Unis: From City Beautiful to Cite-Jardin." *Urban History Review* 29, no. 2 (March 2001).

Gréber, Jacques. *L'Architecture aux Etats-Unis.* Paris: Payot et Cie, 1920.

Hammel, Lisa. "A Vanishing Breed: The Head Gardeners of Newport." *New York Times*, September 3, 1967.

Harley, J. B. *The New Nature of Maps: Essays in the History of Cartography.* Baltimore, MD: Johns Hopkins University Press, 2001.

Harrison, Robert Pogue. *Gardens: An Essay on the Human Condition.* Chicago and London: University of Chicago Press, 2008.

Higginson, Thomas Wentworth. *Oldport Days.* Boston: James R. Osgood and Company, 1873.

Hilderbrand, Gary. *Making a Landscape of Continuity: The Practice of Innocenti and Webel,* Cambridge, MA: Harvard University Graduate School of Design, 1997.

"History Bytes: Newport's Liberty Tree." Newport Historical Society, March 18, 2016. https://newporthistory.org/history-bytes-newports-liberty-tree/.

Hopkins, G. M. *City Atlas of Newport, Rhode Island.* Philadelphia, 1876, 1883.

"The Horticultural Advisor." *Gardener's Monthly and Horticulturist* 24, no. 279 (March 1882).

Howe, Bruce. *The Flora of Berry Hill.* Newport: Berry Hill, 1992.

Howe, M. A. DeWolfe. *The Life and Letters of George Bancroft.* Vol. 2. New York: Charles Scribner's Sons, 1908.

Howe, Walter. *The Garden.* New York: Knickerbocker Press; London: G. P. Putnam's Sons, 1890.

Hull, A. Gerald. "Melons and Their Culture." *Horticulturist* 6, no. 11 (November 1851).

Hunt, Richard Morris. *Drawing of the Southwest Façade of The Breakers,* April 20, 1893. No. 791801.48. American Architectural Foundation, Washington, DC.

Hunter, Sam. ed. *Monumenta: A Biennial Exhibition of Outdoor Sculpture, Newport, Rhode Island, August 17 through October 13, 1974.* Newport, RI: Monumenta Newport, Inc., 1974.

Jacob, Christian. *The Sovereign Map: Theoretical Approaches in Cartography throughout History.* Trans. by Tom Conley. 1st ed. Chicago: University of Chicago Press, 2006.

Jacob, Joseph. Joseph Jacob Probate Inventory, October 3, 1781. NP 1:37. Newport Probate Records. City Hall, Newport, RI.

James, Arthur Curtiss. Olmsted job number 03558. National Park Service, Frederick Law Olmsted National Historic Site, Brookline, MA.

James, Henry. "The Sense of Newport." *Harper's Monthly Magazine* 23, no. 675 (August 1906).

Kelly, Clare Lise. *Montgomery Modern.* Riverdale, MD: Maryland-National Capital Park and Planning Commission, 2015.

Lablaude, Pierre-Andre. *The Gardens of Versailles.* London: Zwemmer, 1995.

Langley, Batty. *Pomona: Or, the Fruit-Garden Illustrated.* London: G. Strahan, R. Gosling, W. Mears, F. Clay, D. Browne, B. Motte, L. Gilliver, J. Stagg, J. Osbourne, and C. Davis, 1729.

Laufer, Gerladine Adamich. *Tussie-Mussies: The Victorian Art of Expressing Yourself in the Language of Flowers.* New York: Workman Publishing, 1993.

Levee, Arleyn A. *The Blue Garden, Recapturing an Iconic Newport Landscape.* Newport, RI: Blue Garden and the Redwood Library and Athenaeum, 2016.

"Life at Newport." *New York Times*, September 3, 1860.

Lin, Maya, Edwina von Gal, and Nicholas Benson. "Artists' Statement." *The Meeting Room: An Installation by Maya Lin.* 2013. https://queenannesquare.com/about/.

"Local Briefs." *Newport Daily News*, September 17, 1895.

Lyndon, Caesar. Accounts and Diaries of Caesar Lyndon. MS. 9004. Rhode Island Manuscripts; Accounts Marriages, and Letters, Newport 1761–1770. Rhode Island Historical Society, Providence.

"Magnificent Newport." *Munsey's Magazine*, 1900.

Maher, James T. *The Twilight of Splendor: Chronicles of the Age of Splendor.* Boston: Little, Brown and Co., 1975.

Major, Judith K. *Mariana Griswold Van Rensselaer: A Landscape Critic in the Gilded Age.* Charlottesville and London: University of Virginia Press, 2013.

Mason, Ellen. Olmsted job number 0257. National Park Service, Frederick Law Olmsted National Historic Site, Brookline, MA.

Mason, George Champlin. "Local Matters: Ocean Avenue." *Newport Mercury*, October 19, 1867.

Mason, George Champlin. *Newport and Its Cottages.* Boston: James R. Osgood and Co., 1875.

Mason, George Champlin. Untitled editorial. *Newport Mercury*, July 26, 1851.

Mason, George Champlin. Untitled editorial. *Newport Mercury*, October 17, 1857.

"Masque of the Blue Garden." *Newport Daily News*, August 16, 1913.

The Masque of the Blue Garden Scrapbook. A compilation of photographs, thankyou notes, and newspaper clippings celebrating the event at the Blue Garden, Beacon Hill House, Newport, RI, August 15, 1913. Gift of Hayward F. Manice. Redwood Library and Athenaeum, Newport, RI.

McCabe, Linda Rose. "Surprise Valley Farm." *Country Life* 45 (April 1924).

Miller, Perry. *Errand into the Wilderness.* New York: Harper and Row, 1964.

Miller, Philip. *The Gardeners Dictionary.* 2 vols. London: Philip Miller, 1743.

Miller, Philip. *The Gardeners Kalendar.* London: John Rivington, 1743.

Minot, S. L. Map of Ocean Avenue. September 9, 1863. Book 35, p. 313. Land Evidence Records. City Hall, Newport, RI.

Morgan, Keith. Introduction. In *Charles Eliot, Landscape Architect.* Amherst: University of Massachusetts Press, 1999.

Morse, Jedidiah. *The American Geography; or A View of the Present Situation of the United States.* Elizabeth Town, NJ: Printed by Shepard Kullock for the author, 1789.

Nash, Roderick. *Wilderness and the American Mind.* New Haven, CT: Yale University Press, 1967.

"Newport Cottages Ready." *New York Times*, June 16, 1879.

Newport Daily News, May 18, 1891.

Newport Directory. Newport, RI: J. A. and R. A. Reid, 1880, 1881.

Newport Directory. Boston: Sampson, Davenport and Co., 1884.

Newport Directory. Boston: Sampson, Murdock and Co., 1886, 1887.

Newport Directory. Providence, RI: Sampson, Murdock and Co., 1888–95, 1899, 1901.

Newport Horticultural Society Records. Redwood Library and Athenaeum, Newport, RI.

Newport Journal and Weekly News, August 23, 1907.

Newport Journal and Weekly News, June 12, 1912.

Newport Journal and Weekly News, July 13, 1914.

Newport Land Trust. Olmsted job number 01070. National Park Service, Frederick Law Olmsted National Historic Site, Brookline, MA.

Newport Mercury, June 28, 1890.

"The Newport Natural History Society." *Newport Daily News*, July 13, 1883.

Newport Town Meeting Records, 1679–1776. Book 2007, p. 27. Newport Historical Society, Newport, RI.

Newton, Norman T. *Design on the Land.* Cambridge, MA: Harvard University Press, 1971.

Nygren, Edward J., and Bruce Robertson. *Views and Visions: American Landscape before 1830.* Washington, DC: Corcoran Gallery of Art, 1986. Exhibition catalogue.

O'Malley, Theresa. "Landscape Gardening in the Early National Period." In *Views and Visions: American Landscape before 1830*, by Edward J. Nygren and Bruce Robertson. Washington, DC: Corcoran Gallery of Art, 1986. Exhibition catalogue.

Olmsted, A. H. Olmsted job numbers 2221, 2261. National Park Service, Frederick Law Olmsted National Historic Site, Brookline, MA.

Olmsted, Frederick Law. Letters from Frederick Law Olmsted to Mariana Griswold Van Rensselaer, May 17, 1887; June 29, 1888. Olmsted Associates Records. Manuscript Division, Library of Congress.

Olmsted, Frederick Law, and John Charles Olmsted. "Plan for the Subdivision of Properties in Newport, Rhode Island belonging to Mrs. Edward King, Mr. J. H. Glover, Esq., the Hon. C. S. Bradley, G. Gordon King," 1885. Plat Book I, pp. 30–31. Land Evidence Records. City Hall, Newport, RI.

Olmsted, Frederick Law. Letter from Frederick Law Olmsted to the Board of Commissioners of Central Park, January 22, 1861.

Olmsted, Frederick Law. Letter from Frederick Law Olmsted to Mariana Griswold Van Rensselaer, May 17, 1887. Olmsted Associates Records. Manuscript Division, Library of Congress.

Olmsted, Frederick Law, and Theodora Kimball, eds. *Frederick Law Olmsted: Landscape Architect, Vol. I* (New York: G.P. Putnam's Sons, 1922).

Olmsted, Frederick Law, Jr. *Proposed Improvements for Newport, Rhode Island.* Cambridge, MA: University Press, 1913.

Omernick, J. M. "Ecoregions of Rhode Island." bplant.org. Accessed March 1, 2021. https://bplant.org/region/1383.

Panaggio, Leonard J. "Thomas Galvin, An Early Professional Gardener." *Newport History Journal 130* (Spring 1968).

"Plant Notes." *Garden and Forest* 7 (August 1, 1894). https://www.biodiversitylibrary.org/item/107742#page/320.

Platt, Charles Adams. *Italian Gardens.* New York: Harper and Brothers, 1894.

Pope, John Russell. Letters from John Russell Pope to the Olmsted Brothers, August 21, 1931; October 1, 1931; and October 30, 1931. Olmsted Associates Records. Manuscript Division, Library of Congress.

Powel, Mary Edith. Diaries. Vols. 1B and 2. Undated. Box 150A. Newport Historical Society, Newport, RI.

Powel, Mary Edith, Journal. Undated. Box 27. Newport Historical Society.

Proceedings of the Newport Natural History Society, 1884–1885. Newport, RI: Davis and Pitman, 1885.

Records of the Island of Rhode Island and Providence Plantations in New England, 1638–1644. Accession number C#00206. Rhode Island State Archives, Providence, RI.

"Rhode Island in 1750." *Rhode Island Historical Society Collections* 13, no. 2 (April 1920). https://catalog.hathitrust.org/Record/008888497.

Richards, L. J., and Co. *Atlas of the City of Newport.* Springfield, MA, 1893, 1907.

Roux, Jessica. *Floriography: An Illustrated Guide to the Victorian Language of Flowers.* Kansas City, MO: Andrews McMeel Publishing, 2020.

Sargent, Charles Sprague. Letter from Charles Sprague Sargent to Dr. Walcott Gibbs, April 28, 1906. Arnold Arboretum, Boston, MA.

Sheldon, George William. *Artistic Country Seats.* New York: D. Appleton and Company, 1887.

Shepheard, Peter. *Modern Gardens.* London: Architectural Press, 1953.

Shurtleff, Nathaniel B. *A Topographical and Historical Description of Boston.* Boston: Noyes, Holmes and Co., 1872.

Smith, Henry Nash. *Virgin Land.* Cambridge MA: Harvard University Press, 1950.

"Society in Fancy Dress." *Vogue,* February 1, 1911.

"Solomon Drowne's Journal." *Newport Historical Magazine* 1, no. 2 (October 1880).

Stowe, Harriet Beecher. *The Minister's Wooing.* New York: Derby and Jackson, 1859.

"Surprise Valley Farm," *Country Life* 45 (April 1924).

Sutton, S. B., ed. *Civilizing American Cities: Writings on City Landscapes.* New York: Da Capo Press, 1997.

Swinburne, Daniel, and Abraham Peckham. Deed: Daniel Swinburne and Abraham Peckham, Grantors, to James Rhodes, Grantee, September 23, 1853. Book 31, p. 218. Land Evidence Records. City Hall, Newport, RI.

Tankard, Judith B. "Rose Standish Nichols, A Proper Bostonian." *Arnoldia* 59, no. 4 (1999). http://arnoldia.arboretum.harvard.edu/issues/206.

Thomas, Keith. *Man and the Natural World.* New York: Pantheon, 1983.

T. J. Brown Day Books, 1905–1945. Private Collection of T. J. Brown, Newport, RI.

T. J. Brown. Interview (interviewer unknown), February 2021. Newport Tree Conservancy, Newport, RI.

Treib, Marc. *Thinking a Modern Landscape Architecture, West and East.* Novato, CA: ORO Editions, 2020.

Tschirch, John R. *Newport: The Artful City.* London: D. Giles Limited, 2020.

Tunnard, Christopher. *The City of Man.* New York: Charles Scribner's Sons, 1970.

Tunnard, Christopher. *Gardens in the Modern Landscape.* London: Architectural Press, 1938.

Tunnard, Christopher. *A World with a View: An Inquiry into the Nature of Scenic Values.* New Haven, CT: Yale University Press, 1978.

Tunnard and Harris. *A Preservation Planning Report on Newport, RI.* Prepared for the Preservation Society of Newport County, January 1960. The Preservation Society of Newport County Archives, Newport, RI.

Turenne, Jim. *Soils of Eastern Rhode Island.* Warwick, RI: Natural Resources Conservation Service, U.S. Department of Agriculture, 2016.

Twain, Mark. "What Paul Bourget Thinks of Us." *North American Review* 160, no. 458 (January 1895).

"The Vanderbilt Greenhouses." *New York Times,* November 8, 1896.

Van Rensselaer, John King, Mrs. *Newport: Our Social Capital.* Philadelphia: J. B. Lippincott, 1905.

Van Rensselaer, Mariana Griswold. "The Artistic Aspect of Trees IV." *Garden and Forest* 1 (October 3, 1888). https://www.biodiversitylibrary.org/item/107709#page/389.

Van Rensselaer, Mariana Griswold. "Landscape Gardening VII." *Garden and Forest* 1 (April 11, 1888). https://www.biodiversitylibrary.org/item/107709#page/91.

Van Rensselaer, Mariana Griswold. "Newport I." *Garden and Forest* 1 (November 28, 1888). https://www.biodiversitylibrary.org/item/107709#page/486.

Van Rensselaer, Mariana Griswold. "Newport II." *Garden and Forest* 1 (December 5, 1888). https://www.biodiversitylibrary.org/item/107709#page/498.

Van Rensselaer, Schuyler, Mrs. *Art Out of Doors: Hints on Good Taste in Gardening.* New York: Charles Scribner's Sons, 1893.

Vaux, Calvert. *Villas and Cottages.* New York: Harper and Brothers, 1872.

Veeder, Paul L., II. "The Outbuildings and Grounds of Chateau-sur-Mer." *Journal of the Society of Architectural Historians* 29, no. 4 (1970). https://doi.org/10.2307/988593.

Voltaire. *Candide.* New York: Boni and Liveright, Inc., 1918.

Vonnegut, Kurt, Jr. *The Sirens of Titan.* New York: Delacore, 1959.

Warren, George Henry, Mrs., and Harold Talbot. Interview (interviewer unknown), July 16, 1970. The Preservation Society of Newport County Archives, Newport, RI.

Weidenmann, Jacob. *Beautifying Country Homes.* New York: Orange, Judd and Co., 1870.

Wharton, Edith. *A Backward Glance.* New York: Curtis Publishing Company, 1933.

Wharton, Edith. *Italian Villas and Their Gardens.* New York: Century Company, 1904.

Wilder, Thornton. *Theophilus North.* New York: Harper Collins, 2019.

Woodward, C. Vann. "The Fall of the American Adam." *New Republic,* December 2, 1981.

Wroth, Lawrence C. *The Voyages of Giovanni da Verrazzano, 1524–1528.* New Haven, CT: Yale University Press: 1970.

Yard, Sally. *Christo Oceanfront.* Princeton, NJ: Art Museum, Princeton University, 1975. Exhibition catalogue.

Yule, Jack. Interview by Thomas Downs. February 7, 2021. Newport Tree Conservancy, Newport, RI.

Yule, John. Obituary. *Newport Daily News,* June 13, 1998.

INDEX

Page numbers in *italic* refer to the illustrations

PICTURE CREDITS

Alexander Nesbitt

Archives of American Gardens

Art Institute of Chicago

Brooklyn Museum

Carnegie Museum of Art

Estate of Christo V. Javacheff

Estate of Gianfranco Gorgoni

Gottscho-Schleisner Collection, Library of Congress

Harry Eudenbach

Jane Burrows

Library of Congress

Mr. and Mrs. S. Matthews V. Hamilton, Jr.

National Gallery of Art

Newport Historical Society

New-York Historical Society

Nick Garcia-Belong

Philadelphia Free Library

Redwood Library and Athenaeum

Robert Yarnall Richie Photograph Collection, DeGolyer Library, Southern Methodist University

Roselle McConnell

The Newport Tree Conservancy

The Preservation Society of Newport County

The University of Rhode Island, Historic Textile and Costume Collection

T. J. Brown

Tommy Downes

Vartanian and Sons

United States Department of the Interior, National Park Service, Frederick Law Olmsted National Historic Site